LAW, ECONOMICS, AND CONFLICT

T0327684

LAW, ECONOMICS, AND CONFLICT

Edited by Kaushik Basu
and Robert C. Hockett

CORNELL GLOBAL PERSPECTIVES

MARIO EINAUDI
Center *for* International Studies

CORNELL UNIVERSITY PRESS

ITHACA AND LONDON

Chapter 4: This is a forthcoming chapter in *Law and Economy in a Young Democracy: India 1947 and Beyond* by Tirthankar Roy and Anand V. Swamy. © The University of Chicago. Reproduced by permission. All rights reserved.

Chapter 7: Sections of this chapter originally appeared in *Law and Macroeconomics: Legal Remedies to Recessions* by Yair Listokin. Reproduced with permission of Harvard University Press, by the President and Fellows of Harvard College. Copyright © 2019.

First published 2021 by Cornell University Press

Library of Congress Cataloging-in-Publication Data

Names: Basu, Kaushik, 1980– editor. | Hockett, Robert, editor.
Title: Law, economics, and conflict / edited by Kaushik Basu and Robert C. Hockett.
Description: Ithaca [New York]: Cornell University Press, 2021. | Series: Cornell global
    perspectives | Includes bibliographical references and index.
Identifiers: LCCN 2020058391 (print) | LCCN 2020058392 (ebook) |
    ISBN 9781501759383 (hardcover) | ISBN 9781501754821 (paperback) |
    ISBN 9781501759284 (pdf) | ISBN 9781501754838 (epub)
Subjects: LCSH: Law and economics. | Law and globalization. | Sociological
    jurisprudence. | Globalization—Economic aspects. | Social conflict—Economic
    aspects.
Classification: LCC K487.E3 L3887 2021 (print) | LCC K487.E3 (ebook) |
    DDC 340/.11—dc23
LC record available at https://lccn.loc.gov/2020058391
LC ebook record available at https://lccn.loc.gov/2020058392

Contents

LAW, ECONOMICS, AND CONFLICT

LAW, ECONOMICS, AND CONFLICT
An Introduction

Kaushik Basu and Robert C. Hockett

We live in the best of times, we live in the worst of times. As we are often reminded by economists and other social scientists, the per capita income in the world today is higher than ever before, and human beings have a longer life expectancy at birth than they have ever had before. We are able to launch rockets into space, observe and track the planets around us, monitor the arctic ice caps, and predict the weather more accurately than we have ever done before. All this is true. But it is also true that we are in one of our most divisive times, with politics polarized as rarely seen outside of a major war and with regions in open conflict, inhabited by people whose lives and life prospects are ruined. There are mass movements of people fleeing from their home countries and continents in search of safety and livelihoods, and, equally, there are efforts to stop them at the gates of where they arrive. Climate change hangs over our heads like the sword of Damocles. Sixty-six million years ago, it must have seemed wonderful for the dinosaurs that had lived for millions of years, grown in size, and ruled the earth. Little did they know that these were also the worst of times for them, that they would see a collapse like never before and be pushed into oblivion.

Unlike the dinosaurs, which did not know that the best of times could also be the worst of times, we human beings in the twenty-first century can fathom this, analyze our own predicament, and try to avert crisis and conflict. There is no doubt that we have done well thus far without much self-analysis. Individuals went about maximizing their own interests and acquisitions, and the invisible hand of the market worked—at least reasonably well—so that societies prospered and our economies grew. From as early as the late eighteenth century, with the publication of Adam Smith's seminal book (Smith 1776), we tried to understand this mysterious invisible hand, and we debated whether this could always be relied on to deliver or whether we needed to marry it with the hand of the state, with its laws and regulations. Just as markets had flourished for thousands of years, we also discovered the importance and the power of the law starting at least five or six thousand years ago. From the Code of Hammurabi through the alleged edicts of Lycurgus in Sparta and the well-articulated laws of Solon in Athens, we have come a long way (Hockett 2009).

The recognition of the importance of the interface between economics and law happened much later. It was recognized in the debates preceding and following the enactment of the Sherman Act in the United States in 1890. It emerged as a formal discipline in the 1960s, with a series of important papers by Coase (1960), Calabresi (1961), Becker (1968), and others.

The rise in global conflict, the dramatic technological breakthroughs of our digital age, and the floundering of traditional law and economics has led to some soul-searching about the fundamentals of law and economics (Posner 2000; McAdams 2015; Basu 2018). It was with these concerns in mind that we set up in 2017 a new research unit at Cornell called CRADLE—Cornell Research Academy of Law, Development, and Economics, the acronym creating a challenge we had to live up to. We decided early on that CRADLE initially should focus on the conflicts around the world mentioned in the opening paragraph. With that in mind, a conference was organized in New York City in April 2018. This book is a selection of papers presented at the conference and some written subsequently that are based on the papers presented and discussions that took place at the conference.

Our focus is on law and economics but more specifically the new challenges arising from globalization, technological advancement, and their concomitant—social and political conflict. In the chapters that follow, we have some of our best minds mulling over the challenges of this new world and how we can steer a course to give individuals the space and freedom to work, innovate, earn, profit, and prosper and the state the wisdom to regulate and ensure that conflicts do not occur, externalities are managed, and some are not marginalized and impoverished while others accumulate and prosper.

The opening chapter, "The Interim Balance Sheet of Democracy: A Machiavellian Memo," by Célestin Monga, goes to the heart of the concern that led to the conceptualization of the conference. The chapter talks to us about the "global economy of anger" and the "great discordance" that has been the collateral offshoot of technological progress and globalization. Drawing on some of his own earlier work (Monga 1996), the author shows that what is often overlooked is that these "advances" have been slowly eroding the foundations of global democracy, enabling political leaders in big and powerful countries to take actions that have no legitimacy or legal basis and are sanctioned by none other than themselves, which is anathema to the very idea of democracy. He talks about the "Tuesday morning meetings" in the White House, where "whoever is the US president" has "the sole power to decide who, among the 7 billion people on earth, must die if suspected of terrorism . . . by a group of nonelected public officers." This chapter raises deep questions about our capacity to uphold fairness, equity, and voice, given these extralegal and subterranean channels of power, enforcement, and punishment.

Given the long history of democracy, which goes back to Athens and its surrounding territories of sixth century BCE, we often act as though we have an adequate understanding of its structure and modalities. Chapter 1 argues that this is far from the truth. Given the intertwining of democracy with technology and institutions that are continuously evolving, our understanding is quite minimal, and the weaknesses are showing up in a stark fashion in today's globalized world. This chapter lays out the importance of independent research and suggests a research agenda for law and economics, which is interesting to read in its own right and sets the tone for much of what follows in this book.

Hope lies in the fact that economics has in recent years (too slowly though, some would say) broadened its approach, dismantling some of the walls around it and opening itself to ideas, concepts, and theories from politics, sociology, biology, and psychology. The second chapter of this book, "The Third Function of Law: Its Power to Change Cultural Categories," by Karla Hoff and James Walsh, is an introduction to how "law and economics" is affected by this broadening of the scope of economics. As such, chapter 2 could provide some of the conceptual foundation stones needed to address the kinds of real-world problems raised in chapter 1. Standard law and economics, as inherited from the writings of the 1960s referred to above, was rooted in the neoclassical assumption of ruthlessly rational individuals, responding to the law based on what it commands, its punishments and rewards. This "command function" of law was partly dismantled and enriched by the new work on the "expressive function," which recognized that the law works not just by command, reward, and punishment but also by triggering social norms and affecting some of our preferences (Sunstein 1996).

In their chapter, Hoff and Walsh introduce a third novelty, what they refer to as the "schematizing function" of the law (see also Hoff and Stiglitz 2016). Lodged in their brains, human beings have cultural categories and concepts that influence what they focus on and what they ignore. At one level, all this happens instinctively and so may seem like innate qualities, but they are influenced and shaped by many social factors (and importantly, in the context of this chapter and this book) by the laws of the nation and also the deliberations surrounding the adoption of laws. The chapter shows how entrenched cultural categories can be used to both reinforce and to block a law. In particular, a law that prohibits discrimination against certain groups can be partly undone by harnessing such cultural forces. The chapter builds on behavioral economics but is also an original contribution in terms of the new concepts and ideas it brings to the field and thus provides the foundations for some of the more everyday policy concerns that later chapters bring to the table.

One enduring theme is corruption. Interest in and writings on corruption go back to ancient times (most notably to Kautilya's *Arthashastra*), and it has triggered a lot of the modern thinking on law, regulation, and economic functioning. Effective corruption control beckons us to take a broader view of economics and look at social norms and psychology, as discussed in chapter 2. It is therefore interesting to read chapter 3, "Fighting Corruption in China: The Roles of Formal and Informal Institutions" by Cheryl Long, as almost a case study of this broader approach to law and economics in contemporary China. As Long notes, corruption is generally made possible by the use of informal ties and links among individuals, since it requires chains of actions for which it is not possible to harness the law, and so one has to rely on trust and also informal channels of punishment and reward. This could explain why nations, such as China and India, in which familial ties and social connections and hierarchies are emphasized, are ones with greater corruption.

It is from this premise that chapter 3 takes off. It is indeed an interesting time to study China. Under Xi Jinping there has been a bigger effort to control corruption than witnessed in a very long time in China. More government officials were arrested on charges of corruption during the four years preceding 2018 than in the four decades before that. But the number of arrests in itself cannot automatically be treated as an indicator of success. In all countries with a corruption control campaign, one has to be mindful of risks. In countries with complex laws and regulations, where virtually everybody, knowingly or unwittingly, infringes some laws, corruption control can easily become an instrument for silencing dissent and opposition. When you have a free pick of whom you arrest for corruption, the temptation is to arrest those who oppose you. There is the further problem of corruption control damaging legitimate business and trade, because people become overly cautious and desist from making decisions. This can drive some of the corrupt activities deeper underground and create the illusion of greater success than is warranted. It can also slow down growth. Long's chapter gives us a bird's-eye view of the full range of connected themes. Though her study is focused on China, it has lessons for all nations trying to curb corruption and illegal business transactions.

Let us move from China to India. A long-standing topic in law and economics, which triggered as much theorizing as did the enquiry into market competition and antitrust law, is that of the functioning of credit markets. There is of course the extensive topic of debt and credit in macroeconomics and monetary policy. But when it comes to law and economics, the management of the rural credit market has been a source of abiding interest to economists and policymakers in emerging market economies. It is arguable that India has been the place of some of the most original research in this field. The fourth chapter of this book, "Overreliance on Law: Rural Credit in India, 1875–2010" is by Anand Swamy, who has done some highly regarded historical research on credit markets in India (see Kranton and Swamy 1999). This chapter is a comprehensive study of rural credit in India, spanning over a century. The focus of the chapter is on why the law has fared so poorly in regulating the rural credit market and enhancing farmer welfare, which is the ostensible aim of the law.

Despite being rooted in history, chapter 4 has important bearings on contemporary India. It discusses in some detail the regulation of rural credit and the rise of the microfinance industry since the celebrated economic reforms of 1991 in India. Commenting on the current situation, Swamy notes that the levels of farmer stress is at an all-time high in India, with many farmers driven to levels of debt that they clearly cannot pay back in their lifetimes, and that there has been a large increase in the incidence of farmer suicides. The chapter brings evidence and analysis to show that the numerous credit laws and regulations have failed to do much to alleviate the problems because of our failure to recognize that credit markets are interlinked with other features of the rural economy. The chapter makes a pointed recommendation—the need to strengthen agricultural insurance and the state's willingness to absorb some of the shocks stemming from productivity fluctuations.

From discussions of China and India, we turn to the developed world and in particular, the United States. A large literature exists on informal credit markets in the developing world, but the topic has attracted less attention in wealthy countries. But for low-income families, even in rich countries like the United States and Sweden, pawnshops and the institutions of pawnbroking can play a crucial role. We are therefore glad to include chapter 5, "Forgotten Markets: The Importance of Pawnshops," by Marieke Bos, Susan Carter, and Paige Skiba, which nicely complements chapter 4's coverage of informal credit in rural India. Studies show that large numbers of poor people and especially those who are unbanked use pawn loans by leaving collateral. This institution has existed for centuries and while attention has shifted away from it—thanks to the rise of the big corporation and the super-rich, who lend and borrow huge sums of money—the informal pawn broker remains a source of survival for the very poor. And this is not unconnected to what happens in the larger, formal economy. As Bos, Carter, and Skiba point out, after the global financial crisis that began in the United States in 2007–2008, quickly engulfed the world, and became the protracted Great Recession, the pawn-broking industry in the United States and Sweden grew by an astonishing 20 percent per year, as poor people were forced to turn to informal credit for their survival. Despite this industry's importance, pawnbroking has characteristically received little attention and also little regulation. This is a chapter that raises a host of questions regarding the welfare consequences of these informal lending markets in rich countries and how they could be regulated. This is a chapter that has the potential to spur new research.

One specific area in which the technological advances of recent decades re-ferred to in chapter 1 is having a deep impact is the effectiveness of antitrust laws. There has been a lot of soul-searching in recent times on how large tech compa-nies and digital platforms have been able to use technology and global dispersion of their activities to circumvent antitrust laws, most notably in the United States. That country had played a pioneering role in promoting competition and curb-ing collusive pricing, beginning with the enactment of the Sherman Act in 1890 (see Khan 2016). Chapter 6, "New Technology, Increasing Returns, and the End of the Antitrust Century" by Kaushik Basu, shows that the challenge is not merely a matter of determination and the willingness to use the laws. It argues that the changing modalities of production, inspired by the digital revolution, are funda-mentally altering our capacity to use antitrust laws and nurture competition with-out severely damaging productivity.

The chapter develops the idea of "vertically serrated" markets. These are mar-kets where, for example, the hundred firms involved in the automobile industries are not organized like they were in the olden days, when each one of them pro-duced complete cars. Instead, the hundred firms now are typically specialized: one for producing the braking system in its entirety, one for the chassis, one for the wheels, and so on. In the polar case, each one of them produces all of one part of the car. Chapter 6 characterizes the equilibrium of these vertically serrated in-dustries. It shows how there will be a tendency for all surplus to collect in few hands and for a possible exacerbation of price discrimination. It is then shown how, thanks to increasing returns to scale, it is difficult to use antitrust laws to curb these inequities. The chapter closes with a discussion of how we may have to use other kinds of laws, including those pertaining to dispersed shareholdings and profit sharing to take on this new challenge of our times.

Rich countries and advanced economies, poor countries and emerging-market economies are all subjects that deserve individual scrutiny and analysis, as the next three chapters show, but in a globalized world what one nation does can have pro-found effects on other economies. This recognition brings us back to the topic discussed in the opening chapter, that of global interactions and the scope for reg-ulating them. The focus of chapter 7, "Law and International Monetary Regimes" by Yair Listokin, is on one aspect of the large political economy of multi-country policy interventions, that which works through the money markets, liquidity, price controls, and overall macroeconomic policy. This is an important area of research and policy activism involving important multilateral organizations, like the International Monetary Fund and the Bank of International Settlements. There have been debates about exchange-rate policies (which by definition, have effects on other countries), about capital controls (which may block money from entering your nation but also blocks the movement of money from other countries), and price controls (which is often treated as a no-go area). Capital controls and interventions in the price system have also been politically divisive topics. The creation of the European Union helped stimulate these debates, since there were immediate policy spillovers that directly affected human well-being, from Britain and Germany to Greece and Ireland. This chapter discusses these topics and puts forward some radical proposals with special commentary on the European Union.

Chapter 8, by Gael Giraud, takes us back to some of the moral and philosophical questions that underlie a lot of law and economics and were touched on in the opening three chapters: What role do our moral preferences play in our choices? And what is the relation between economics and moral science? These are important matters that underlay a lot of the founding ideas of economics. It is worth remembering that, starting in 1752, Adam Smith held the Chair in Moral Philosophy at the University of Glasgow and would soon be working on *The Theory of Moral Sentiments*, which would be published in 1759. At first sight, there seems to be a sharp contrast between the way human beings make moral choices and the way in which *homo oeconomicus* makes individual choices. The former is meant to be made from behind the veil of ignorance or with the objectivity of Smith's impartial spectator and is subject to contestation, whereas the latter is a person's personal preference and not a matter of contestation. But there are connections between ethical preferences behind the veil of ignorance and personal preferences. This chapter takes a relatively unusual line by showing how our ethical preferences can affect our personal preferences and choices. By this intertwining of ethical and personal choices, Giraud takes us back to some of the earliest concerns of economics and tries to rehabilitate economics as a moral science.

The last three chapters of this book are commentaries that were written by participants at the conference, using the hindsight of ideas and data presented by the speakers.

Much of the early interest in the interface between law and economics arose from the realization that, while markets are a powerful instrument for delivering goods and services (and ultimately, well-being) to our doorstep, we also need to contend with market failures. Rural credit markets (as discussed in chapter 4) are rife with market failures because of asymmetric information. Corruption of the kind discussed in chapter 3 flourishes in many countries because of the failure of markets to deliver. Antitrust laws are needed, because monopolies and oligopolies often cause markets to be inefficient and consumers and workers to suffer. Chapter 9, "Exchange Configurations and the Legal Framework," by Peter Cornelisse and Erik Thorbecke, develops the idea of "exchange configuration" to look at some of these diverse matters through a unifying lens. Briefly summarizing important prior developments, such as New Institutional Economics and Transactions Cost Economics, Cornelisse and Thorbecke discuss the role of law and regulation for tackling not just market failures (such as the inadequate provision of public goods and our inadequate handling of the environment) but also equity and income distribution.

Chapter 10, "Reimagining Governance through the Role of Law: A Perspective from World Development Report 2017" by Luis-Felipe Lopez-Calva and Kimberly Bolch, draws on the ideas and concepts presented in the first seven chapters. It evaluates them based on the framework in the report on law and governance that was the focus of the 2017 World Development Report of the World Bank. That report had attracted a huge amount of attention from both policymakers and the academic community (see World Bank 2017). Lopez-Calva and Bolch argue that although we use the word "law" in a rather generic fashion, in reality, there are various types of laws, and it is important to classify them. By using illustrations from the chapters in this book, Lopez-Calva and Bolch show that laws often have a hierarchy. They can be ground-level rules pertaining to how individuals relate to one another, and at the other extreme, they can be rules about how rules are to be created and enforced. This chapter also draws special attention to understanding the role of law as an instrument for resolving disputes and contestation. During major shifts in technology, such as the one the world is witnessing now, this becomes key to the peaceful resolution of conflict, as discussed in several chapters, and, in the context of the global theater, is especially emphasized in chapter 1.

Chapter 11, "Beyond Law and Economics: Legitimate Distribution without Legislation?" by Nicole Hassoun, brings the curtain down on the project by evaluating and commenting on various special themes and policy problems discussed in this book using the broader brush of moral philosophy. She argues that law and economics, while themselves multidisciplinary, have a basis in an even broader disciplinary mooring, that of philosophy. Drawing on classic works in law, economics, and philosophy, such as Dworkin (1986) and Raz (1986), and on some of her own research (Hassoun 2008), she raises important questions about the concept of legitimacy in the context of the kinds of interventions discussed elsewhere in this book, such as central bank policies (chapter 7) and antitrust regulations (chapter 6).

While much of standard law and economics deals with the direct economic consequences of legal interventions, we often overlook the fact that many of these decisions taken by lawyers, policy economists, and technocrats can have sweeping consequences. A central bank's act of lowering interest rates can enrich thousands of people and also cause prices to rise and put the livelihood of thousands of people in peril. What gives technocrats the legitimacy to take these actions? What makes these kinds of sweeping decisions, with large human consequences, "morally permissible"? These are the questions that Hassoun raises in this compelling closing chapter. Some of these big topics do not have easy answers and are, by their nature, open ended. But she also posits some minimal necessary conditions that must be fulfilled for these big legal and other policy decisions with large allocative consequences to be considered morally legitimate. This and the many open-ended questions raised in this chapter are of value both in giving deeper roots to the ideas discussed in the present book and in doing the spadework for further research and sequels to it.

References

Basu, K. 2018. *The Republic of Beliefs: A New Approach to Law and Economics*. Princeton, NJ: Princeton University Press.

Becker, G. 1968. "Crime and Punishment: An Economic Approach." *Journal of Political Economy* 76: 169–217.

Calabresi, G. 1961. "Some Thoughts on Risk Distribution and the Law of Torts." *Yale Law Journal* 70: 499–553.

Coase, R. 1960. "The Problem of Social Costs." *Journal of Law and Economics* 3: 1–44.

Dworkin, R. 1986. *Law's Empire*. Cambridge, MA: Harvard University Press.

Hassoun, N. 2008. "The Evolution of Wealth: Democracy or Revolution?" in J. Knight (ed.), *Wealth, NOMOS, LVIII*. American Society for Political and Legal Philosophy.

Hockett, R. 2009. *Law*. Chicago: Chicago Review Press.

Hoff, K., and J. Stiglitz. 2016. "Striving for Balance in Economics: Towards a Theory of the Social Determination of Behavior." *Journal of Economic Behavior and Organization* 126: 25–57.

Khan, L. 2016. "Amazon's Antitrust Paradox." *Yale Law Journal* 126: 710–805.

Kranton, R., and A. Swamy. 1999. "The Hazards of Piecemeal Reform: British Civil Courts and the Credit Market in Colonial India." *Journal of Development Economics* 28: 1–24.

Kautilya. ca. 300 BCE. *Arthashastra*. Penguin edition.

McAdams, R. 2015. *The Expressive Powers of Law: Theories and Limits*. Cambridge, MA: Harvard University Press.

Monga, C. 1996. *The Anthropology of Anger: Civil Society and Democracy in Africa*. Boulder, CO: Lynne Rienner Publishers.

Posner, E. 2000. *Law and Social Norms*. Cambridge, MA: Harvard University Press.

Raz, J. 1986. *The Morality of Freedom*. Oxford: Oxford University Press.

Smith, A. 1776. *An Inquiry into the Nature and Causes of the Wealth of Nations.* 1976 edition. Oxford: Clarendon Press.

Sunstein, C. 1996. "On the Expressive Function of Law." *University of Pennsylvania Law Review* 144: 2021–2053.

World Bank. 2017. *World Development Report, 2017: Governance and the Law.* Washington, DC: World Bank.

THE INTERIM BALANCE SHEET OF DEMOCRACY

A Machiavellian Memo

Célestin Monga

Every Tuesday morning, the heads of intelligence agencies and the national security advisor of the United States gather around the US president in the Situation Room at the White House in Washington, DC. They discuss the most confidential document in American politics: the list of people in various places in the world who are considered dangerous "threats" or "terrorists," cannot or should not be captured, and are recommended for secret assassination. Sometimes the list includes the names, pictures, and profiles of American citizens and even minors whom national security experts in the executive branch of the US government believe should simply be killed—not arrested and brought to trial in the United States or elsewhere. The evidence against these suspects is classified and therefore not to be shown in court.

Sipping coffee or tea, drinking orange juice, and perhaps sharing cookies, participants at these meetings discuss counterterrorism strategies and plans, and casually advise the US president on which suspects should be killed according to a priority list, even when the suspects are far from any battlefield. The confidential list of suspects is officially called the "Disposition Matrix"—a name that even George Orwell could not have imagined in his famous novel *1984*. Decisions are made quickly, after the president has listened for a few minutes to the opinions of his small staff around the table.

These Tuesday morning meetings were initiated and formalized during the administration of Nobel Peace Prize winner Barack Obama. Its members institutionalized the practice known as "targeted killings" and adopted new rules and regulations that grant whoever is the US president the sole power to decide who, among the nearly 8 billion people on earth, must die if suspected of terrorism. This group of nonelected public officers has been entrusted to make such uncontested and irrevocable decisions.[1] Regardless of the country in which one lives, all citizens of the world are required to trust the sovereign, ultimate judgment and wisdom of the US president. The president takes the oath to protect the United States against terrorism and is entitled to unilaterally kill anyone anywhere in pursuit of this sacred mission.[2] As noted by Greenwald, "The president's underlings compile their proposed lists of who should be executed, and the president—at a charming weekly event dubbed by White House aides as 'Terror Tuesday'—then chooses from 'baseball cards' and decrees in total secrecy who should die. The power of accuser, prosecutor, judge, jury, and executioner are all consolidated in this one man, and those powers are exercised in the dark" (Greenwald 2013).

Since this information was made public, the world has learned that it was only the tip of an iceberg: The world has witnessed the deaths of countless civilians, often women and children, killed by drone strikes in Yemen, Pakistan, Somalia, Afghanistan, and elsewhere, who are simply referred to as "collateral damage." Under a global-war theory, the entire planet is a battlefield. Targeted assassinations routinely take place in countries far from any war zone.

The fact that President Barack Obama, a Harvard-trained lawyer and a former constitutional law teacher at the University of Chicago, felt empowered and entitled by American laws and regulations to make these life-and-death decisions in secrecy, and to select who should be executed without any charges in the court of law or due process, sheds light on the status of habeas corpus, liberty, and the implementation of the Bill of Rights in the country still widely viewed as the most "democratic" in the world.[3] Perhaps not surprisingly, it has also been revealed that many secretive practices considered illegal, undemocratic, and unethical by human rights organizations had been going on in democratic countries. For instance, it was revealed that the US National Security Agency had wiretapped top German officials and many world leaders (including from democratic countries) for long-term surveillance during several decades and had eavesdropped on several French finance ministers and collected information on French export contracts, trade, and budget talks (*Guardian* 2015).

These revelations emboldened authoritarian political leaders around the world to assert and defend their own brand of democracy—many of them using the real or imaginary threats of global terror to justify the adoption of liberticidal measures. After all, if US presidents could unapologetically grant themselves the power to order the killing of anyone on earth without having to explain the reasons or provide evidence of guilt before any court of law, or secretly "dispose" of some people as they deemed appropriate—with indefinite imprisonment or death, why couldn't other world leaders? If whoever holds power in the Oval Office can serenely wiretap the cell phones of several German chancellors or that of the president of Brazil, none of them suspected of being a potential "terrorist," what would prevent the leaders of Russia, China, Indonesia, Venezuela, or Burundi from using similar tactics? If intelligence agencies in Western countries self-proclaimed as "democratic" could routinely conduct intelligence-gathering operations against foreign companies in the name of national security, why should other self-proclaimed democratic countries in Asia, Latin America, or Africa not do the same?

These questions go well beyond legal debates over the extraordinarily broad powers of the "leader of the Free World." The issues underlying them also transcend the philosophical debates over the ethics of rules and practices by "democratic" governments expected to define themselves, in all circumstances, as nations where transparent and strong institutions are in place to ensure that the most sacred of all decisions (taking anyone's life) are made within a system of checks, balances, and restraint. They are at the heart of the legitimacy and validity of democracy and freedom. Yet, despite some outrage (expressed mainly in intellectual circles), the dominant political reaction to these revelations and much of the literature on global political developments has generally been limited to analyses and commentaries on the mechanics of democracy. The focus has often been on problems with alternative, totalitarian systems of democracy (Lefort 1994), on problems with the process of democratic consolidation, on symptoms of its subversion by cynical political entrepreneurs (Levitsky and Ziblatt 2018), on "the rise of illiberal democracies" (Zakaria 2007, 2019), the functioning of political institutions, and so forth. Most recent studies of contemporary political events have not examined democracy itself, its relevance and feasibility after several centuries of implementation in an increasingly globalized world, where issues of economic governance have become more prevalent than almost anything else.

A few authors have recently acknowledged the theoretical challenges of democracy and its zigzagging path in recent decades (Gauchet 2002). Some have questioned its founding myths, highlighted its contradictions, and suggested its reinvention (Canfora 2006). Others have highlighted its superficiality, its high emotional content, its obscenity and even naiveté (Debray 2007). Optimists have recommended that democracy be freed from suspicion of being a mainly Western concept and instead be viewed as a credible organizing tool for the polity, beyond universal suffrage or even elections (Sen 1999; Agamben et al. 2009).

In the context of accelerated social transformations and a fast-changing world economy,[4] with landmark technological innovations, the banalization of artificial intelligence, and the circulation of unprecedented amounts of capital across borders in search of returns, the proposition that democracy is an *operationalizable* ideal deserves closer scrutiny. Digital computation is "a force that produces and serializes subjects, objects, phenomena, but also consciences and memories and traces, which can be coded and stored and which are capable of circulating" (Mbembe 2019). Big Data and laws adopted by governments in powerful countries to have extraterritorial access to data offer new, easier possibilities for illegal political hacking and for legal political interference across boundaries—beyond the traditional, old-fashioned political interventions that have always taken place among nations.[5] With the interconnectivity of economic and financial systems, increasingly sophisticated algorithms, faster and more powerful computational instruments, and progress in artificial intelligence, almost all countries now have unbridled access to national databases in other countries. This makes all nations vulnerable and all governments concerned.[6]

The largely muted reactions to revelations about the existence of the "Disposition Matrix" (also known as the "Kill List"), the general indifference to global eavesdropping of political and business leaders, the global acceptance of the death of privacy so that Big Data conglomerates can share information with totalitarian "democratic" governments in return for business opportunities,[7] and the relativism (if not outright confusion) about standards of freedom across countries should force a rethinking of the meanings of democracy and even its possibility.[8] Such idiosyncrasies are not taking place in Honduras, Equatorial Guinea, or Bhutan, but in the most "advanced democracy" and the most powerful country in the world—a country whose democratically elected president, Donald Trump, branded himself as a "stable genius" after doubt was expressed by his political opponents about his mental stability.

Some "totalitarian democracies" have emerged and are relying on these new, subtle forms of violence to perpetuate political and economic dominance. There is also a global uprising of angry, populist movements using digital means to express political opinions and to sway public opinion or even try to achieve political goals that they could not reach through the ballot box. The world is therefore getting used to violent forms of "freedom" and "democracies," from above (totalitarian elites) and from below (populist movements). Both the new "democratic" totalitarianism and the "riot democracies" (*démocracie de l'émeute*, as French President Emmanuel Macron referred angrily to the Yellow Vest movement[9]) are fueled by economic and identity fears.

The issue here is not that democracy is under attack, as is often stated in the mainly nostalgic literature devoted to recent global developments. Some researchers and commentators appear too afraid to seriously consider what has become self-evident: Democracy is both a great moral horizon and an impossible system of governance to conceptualize, apply consistently, and rigorously across time and places. This is especially relevant in a world where perceptions of economic inequality are growing, a world with an ineffective system of global governance (Crozier et al. 1975) and persistent imbalances in voice and power distribution between advanced industrialized nations and developing countries.

This chapter is about the need for intellectual reckoning. It starts with a commentary on what I call the "great discordance"—the paradoxical gap between secular improvements in democratization and economic well-being and the still-high levels of citizen anger and disillusion around the world (section 1). It then discusses the global, unsustainable democratic deficit, and explores its foundations—from the original sins of democracy to today's democratic trilemma, (i.e., the impossibility of building democratic systems that are ethical, based on efficient political institutions, and promote universal suffrage; section 2). The chapter ends with the conclusion that the main law of economics is to constantly subvert politics in ways that cannot allow democracy to be more than an abstract ideal (section 3).

1. The Great Discordance

Human societies everywhere are experiencing a great malaise. Despite the indisputable acceleration of the pace of technological innovations in the past three centuries, which has brought enormous economic gains to the world, raised global income, and improved welfare and the quality of life globally, despite improvements in self-reported levels of happiness in a handful of countries, the planet is still filled with rage and anger. People in countries at all income levels are expressing deep levels of mistrust and dissatisfaction vis-à-vis the quality and effectiveness of their elected political leadership, their formal institutional systems, and the prevailing rules of the game—which they have often validated through free and fair elections. This section discusses the new global economy of anger and its paradoxical explanations, mainly in economic terms (the feeling of rising inequality).

The New Economy of Anger

Anger and discontent levels around the world are high, even though most available indicators of political and economic progress are better than they have even been. This deep paradox reflects a great discrepancy: By all accounts, the world has never been a "better" place in which to live. On the broad historical front, empirical research in archeology, psychology, cognitive science, economics, and sociology suggests that things have never looked better for the human species. Any human being living today is much less likely to meet a violent death or to suffer from violence or cruelty at the hands of others than were people living in any previous known period of world history. Studies of the causes of death in different

eras and regions yield surprising results: Analyses of skeletons found at archaeo-
logical sites suggest that 15 percent of prehistoric humans met a violent death at
the hands of other persons (Pinker 2011).

By contrast, in societies organized around states with some forms of government,
the most violent appears to have been Aztec Mexico, in which 5 percent of people
were killed by others. The violent thirteenth-century Mongol conquests alone
caused the deaths of an estimated 40 million people—equivalent to 280 million
people today. During the bloodiest periods of European history (the seventeenth
century and the first half of the twentieth century), deaths in war were "only" around
3 percent. This "pacification process" (Pinker) was brought about by the state
monopoly on the legitimate use of force. It confirmed Hobbes's (1651) view that in
the absence of a state, life is likely to be "solitary, poor, nasty, brutish and short"
(*Leviathan*, xiii. 9). Empirical evidence shows that today's world is less violent, less
cruel, and more peaceful than during any previous period of human existence. The
decline in violence holds for deaths in war, murders of all sorts, fights in the family,
brutal tensions in neighborhoods, and the like. For instance, the chance of anyone
living in Europe being murdered is now less than one-tenth, and in some countries
only one-fiftieth, of what it would have been if they had lived 500 years ago.

On the political front, social science research also paints a good background
for optimism. Empiricists have described a generally positive democratic trend
over the past three centuries. Huntington (1991) famously identified three major waves, starting in the 1820s with the widening of suffrage to a large proportion of the male population in the United States, and continuing for almost a
century until 1926, bringing into being some 29 new democracies. In Huntington's view, the ascent to power of Benito Mussolini in Italy in 1952 marked a reverse of democratization in the world. A second wave of democratization
occurred after the triumph of the Allies in World War II, and a third one was initiated after the Portuguese military staged a coup against their authoritarian government, initiating profound political change that culminated in the emergence
of a democratic regime. This last wave was enhanced by the fall of the Berlin Wall
and the collapse of the communist regimes of East-Central Europe, and the spread
of democratic ideals around the world.

Huntington's thesis has gained worldwide influence despite its weak theoretical basis, the conceptual flaws underlying his analysis, and the arbitrary classifica-
tions of political regimes he used (Monga 1996). More recently, political scientists
have observed that even though many countries have succeeded in bringing down
authoritarian regimes and replacing them with freely elected governments, few of
them can actually be considered stable democracies. In the early 1970s, political
scientists observed that there were roughly 40 countries in the world that could be
rated as more or less democratic. As Diamond (1997, 2) explains:

The number increased moderately through the late 1970s and early 1980s as a number of states experienced transitions from authoritarian (predominantly military) to democratic rule. But then, in the mid-1980s, the pace of global democratic expansion accelerated markedly, to the point where as of 1996 there were somewhere between 76 and 117 democracies, depending on how one counts. How one counts is crucial, however, to the task of this essay: thinking about whether democracy will continue to expand in the world, or even hold steady at its current level. In fact, it raises the most fundamental philosophical and political questions of what we mean by democracy.[10]

Most of the countries labeled as "democratic" in recent decades still struggle to consolidate their new and fragile democratic institutions (Diamond 2015).

Parallel to the struggle to consolidate democracy is the well-observed disillusionment: participation in politics and in elections has been lower than one would have expected in many countries, while the ability of political parties and trade unions to mobilize voters and citizens has been declining.[11] The high levels of mistrust of political leaders and disillusionment with democratic institutions in countries labeled "new democracies" is surprising, given the significant reported improvements in the development of liberal democratic institutions, the extension of political rights and freedoms, and peaceful turnovers of power (Paller 2013). This great discordance appears to be even more puzzling when analyzed against the background of empirical research on the evolution of liberty and the effectiveness of political institutions, which consistently claims that democracy has taken root in all corners of the world: Long-term trends in "democratization" (regardless of how it is defined) show generally positive developments over the past half-century, despite some hiccups (figure 1.1).

The great discordance is also notable on the economic and social front. Empiricists provide strong evidence to support the thesis that things have also been moving in a positive direction. Living conditions around the world have improved over the past 200 years, at least at the global level. Figure 1.2 shows that in 1820, the vast majority of the world population lived in what would be considered extreme poverty today, while only a small fraction of the elite enjoyed higher standards of living (using the most common approach to poverty measurement sets, that is, a line with constant real value over time and space).[12] Since then, the share of extremely poor people has declined steadily, falling below 10 percent in 2015 (though global extreme poverty rose in 2020 for the first time in several decades as the disruption of the Covid-19 pandemic aggravated the negative impacts of conflict and climate change).

Similar positive trends can be observed on social issues: In 1820, 12.05 percent of the world population aged fifteen years and older was literate. In 2016, it was

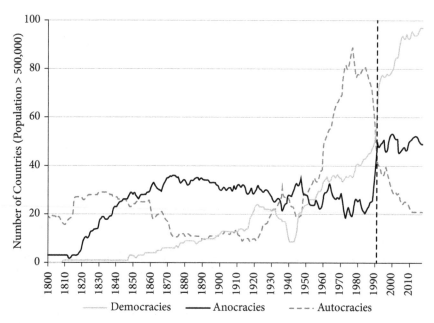

FIGURE 1.1.   Global trends in governance, 1800–2017.

Source: Center for Systemic Peace (2020).

86.2 percent (Roser 2017). During the same period, the proportion of the world's newborns that died before their fifth birthday declined from 43 percent to 4 percent, illustrating remarkable improvements in global health conditions.

Stressing such "astonishing progress," which he attributes primarily to policies supported by the world's elites, Zakaria (2019) sums up enthusiastically how things can be viewed from the perspective of the United States: "After 400 years of slavery, segregation and discrimination in America, blacks have been moving up. After thousands of years of being treated as structurally subordinate, women are now gaining genuine equality. Once considered criminals or deviants, gays can finally live and love freely in many countries. The fact that these changes might cause discomfort to some is not a reason to pause, nor to forget that it represents deep and lasting human progress that we should celebrate." Zakaria's very positive assessments of the evolution of the quality of life is consistent with Pinker (2011)'s praise of the "rights revolution," the revulsion against violence inflicted on ethnic minorities, women, children, homosexuals, and animals, which has developed in the second half of the twentieth century.

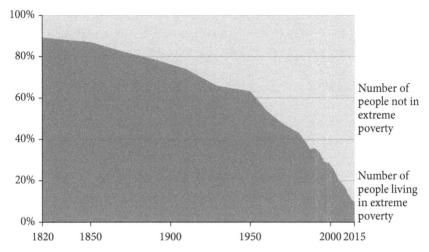

FIGURE 1.2.   World population living in extreme poverty, 1820–2015.
Extreme poverty is defined as living on less than 1.90 international-$ per day.
International-$ are adjusted for price differences between countries and for price
changes over time (inflation).

Source: Data published by World Bank and Bourguignon and Morrisson (2002).

In sum, just looking at the deep trend as measured by empiricists, global happiness should be on the rise, perhaps even exponentially. Yet sociopolitical well-being in various places around the world (in high- and low-income countries) has been marked recently mainly by anger, resentment, fears, identity conflicts, and the resurgence of populism and xenophobia.

How could this be? What explains the great discordance between the steady improvements in global political, economic, and social welfare reported by empiricists and the recent eruptions of anger observed in many places around the world? First, social and cognitive scientists are still struggling with theoretical and measurement issues surrounding comparative analyses of political well-being (Monga 2017). Various methodological problems must be addressed to elaborate intellectual and policy frameworks for making socially acceptable political decisions. One must obviously start with valid methods for defining, understanding, capturing, and measuring the notion of individual political well-being. The methods used for individual assessments should also be extended to social groups in ways that make such measurements meaningful and credible. All this supposes that individual preferences can be measured at a satisfactory level of confidence and that the intrinsic "subjectivity" in such exercises is more than compensated by the "objectivity" of the methods used. Yet the innate inability of human beings to look past their intrinsically self-centered natures, their shifting egos and psyches, and their unstable preferences; the impossibility of consistently defining their own tastes, feelings, and opinions; and the structural limitations of any attempt to consistently capture and aggregate the criteria for common well-being make interpersonal comparisons of political well-being a permanent challenge.

Second, it is difficult to determine rigorously whether the past was "good" or "bad," or to assess whether life is getting "better" or "worse." Milanovic (2017) explains this difficulty quite well. He points to the dominant narrative about the exhilarating days at the end of the Cold War and the longing "for a time when unstoppable victory of democracy and neoliberal economics was a certainty and liberal capitalism stood at the pinnacle of human achievement." He then contrasts that intellectual consensus with his own experience. He saw the end of the Cold War as an ambivalent event, which brought national liberation and the promise of better living standards to many people in Eastern Europe, but it was also traumatic for others because of the rise of vicious nationalism, wars, unemployment, and disastrous declines in income. His discomfort with triumphalism surrounding the fall of the Berlin Wall was compounded by the rather enjoyable memories he had of his childhood in former Yugoslavia: He never had to deal with collectivization, killings, political trials, endless bread lines, imprisoned free thinkers, and other stories that are currently published in literary magazines. On the contrary, he remembers "long dinners discussing politics, women and nations, long Summer vacations, foreign travel, languid sunsets, whole-night concerts, epic soccer games, girls in mini-skirts, the smell of the new apartment in which my family moved, excitement of new books and of buying my favorite weekly on the evening before the day when it would hit the stands" (Milanovic 2017).

Yes, indeed, comparing various periods in history may seem like a straightforward exercise when relying on empirical data. In fact, it is a rather subjective task. Although lots of historical and statistical evidence confirms that life on earth used to be shorter, sicker, riskier, and less free (with citizens generally having fewer options to express themselves), it does not necessarily follow that things are "better." As Rothman (2018) put it, "if being alive now doesn't feel particularly great, perhaps living in the past might not have felt particularly bad. Maybe human existence in most times and places is a mixed bag. . . . By an obscure retrospective calculus, the good appears to balance out the bad. Frightening events seem less so in retrospect. Memory is selective, history is partial, and youth is a golden age. For all these reasons, our intuitive comparisons between the past and the present are unreliable." Interpersonal comparisons of (political) well-being across time and place are conceptually as challenging as comparing a painting by nineteenth-century romanticist Eugène Delacroix to a book by Dante or García Márquez or

Pablo Neruda. This may partly explain why many attempts to explain the great discordance have focused on the economics of political disillusionment.

The Political Economy of the Elephant Curve

Why is there so much intellectual disappointment and popular anger with the political, economic, and social outcomes of "democratic" regimes, including in industrialized countries, such as the United States or the United Kingdom, with the oldest and strongest institutions? The most widely accepted explanation is the complex story of the dynamics of poverty and inequality, mainly within countries. "Inequality has been named as a culprit in the populist incursions of 2016 and 2017. But what is inequality, and what role does it play in inhibiting or encouraging growth, or in undermining democracy?" (Deaton 2017).

Let's start with the global story of poverty. It has declined around the world in recent decades, and this decline should generate higher levels of life satisfaction and perhaps enhance acceptance of the prevailing political institutions, at least in countries where strong progress has been recorded. Globally, economic growth typically comes with lower absolute poverty rates (figure 1.3).

The story of global inequality is different. It rose from 1820 to about 1990, driven mainly by divergent growth processes: with the Industrial Revolution, many of today's rich-world countries took off in the early nineteenth century (though there

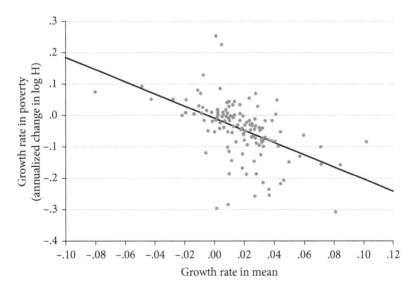

FIGURE 1.3.   Growth and absolute poverty. Slope = −2.2 (= 0.27).

Source: Ravallion (2016).

were some late starters). The pattern changed dramatically toward the end of the twentieth century (Ravallion 2020). High growth in Asia ignited a convergence process, which stimulated a decline in global *relative* inequality (measured using the ratios of incomes relative to overall mean) in the new Millennium (figure 1.4)

The decline in global inequality has meant that economic growth has had a larger impact on absolute poverty. But in itself, this is not enough to prevent popular anger and political protests. People are concerned about both absolute inequality (the absolute differences or the gap between rich and poor), and about the extremes. To understand how this can happen, let's consider two cities with only three inhabitants each, with the following wealth distribution:

- City A: $3, $6, and $9
- City B: $6, $12, and $18

Most relative inequality measures (such as the Gini index) would indicate that there is no difference between the two cities. Yet survey results of opinions about these two distributions would show that many respondents consider City B to have higher inequality. That is the power of popular perceptions and collective beliefs, which can lead to sociopolitical tensions and even social conflicts.

Looking closely at the story of changes in income distribution in the world over the two decades preceding the 2008 Great Recession, Lakner and Milanovic (2013) offer an "Elephant Chart" (figure 1.5), which has often been used to explain the disappointment with democratic political systems and the rise of populist

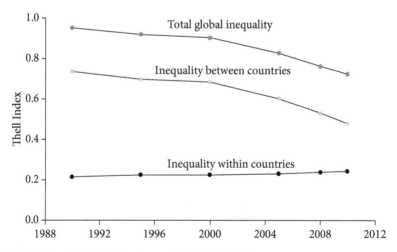

FIGURE 1.4.   Global relative inequality, 1990–2010.

Source: Bourguignon (2016).

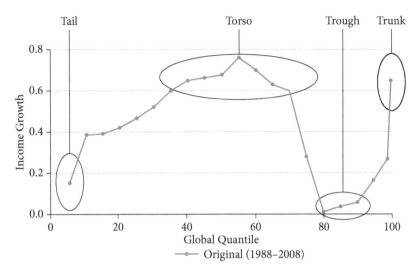

FIGURE 1.5.   Changes in income distribution in the world, 1988–2008.

Source: Lakner and Milanovic (2013).

movements.[13] Examining the income growth of each percentile of the global income distribution over two decades, the chart sheds light on which one has benefited the most from globalization (the world is viewed here as one country). The line on the chart starts low on the far-left end (the elephant's tail), then climbs to a peak (torso) before falling (trough) and then rising again to near-peak levels (trunk). It climbs sharply on the left to reflect how outcomes improved in the developing world from the fall of the Berlin Wall to the Great Recession. However, it also shows that the world's poorest—most of whom reside in Africa—are only slightly better off than in the past (the elephant's slumped "tail").

The world's middle class rose substantially and recorded gains, mainly because of the good catching-up performance of large emerging countries such as China— this is illustrated on the chart by the peak at the elephant's "torso." By contrast, the global upper middle class did rather poorly, with roughly zero growth in income over two decades—this is reflected by the depth of the trough at the bottom of the elephant's "trunk." The biggest winners are the top 1 percent, the elites among the world elites (mostly from industrialized countries), who have reaped massive income growth—shown by the elephant's upward "trunk." In other words, the right side of the chart shows how incomes declined dramatically for the working and middle classes in the developed world but soared for the planet's wealthiest people.

Some researchers chose to focus on the group in the middle of the Elephant Chart (a group assumed to represent mainly the low and middle classes of industrialized Western countries). The stagnant income at a time of increased global trade and investment was thought to be the main source of popular anger and rising identity politics in rich countries. Political conclusions were then drawn about the negative consequences of globalization (Krugman 2016). Yet there is no evidence or claim in the Lakner-Milanovic empirical analysis that workers in rich countries lost ground because of globalization. In fact, the evidence suggests that most workers in industrialized countries in all percentiles actually did well over the period analyzed, and that several fundamental changes other than globalization were important factors in income growth over time.

A subsequent study of the shape of the Elephant by Kharas and Seidel (2018) following the Lakner-Milanovic approach but using a different methodology[14] and extending the coverage with new data five years into the post–Great Recession era yielded broadly similar results, with some important caveats: Their version of the Elephant Chart depicts primarily a story of convergence, with poorer countries, and the lower income groups in those countries, having grown most rapidly in the measured two decades. Their analysis does not support the conclusion that the poorest people are being left behind, nor that the rich are taking all the income gains.

Inequality as Cholesterol: The Good and the Bad

In fact, the original Elephant Chart does not show how a specific group of people in the 80th percentile from 1988 fared over time. Rather, it compares *whoever* is in the 80th percentile in 1988 to *whomever* is in the 80th percentile in 2008, which may refer to completely different groups of populations (again, the chart takes the world as one country). To understand which groups are responsible for the shape in the chart, one must examine how the curve changes when holding populations constant and removing various countries.

Corlet (2016) digs deeper in that direction, focusing specifically on the experience of low- and middle-income households in the industrialized world. His analysis shows the dangers of using a global, multidecadal graph such as the Elephant Chart to draw conclusions about particular countries and particular groups within them. He finds that overall income growth is understated because of changing country selection (the globally poor in 1988 and those in 2008 are not necessarily the same groups of people; different countries are included in the datasets that underpin the chart over the two decades). For example, a percentile could include primarily Japanese households in 1988 and Russia in the next decade, because both countries recorded major changes in the composition of income distribution and population growth. Corlet also observes that population changes, rather than just income changes, have driven the income growth distribution in the Elephant Chart. Furthermore, the aggregate data hide big variations between advanced economies. In sum, "the zero growth doesn't imply that the incomes of the 80th percentile did not grow. Rather it shows that the 80th percentile in 1988 has roughly the same income as the 80th percentile in 2008. But these two groups may be composed of different populations" (Freund 2016).

Other factors may have determined changes in the income distribution curve. The fall of the Berlin Wall, followed by the fall of the Soviet Union, or the economic stagnation of Japan (caused mainly by its rapidly aging population) accounted for the stagnation or decline in income in those countries, irrespective of globalization. Policy shifts in some industrialized countries (especially on taxes) may also have played a role on the evolution of income for some social groups. It is therefore a leap of faith to use the Elephant Chart as evidence that globalization allowed poor countries to grow to the detriment of workers in rich countries, or to use it as a rigorous explanation for some of the unpredicted major political events the world has witnessed (Brexit, the Donald Trump election as US president in 2016, etc.).

This brings us back to the initial questions on the political significance of inequality and its potential relationships with democratic systems and the distribution of power in social institutions. "Inequality is not so much a cause of economic, political, and social processes as a consequence," says Deaton. "Some of these processes are good, some are bad, and some are very bad indeed. Only by sorting the good from the bad (and the very bad) can we understand inequality and what to do about it. Moreover, inequality is not the same thing as unfairness; and, to my mind, it is the latter that has incited so much political turmoil in the rich world today. Some of the processes that generate inequality are widely seen as fair. But others are deeply and obviously unfair, and have become a legitimate source of anger and disaffection" (Deaton 2017).

In other words, inequality can be viewed like cholesterol: There is the good and the bad. People happily accept differentials in income or wealth that originate from perceived hard work, a brilliant innovation by an inventor, or from a great idea that makes one person or group richer than others. Examples of such generally accepted sources of inequality include the inventions that spurred the industrial and health revolutions in the eighteenth century, making families and a few countries in northwestern Europe well off, but eventually also improving the living conditions and health outcomes for billions of people around the world. As Deaton puts it, "it is hard to object to innovators getting rich by introducing products or services that benefit all mankind" (Deaton 2017).

By contrast, Deaton argues, people object to inequalities that they attribute to unfairness. This is the case when the genesis of wealth is perceived to be from state capture or other unethical activities, or even from intergenerational inheritance that is perpetuated or amplified by tax systems and regulations. He also suggests that another reason for growing public discontent in the United States in particular is that median real (inflation-adjusted) wages have stagnated over the past fifty years (Guvenen et al. 2017), and people in the Western world object to government or university-sponsored programs that seem to favor particular groups, such as minorities or immigrants. "This helps to explain why many white working-class Americans have turned against the Democratic Party, which they view as the party of minorities, immigrants, and educated elites" (Deaton 2017).

The empirical evidence supporting such arguments is mixed, at best. To a certain extent, the divergence between median and top incomes in old democracies like the United States could indeed be the result of impersonal processes, such as globalization and technological innovation, which have devalued low-skilled labor and favored the well-educated.

Deaton is right in suggesting that inequality is not always unfair. However, his analysis leaves out the hysteresis effects of enrichment, and the subjective ways in which political anger often expresses itself—including in old democracies. Only an extremely small number of today's rich, educated elites were actually involved in any invention or innovation that improved life on earth. Even for the handful of families that may be associated with particular technological or scientific advances known to have created wealth, only an infinitesimal number can be viewed as benefiting from the fruits of their personal genius, talents, or luck. Then the question becomes whether intergenerational wealth and inequities should be widely accepted. For instance, Bill Gates or Steve Jobs have indeed found new ways of using computers and boosting productivity and human welfare. Should their accomplishments grant (almost) infinite intergenerational wealth to their descendants, even the laziest of their heirs? By such standards, anyone with Einstein's lineage should be entitled to lifetime riches and the potential for disproportionate levels of political and social influence.

In sum, Deaton's elegant conceptual distinction between the understandable (good) inequality and the unfair (bad) type is difficult to operationalize. It is based on the assumption that sources and uses of wealth, and the perception of wealthy people by the majority of the population, remain linear through time. That is rarely the case. Throughout human history, some deeply unethical practices have often yielded wealth that has been converted to good use. Trying to entangle which types of enrichment may be ethical and fair from the ones seen as unfair is not what angry protesters against injustice and the prevailing democratic systems do when they take to the streets, or when they choose not to vote and therefore raise abstention to levels, which may lead to questioning the legitimacy of certain elections. Empirical arguments and explanations linking political disaffection to inequality have some merit, but they remain insufficient to explain the deep levels of disillusionment observed around the world. Something more fundamental is going on: the unraveling of democratic myths in an era of global economic challenges, and the recognition that the ideals of democracy rooted in the law carry some intrinsic contradictions.

2. An Unsustainable Democratic Deficit

There has always been broad intellectual consensus about the primacy of the law, especially in its role as a codifier and underwriter of democratic political systems. Even people who disagree over everything tend to agree on the necessity of the law and the need to underpin it with some ethical foundations. This collective reverence for the law goes back at least to Plato's last and longest chapter in *Dialogues*, which is about laws. But why is it that the perceived virtues of the law do not translate into strong collective beliefs in "democratic" countries, where laws supposedly organize public life and few doubt the wisdom of a well-informed citizenry freely picking and choosing their systems of government and their leaders? Why is there so much disappointment and anger with democratic outcomes in "democratic" countries?

Recent political history in the Western world is particularly fascinating. In 2016, the great and well-educated people of the United Kingdom voted in a referendum to withdraw their country from the European Union. The minority who did not like the results still managed to slow down the implementation of the popular will and reopen the debate with the clear goal of reversing the outcome of a "democratic" exercise. The same deep feeling of dissatisfaction was observed after elections that were considered "free and fair" by the losing candidates led to power Presidents Donald Trump in the United States and Emmanuel Macron in France, and Prime Minister Victor Orban in Hungary. In all three countries, angry groups of citizens took to the streets to demonstrate their refusal to recognize these elected leaders, whom they viewed as illegitimate when they started implementing the political programs on which they had campaigned and won. In the United States, some important political leaders called for the impeachment of President Trump right after he took office, while the so-called Yellow Vest movement spread across France to call for the resignation of President Macron.

Yet the problem, if any, may not be with any one of these elected leaders but with the electoral system (Maskin and Sen 2017a,b), with the rules of the game, or even with the constitutions of these countries, which have been in force for decades and centuries and are generally considered as settled framework not to be amended, except in exceptional circumstances.[15] While the rationale for restraining the propensity to change constitutions and laws is understandable, as societies set rules to build enduring institutions, it also highlights one of the intrinsic contradictions of democratic consolidation: Why should people be bound by political principles and even institutions designed centuries earlier, in a world in constant flux? Chesterton once wrote: "Tradition means giving a vote to most obscure of all classes, our ancestors. It is the democracy of the dead" (1908, 85). A modern-day autocrat would probably welcome the opportunity to change a country's constitution and the rules of the political game any time, as often as necessary, to accommodate the political majority of the day, under the justification that such a system would ensure that the political architecture reflects the will of the people at any given moment. The ensuing political instability may just be the trade-off and the cost to bear to ensure that the citizens always have their say in how to continuously improve a democratic system.

Intriguing questions on the relationship between democratic systems and economic governance also arise when mainstream political leaders in "matured" democracies publicly state their strong belief that their country has turned to authoritarianism. Less than two years after leaving office, former French President Nicolas Sarkozy publicly accused his successor François Hollande of using the judiciary to pursue a personal vendetta against him. Sarkozy criticized the government and compared his country's judiciary to the East German Stasi (secret police). Judges had ordered Sarkozy's telephones tapped in the context of an investigation into his campaign finances.

In an open letter titled "What I Want to Say to the French," Sarkozy (2014) wrote:

> It is my duty today to break this silence. If I do so, it is because the sacred principles of our republic are trampled underfoot with unprecedented violence and absence of scruples. . . . Who could have imagined that, in 2014 in France, the right to privacy would be violated by telephone taps? The right to secret conversations between a lawyer and his client willfully ignored? . . . The right to presumption of innocence desecrated? Calumny established as a government method? The justice of the republic manipulated through calculated leaks? . . . Even today, anyone who calls me knows they will be listened to. You're reading correctly. This is not an excerpt from the wonderful film *Other People's Lives* about East Germany and the activities of the Stasi. It's not about the abuses of some dictator. . . . It's about France. . . . It would be laughable if it weren't a question of fundamental republican principles. The France of human rights has clearly changed. (Translation mine)

Similar public statements of disbelief vis-à-vis the validity of democracy with independent judiciaries were also made recently by former presidents of Brazil

(Luiz Inácio Lula da Silva and Dilma Rousseff) and South Korea (Park Geun-hye and Lee Myung-bak) when they were removed from office or sentenced to jail. The fact that they presided over very successful tenures at the helm of their nations did not protect them from what they considered to be politically motivated charges by perverted political and judiciary institutions. How can such strong, contradictory statements by credible political leaders who held the highest office in democratic countries be understood?

The Original Political Sin

Researchers around the world have struggled to make sense of the troubling recent political developments, their meaning, and their significance. A very large body of literature has erupted not just in the social sciences and the humanities but also in the "hard" sciences, with a wide range of commentaries and explanations of the reasons behind the so-called "crisis of democracy." Some have gone back to the appropriate scope of democracy and democratic systems, reopening the old debate on whether they should be limited to the design and implementation of institutions and rules for political governance and freedom, or whether they should also cover issues of social and economic equity to foster the development of inclusive societies (Held 1987). Others have attributed recent turmoil to the exponential development of technology in the age of enhanced globalization, with the infinite new ways of using new digital tools and platforms and even artificial intelligence to heavily influence and manipulate political actors and determine political outcomes.

Few researchers have questioned the continued validity and relevance of the highly abstract notion of democracy in a world where all its theoretical foundations and assumptions and its practical prerequisites (clearly defined citizenship acting freely on the basis of accurate information, well-functioning and neutral judiciary and administrative technostructure, etc.) are clearly unstable and often unreliable. Without a reexamination of the preconditions and requirements for democracy to mean more than a nice ethical horizon, analyses of the current "crisis" mainly reveal a broad intellectual malaise.

In their puzzled assessment of the state of democracy in the world, Pinker and Muggah (2018) observe that democracy has spread from one country to more than 100 countries in the space of two centuries but has also suffered setbacks along the way, and it continues to face resistance to this day. They conclude with the Churchillian statement that "democracy, after all, is not inevitable, and yet it remains the best system of governance compared to the known alternatives." It's a valiant and elegant attempt to rescue what is clearly one of the boldest human ideas. But it is also a naïve statement: The disappointments with the idea of democracy have been around since its inception.

In his exploration of effective and ethical forms of government, Plato noted in *The Republic* that democracies emerge as a result of discontent with oligarchy. But he quickly warned that democracies are susceptible to "tyranny of the majority" and rule by demagoguery for those who can subvert and use the institutions to their advantage (Sterling and Scott 1985). Plato even saw democracy as potentially more dangerous than oligarchy, as it motivates the anger of the poor (the largest social group) against the wealthy rulers, which eventually leads to anarchy and chaos. In fact, he pessimistically predicted modern-day populism and its poisonous effects on "democratic" systems. While the descent into tyranny has not occurred in countries that have credibly labeled themselves as democratic and have been largely viewed as such, the various degrees of popular discontent after democratic consultations in such places as the United States, the United Kingdom, or even the Philippines and Venezuela, point to the deep dissatisfaction with political systems that on paper are viewed as ideal.

There have always been mixed feelings about democracy, including from its strongest proponents. On one hand, its ideals are compelling and generally viewed as highly ethical, regardless of place and time. On the other hand, its implementation blueprint has often led to disagreements and impasses. Centuries ago, based on doubts about the optimality of universal suffrage and the recognition that not all citizens could ever have the same levels of understanding of critical issues (and the Bell curve distribution of educational levels in all countries), some societies came up with various strategies and mechanisms for making their representative democracies less vulnerable to and less dependent on the views of uneducated citizens.

One of the intrinsic contradictions of the democratic utopia is the basic fact that all voices are supposed to be given the same political weight, as all voters are considered equal, regardless of their backgrounds, understanding of the issues on the ballot, and even though they may hold different or even opposite beliefs and degrees of commitment to the ethics of democracy. With this postulate, the result of a democratic election is by definition the mere summation of opinions expressed in votes cast by people who may disagree even on the need for a democratic system, and certainly on the meanings and ideals of what that system should be. The rather primitive accounting exercise of amalgamating random thoughts and preferences that are often poorly developed by voters with a wide range of views on what citizenship is (or should be) is the original sin of democracy.

Throughout human history, taxation has been used not only as a means to fund the state but also as a criterion for legitimating citizenship.[16] Political philosophers and theorists, struggling with the challenge of operationalizing the ideal of democracy (power to every citizen) in a way that does not give the same weight to the votes of citizens of different levels of understanding of the issues of the polity, thought they could use the capacity to pay taxes as a justifiable and morally accept- able discriminant. By setting a certain level of tax contribution as a threshold of eli- gibility to be a voter, they could differentiate among citizens and ensure that only those able to pay would be voters. People in this category (mainly landowners, aristocrats, businessmen, and nobility) were assumed to be informed and educated enough to grasp and make good choices in the issues in play during elections.

To ensure high-quality debates without excessive conflicts among policymak- ers, John Locke recommended in the late seventeenth century that a smaller and more homogenous section of the people be allowed to participate in legislation "in proportion to the assistance which it affords to the public" (Sigmund 2005, 79). A by-product of this decision was often the logically limited amount of tax revenue available for redistribution and the relatively small size of the public sector.

At the 1787 Philadelphia Constitutional Convention, the same approach was considered, with several delegates suggesting the adoption of multiple voting rights depending on wealth. It took Madison's skills of persuasion to convince the framers of the US Constitution that the creation of the Senate with equal pow- ers was a better mitigating tool for the propensity to tax by the House of Repre- sentatives (Schön 2018).

Systems of suffrage based on a tax threshold (*suffrage censitaire*) were also adopted during the French Restoration and were praised as a balanced approach to liberal democracy by many influential thinkers. Even great minds such as Toc- queville (2004 [1835], chapter V) and Stuart Mill (1873 [1861], chapters 8 and 15) advocated such a discriminatory electoral system, not realizing that the very idea of making voting rights contingent on a particular level of wealth was a vio- lation of the basic principle of *demos-kratos*: Excluding some people from full citi- zenship because they cannot afford to pay tax is an undesirable way of giving them voice and achieving democracy.

These conceptual challenges have not yet been addressed satisfactorily—not even in the most advanced democracies. In some mature democracies, the proper criteria for assessing the degree of fairness of the voting process itself is still marred with controversies. In the United States, each major election is still tainted with charges of voter suppression.[17] In Europe, the politics of taxation and citizenship is still generating heated debates and anger, especially in an era when globaliza- tion of the world economy and the complexification of rules allow some of the largest international corporations to "optimize" their accounting strategies and minimize their contribution to public finances.

In sum, several centuries after the Enlightenment and despite nearly universal consensus on the ideal of democracy, the world is still nowhere near a basic common understanding of how it should be defined, implemented, and customized to a country's circumstances to reflect changing voter preferences. As noted by Engerman and Sokoloff (2005), extreme variation in the extent of political inequality among citizens in the same countries emerged early across the colonies established by the Europeans around the world. These contrasts have persisted over time through systematic differences in the ability and inclination of elites to shape legal frameworks to advantage themselves.

A Democratic Trilemma

It is tempting to consider the observed lapses in "democratic" countries as resulting only from poorly designed social and political institutions, as being the consequences of capitalism and globalization gone wild, or as reflecting the behavior of cynical political entrepreneurs who can cleverly engineer ways of riding popular anger and discontent about inequality or about "threatening" illegal migrants. Such analyses assume that democracy is a reasonably well-understood ideal, and that several centuries of intellectual debates and experiments (mostly in advanced industrialized economies) have led to a widely shared agreement on how to implement it successfully (a set of concepts, institutions, rules and regulations, and policies and practices). Nothing could be further from the truth. Despite numerous "foundational" documents, international covenants, and treaties, and a general agreement on a few basic, first-order principles, there is still no framework for credibly assessing democratic progress and consolidation in ways that are comparable across countries (Monga 2015).

All popular indices measuring democratization in the world (Polity IV, Freedom House Index, etc.) are based on subjective and often random assessments of what a mainly Western concept of democracy is supposed to mean across time and space. As a result, some version of habeas corpus (which has evolved considerably even in the United Kingdom since 1215) is subjectively evaluated by outside observers in twenty-first century Alaska, Angola, or Afghanistan. Not surprisingly, strong authoritarian leaders in Bolivia, Burundi, or Bhutan, who reject universalism and base their own judgment on relativism, oppose both the vague (Western) definition of democracy and the false "conventional wisdom" on how it should be implemented and monitored. Many political leaders in Asia also disregard Western approaches to democracy and articulate their own approaches to it, often focusing on meritocracy.[18]

Even in the Western world, where one would expect a strong, stable consensus on democracy, its scope, modus operandi, and criteria for validation, the disagreements among the players in the polity are regularly so deep that political arguments are still often settled through the instrumentalization of the courts or

through violent protests. That is why a French president elected on a clear platform of reform can be forced by a minority of violent protesters to make major
policy reversals. It is also why a former French president can publicly accuse the
government of his country of Stasi-like methods of government. That is why a
majority of the people of the United Kingdom can vote in a referendum to leave
the European Union (Brexit) and yet have their democratically expressed request
overruled by a political class not eager to act on it.

The main reason for the disappointments and constant uneasiness about the
democratic ideal is the trilemma preventing its full implementation. It is indeed
impossible for any society to achieve ethical democracy, as stated for centuries
by political philosophers and theorists and codified in a set of general principles
by the international community since the 1948 Universal Declaration of Human
Rights, while also having efficient political institutions and giving full voice to all
the people's choices (through universal suffrage). These three objectives are impossible to achieve simultaneously.

First, as stated in most constitutions around the world, ethical democracy
would require a well-informed citizenry committed, if not to high morals, then
at least to the highest standards in their quest for truth. This in itself is hard enough
to achieve, given the challenges of defining what the truth is or getting accurate
information that all citizens can process independently in the era of "fake news."

Second, the goal of efficient political institutions—defined as delivering in a
timely and cost-effective manner a set of widely accepted laws, rules, and regulations, ensuring that they are actually implemented and effectively monitored—
would entail more than the traditional forms of representative or participative
democracy currently in existence. In principle, representative democracy provides
a second layer of protection and safety mechanisms to ensure that not all wishes
of the people are taken at face value and that the political system is stable. Yet in
both "democratic" and "undemocratic" countries, voters and citizens are often
deeply disappointed with the quality of their political representatives, as evidenced
by the often very low approval ratings of their parliamentarians. Participative democracy allows citizens to get more directly and more often involved in setting
national priorities, selecting key policies, and deciding how to implement or stop
them. However, it can slow down the functioning of the political system or create
an atmosphere of constant uncertainty and fears of policy reversals that reflect
the shifting public mood.

Third, reliance on universal suffrage to give voice to every citizen and the
broadest legitimacy to the strategic choices and policies made in the polity entails granting every voter the absolute same level of trust in their "good" judgment. It also assumes that well-informed (and hopefully well-educated) voters
will wisely and honestly make "good" decisions—whether for themselves or for

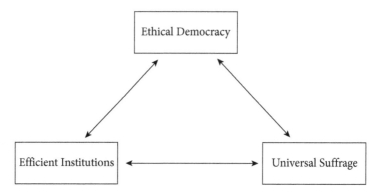

FIGURE 1.6.   A democratic trilemma.

society as a whole, without giving in to popular fantasies. Yet this objective is unrealistic, at least beyond a population of a certain size. Even in well-educated social groups, exit polls after elections always show a very wide range of preferences and determinants to their political choices. Following Rodrik (2011), it can be said that a democratic trilemma makes it impossible to achieve three of the major goals that constitute democratic ideals (figure 1.6). They are mutually incompatible: One can combine any two of the three, but never have all three been combined simultaneously and completely. This is a major reason for the global disenchantment with politics, the law, and globalization.

Market Failures in Democracy

In the memorable opening sequence of the movie *Spectre*, James Bond is chasing a hitman trying to bomb a major parade in Mexico during a celebration of the "Day of the Dead." In a rational quest for survival, they exchange fire as they try to kill each other, but only end up demolishing buildings, which fall on them. After miraculously escaping from the ruins, they keep fighting in a flying helicopter, which hovers and swoops in the air, both protagonists again making rational individual decisions that can only lead to bad outcomes for both of them.

Citizens and voters act in the same way. That is why political markets are messy everywhere—including in the so-called "advanced democracies." Both on the supply and demand sides, actors are often selfish and unstable in their preferences, and the rules (written and unwritten) are therefore unpredictable and unreliable. Social norms, group beliefs, and irrational fears play out in unexpected ways and are often compounded by external interference (by powerful international financial institutions imposing painful economic policies, influential countries seeking to promote their preferred candidate, or malevolent stakeholders and malicious hackers manipulating voters through fake news). Yet theories of democracy generally assume the existence of well-functioning institutions and systems, through which the supply of political ideas by rational political entrepreneurs (or other actors) and demand for such goods and services from citizens are mediated in political markets. These markets are assumed to have accurate and adequate information and are refereed by free media and other honest (if not "neutral") brokers. It is surprising that several centuries of political thought have relied on such an improbable set of assumptions.

Democracy market failures occur everywhere and can be defined as inefficient production and distribution of political goods and services in supposedly free countries, resulting in net political and social welfare loss. Political markets exhibit externality problems, even when they are deemed free (and therefore subject to the equalizing laws of supply and demand). These externalities make the quest for democracy and the process of democratic consolidation always chaotic or random. The individual incentives for "rational" behavior do not lead to "rational" outcomes by various groups or for the society. In other words, even when each citizen or voter makes what he/she perceives subjectively as the "appropriate" decision for him/herself, those decisions often prove to be suboptimal or even wrong and disruptive, in a steady state disequilibrium. A good indication of this is the trivial fact that few candidates would be elected to high office in any advanced democracy by campaigning on a fully truthful platform about the policies they actually intend to implement if elected.[19]

The emergence, spread/dissemination, legitimation, and consolidation of democracy can be fostered or impeded by positive and negative externalities. In all political markets—whether they are classified as democratic or not—positive political externalities arise when some citizens benefit from the actions taken by the few who are willing to take risks and even pay a high price to successfully advance the agenda of freedom. Of course, the risk-taker citizens cannot charge others for these benefits and might therefore not go as far as they would like. The quest for democracy should therefore account for the free-rider problem. Negative externalities also occur when one person's actions harm another. When polluting, factory owners might not consider the costs that pollution imposes on others.

More often than not, externalities undermine the political and social benefits of individual selfishness in the quest for democracy. If selfish citizens do not have to pay any price to enjoy the benefits of freedom and democracy, they will not pay. And if selfish political leaders do not believe that they will be rewarded for political works and risks, they will not devote their time, energy, and resources to the fight for democracy and freedom. An invaluable individual good, such as democracy or freedom, would not then materialize. As Friedman (1996, 278) states, the externality problem "is not that one person pays for what someone else gets but that nobody pays and nobody gets, even though the good is worth more than it would cost to produce."

"Democracy is for the Gods," Bradatan (2019) asserts. "Just scratch the surface of the human community and soon you will find the horde." He adds:

> Fundamentally, humans are not predisposed to living democratically. One can even make the point that democracy is 'unnatural' because it goes against our vital instincts and impulses. What's most natural to us, just as to any living creature, is to seek to survive and reproduce. And for that purpose, we assert ourselves—relentlessly, unwittingly, savagely—against others. We push them aside, overstep them, overthrow them, even crush them if necessary. Behind the smiling façade of human civilization, there is the same blind drive towards self-assertion that we find in the animal realm.

Such a somber prognostic echoes the analysis of zoologist Lorenz, who studied the aggressive behavior of animals and related his findings to the complicated nature of humans and modern society. It is "unreasoning and unreasonable human nature" that leads "two political parties or religions with amazingly similar programs of salvation to fight each other bitterly" (Lorenz 1966, 228–229). It is also that same animal, bestial, self-destructive drive that explains why an estimated 480,000–507,000 people have been killed in the post-9/11 wars in Iraq, Afghanistan, and Pakistan (Crawford 2018, 1).[20] This tally of the counts and estimates of direct deaths caused by war violence does not include the more than 500,000 deaths from the war in Syria, raging since 2011. The tally is an incomplete estimate of the human toll of killing in these wars. As Crawford also notes, it does not include "indirect deaths." Indirect harm occurs when wars' destruction leads to long-term, "indirect," consequences for people's health in war zones, for example, because of loss of access to food, water, health facilities, electricity, or other infrastructure.

Democracy is not a bad idea or an unworthy ideal. On the contrary. The point here is that it may just be too noble a horizon for humans to achieve, given their consubstantial taste for violent conflicts and oppressive manners, the genetic incompetence to address their own shortcomings, and their innate ability to credibly cast themselves as ethical creatures. Human societies have tried to mitigate the risks posed by their basic instincts and to mediate the disorderly political processes of conflicting claims from individuals and social groups by setting up various democratic institutions and adopting written and unwritten rules and other social norms.

In any political system, policies reflect the institutions and rules that determine resource allocation. Political actors choose to support, resist, or distort particular institutions or policies, depending on their interests and capabilities. As noted by Khan (2018, 636), "the distribution of organizational power can therefore determine the institutions and policies that are likely to persist as well as the ones most likely to be developmental in that context. This directs our attention to the importance of accurately identifying the relative power and capabilities of relevant organizations that describe a particular political settlement and how these may be changing over time."

The starting point of the reasoning here is that institutions function very differently across countries, because their political contexts are different. This has important implications for the design of governance priorities in different countries. The critical "democratic" questions then become the identification of the powerful and influential social groups, the criteria for the distribution of power among them, and how both the groups and the rules must change and evolve over time—hopefully as the economy grows and there are more income and rents to be shared. Holding power is partly based on income and wealth but also on historically rooted capacities of different groups to organize. "A political settlement emerges when the distribution of benefits supported by its institutions is consistent with the distribution of power in society, and the economic and political outcomes of these institutions are sustainable over time" (Khan 2010, 25).

In advanced countries, the distribution of power largely reflects the distribution of incomes generated by formal institutions and rights. In contrast, the distribution of power in developing countries is essentially a competition among informal sociopolitical institutions. This is the justification for a political settlements framework, which acknowledges that the distribution of organizational power is important for understanding the economic and political effects of institutions and policies (Khan 2018).

Self-proclaimed advanced democracies typically address these problems in two ways. The first is by setting rules for lobbying, defined as "the process of political influence by corporations and other business interests on elected officials or appointed bureaucrats through means of information or other resources—e.g., campaign contributions or employment opportunities—in the adoption, retention, or amendment of public policy" (Bombardini and Trebbi 2019, 2). The second way is by trusting that their independent judiciary serves as a referee of last resort to rule on political fights and disagreements.

While these solutions seem ethical and elegant, they fall short of addressing the core problem of fairness and equality among all citizens, which is the cornerstone of democracy. The main question about lobbying is whether it is a legitimate and valid political mechanism "to represent their client's interests by educating lawmakers and their staff about the effect any proposed legislation or regulation will have on their client . . . [and] to petition the government," as the US National Institute for Lobbying and Ethics (a trade association representing American lobbyists) indicate in their mission statement (n.d.), borrowing from the First Amendment of the US Constitution. Or is it a mechanism allowing powerful businesspeople to legally distort public policy from the social optimum, subvert democracy, and create opportunities for state capture and corruption?

Regardless of how transparent and stringent the rules on lobbying are, empirical studies show that they almost always lead to suboptimal and often unethical outcomes.[21] As for the independence of the judiciary, it has been challenged regularly in all so-called advanced democracies, often by the very people at the highest levels in government whose primary responsibility is to monitor the rule of law: world leaders US President Donald Trump, French President Nicolas Sarkozy, and Brazil's Presidents Dilma Rousseff and Lula da Silva, among others, have publicly expressed strong opinions about the politization ("weaponization") by their opponents of the judiciary in their own countries. Whether their claims were factually accurate matters little. If the first magistrate of an "advanced democracy" is of the view that the country's democratic system is not functioning well or has been hijacked by his/her political opponents, the end result will be disappointing: large fractions of voters and citizens in the United States, France, and Brazil feel the same about their political systems as do many people in Venezuela, Burundi, or Myanmar.

Democratic market failures are also obvious in the structural problems exhibited by judicial systems everywhere. Some "advanced democracies" claim colorblindness but enact policies that scapegoat marginalized social groups. For instance, in the United States, an increasingly high number of citizens lose their voting rights and are disenfranchised by the inimical legal system that is supposed to protect them from political abuse. Since the 1980s, the US prison population has risen from about 300,000 to more than 2 million. This trend has been fueled by drug convictions, with a disproportionate number of new felons being African Americans.

Legal scholars have shown that this is not coincidental: Because first-time drug offenders can face ten years imprisonment in many states, thousands of African-Americans, fearing these mandatory sentences, enter plea bargaining and find themselves in jail for crimes they did not commit (Alexander 2010). On release, they are pushed into a shadow society, where employment opportunities are nonexistent, and trapped in "a closed circuit of marginality." Evidence of discrimination by the judicial system is provided by the following facts. In 2000, the National Institute on Drug Abuse reported that white students used crack cocaine at eight times the rate of black students; and while cocaine is indeed a scourge in

US society, drunk driving (by white men 70 percent of the time) results in far more violent deaths, yet drunk drivers are often charged only with misdemeanors. Such structural problems in the judicial system—which is the main monitoring and regulatory institution in all political markets—make the quest for sustainability and validity of democracy everywhere almost a matter of subjective appreciation.

Myths of the Representative Citizen and Omniscient Political Agents

The scene, broadcast live on television worldwide in November 2011, shocked the world. Standing on the podium among eight fellow Republican presidential candidates at Oakland University in Michigan, Texas Governor Rick Perry sought to prove he had the best ideas, know-how and leadership skills to pull the United States out of its worst period of economic stagnation since the Great Depression. He turned toward his toughest opponent, fellow Texan Senator Ron Paul, looked him in the eyes, extended his left arm in a very compelling manner and gestured to highlight his argument:

> "I will tell you: it's three agencies of government when I get there that are gone," he stated forcefully. Counting with his fingers: "Commerce [*raising his thumb*], Education, [*raising his index finger*], and the . . . [*raising his middle finger*] what's the third one there? . . . Let's see . . . [*touching his forehead in embarrassment*]." (Reilly 2016)

The crowd erupted in laughter and disbelief. It was terrible optics for the governor of one of the largest states in the United States running for president and not being able to remember the three departments of government that he had identified as deserving to be shut down if elected. In his stump speech on the campaign trail in the previous weeks, he had mentioned the Energy department as the third one to be abolished.

That evening, on live television, Governor Perry was pushed by the moderator of the debate to finish his thought:

> "But you can't name the third one?
>
> "The third agency of government . . . I would do away with Education, the . . . Commerce [*after one of his opponents came to his rescue and reminded him*], and . . . let's see . . . [*looking at his note while grimacing*] I can't . . . the third one . . . Sorry. I can't . . . Oops!"

It was a painful episode to watch, regardless of how one felt about Governor Rick Perry. The video clip of the sequence went viral. The following days, the headlines were about "the worst stumble of the presidential campaign." Governor Perry quickly dropped out of the race.

Fast forward, five years later. President Donald Trump, newly elected, picked the former Texas Governor as Energy secretary, the very department whose name he famously forgot in the television debate. During his tenure as governor, Rick Perry called for lighter regulation of the oil industry and referred to the science around climate change as "unsettled." He was picked to oversee the development, stewardship, and regulation of energy resources, safeguard the nuclear arsenal, and promote America's energy policy. Environmental groups reacted angrily to his nomination and confirmation by the US Senate, calling his selection "an insult to our functioning democracy."

Fast forward, two more years. US Secretary of Energy Rick Perry talked for 22 minutes on the phone with a man he thought was the prime minister of Ukraine. In fact, he was actually speaking to a Russian prankster known for targeting high-profile politicians and celebrities. During the call, the man in charge of the world's biggest stockpile of nuclear warheads was misled to discuss with hackers US coal exports to Ukraine, a proposed energy pipeline across the Baltic Sea, and a (fake) new source of fuel derived from manure and homemade alcohol (Wootson 2017). Such a level of vulnerability for a country whose democratic institutions are supposed to be the strongest and have been functioning for centuries is surprising. Again, one must remember that this was not happening in Azerbaijan, Bolivia, or South Sudan, but in the United States of America, the country whose defense budget is the largest in the world.

Perhaps no one should have been surprised about how all this unfolded in one of the world's oldest democracies. First, that Governor Rick Perry struggled to recall the name of one of the three government agencies he vowed to cut if elected president should not have been disqualifying: His disastrous brain-freeze on live television in 2011 simply showed that he was only human, despite being a major political figure. After the debate, Perry's campaign advisors had sought to contain the damage by describing the stumble as "a human moment" and "authentic." They could have just explained that Rick Perry was an ordinary human being.

Likewise, the outrage at his intellectual meltdown under pressure in front of a global television audience mainly reflected the unrealistic expectation of constant brilliance and infallibility, which viewers, voters, and citizens have vis-à-vis political figures. Democracy is supposed to function well with good and ethical leaders who have emerged from a competitive process mediated by legitimate institutions and social norms. Yet political markets are structurally dysfunctional everywhere in the world, because they involve fallible and often unreasonable actors, both on the demand and the supply sides, and there are no neutral "regulatory" authorities to ensure predictable outcomes of the interactions. In economics, the price mechanism and the often clearly identifiable interests of the various agents can help predict the outcomes with a high degree of accuracy. That is rarely the case in politics, where the heterogeneity of agents is acute, and their stated individual goals and preferences are more unstable (Monga 2017).

The rational choice models used by political scientists and democracy theorists to study political markets often assume the existence of a mythical representative citizen (or political leader or voter). All such rational citizens are supposed to behave and act in such a manner that their cumulative actions might as well be the actions of one agent maximizing his/her expected political utility function. Researchers construct representative agents to deal with the complicated issue of aggregation (the summing up of individuals' behaviors to derive the behavior of a political market or an economy). The biggest assumptions underlying such a reasoning is that political markets are complete (in the economic sense; that is, they offer at least as many assets with linearly independent payoffs as there are states of the world, and every political agent can exchange ideas, services, or goods, with every other agent without substantial transaction costs). Theories of democracy also assume that political markets are competitive and that citizens and voters have homogeneous beliefs and time-additive, state-independent utility functions that are strictly concave, increasing, and differentiable. This is obviously not the case, not even in "advanced democracies."

Modeling the behavior of one person given some preferences and constraints is a rather straightforward exercise. Modeling the behavior of a group of people, or an entire economy, is a more challenging and less elegant task. Still, it is an unrealistic assumption to consider that the choices of all the diverse voters, citizens, and political leaders in the polity—even in one small village—can be viewed as the choices of one "representative" standard utility–maximizing individual whose choices coincide with the aggregate choices of heterogeneous individuals.

Real-life political stories of the Rick Perry type also show why democracy theories—based on the reduction of the behavior of heterogeneous agents (politicians and citizens) to a single, stylized version of what it should be—may be analytically convenient but are utterly unrealistic and lead to misleading conclusions, even if all these agents are utility maximizers. Such models are particularly ill suited to studying politics, which often involves coordination failures. Unfortunately, the more promising analytical approaches, which focus on heterogeneity of agents and interactions among individuals, are still rarely used in the study of politics and democracy (Kirman 1992; Maliar 1999). Rick Perry was a "representative" political agent only in the sense that all his competitors supplying political goods and services could have exhibited the same flaws that he displayed on television. He was not a stylized, imaginary, well-informed and infallible utility maximizer in the supposedly free market of politics.

There is wide consensus among political theorists that an educated, well-informed, and well-meaning citizenry aware of and concerned with individual (personal) and collective (social) interests is indispensable for democratic consolidation. Yet little empirical evidence supports that proposition. Nations with the largest share of highly educated citizens do not necessarily fare well on measures of democratization—regardless of the validity of these indicators. Countries such as the United States and the United Kingdom exhibit the highest mean years of schooling in the world (13.4 and 12.9 in 2017, respectively).[22] Yet their electorate is prone to abrupt shifts in mood due to the sirens of populism, for instance, and their supposedly educated voters and citizens appear as vulnerable to fake news and political manipulations as those living in countries with low levels of mean years of schooling, such as Afghanistan (3.8) or Burkina Faso (1.5). The embarrassing question then becomes whether even highly educated citizens can be trusted to make "good" and "free" judgments in their important civic duties and to make their legitimate democratic systems function properly.

The weak correlation between schooling and democratic ethics is even more apparent when one looks at India, the most populous and therefore "largest democracy in the world." One can only be puzzled by the deep sociopolitical trends observed there in recent decades. Despite failing to deliver on his 2014 campaign promises to bring stronger economic growth to India and rid the country of corruption and dynastic politics, Prime Minister Narendra Modi was reelected in 2019 with an even greater mandate. During his first term, his government had to weather the fallout from a disastrous demonetization scheme. Ethnic violence also increased significantly—fueled by the rise of Hindu nationalism (Hindutva). As perplexed political experts searched for explanations, Sharma (2019) commented: "We do not live in Modi's India. We live in Indians' India, and the reason so many Indians adore Modi is because he represents their preferred conception of the Indian nation. No other explanation for [his] results is as compelling."

Modi's reelection against the backdrop of lower-than-anticipated economic performance and heightened political violence can also be analyzed as evidence of the breakdown of the unethical political equilibrium, which has been part of Indian politics for decades. On one side are some extreme proponents of Hindu nationalism who have been trying to create a dominant Hindu identity; on the other side are caste-based parties or region-based parties opposed to the emergence of Hindu majoritarianism. Modi's success reflects the prominence of the former group—and his ability "to mobilize a fairly wide cross-section of Indians across different castes into a larger Hindu narrative" (Pratap Bahnu Mehta, quoted in Chotiner 2019).

It is perplexing that these two forces—neither of which would be described as truly embodying the democratic ideals and values as articulated, for instance, by

Sen (1999)—helped keep India's political system stable only by neutralizing each other. It is even more bewildering to notice that both groups have been striving and sustained with support from well-established and deeply entrenched local, traditional, religious groups and nongovernmental organizations. After all, such civil society organizations are expected to serve as backbone for the design, implementation, and monitoring of democratic institutions (Diamond 1994; Monga 1996; Putnam 2000; Tocqueville 2004). The battle of narratives between proponents of Hindu cultural majoritarianism and those protecting "lower" caste identities complicates the quest for ethical, altruistic forms of democracy. In fact, many of these groups are uncivil societies, as they can produce negative social capital (Monga 2009).

All these examples illustrate a global picture of democracy as one of the brightest human ideas but still more abstract than practical, and certainly not rooted in a valid theory of free political markets with representative citizen and omniscient political agents.

3. The Law of Economics: How to Gain Democratic Credentials

One would have thought that some 2,422 years after the Greeks articulated the need to associate the notions of "demos" and "kratos," more than 800 years after the Magna Carta, 243 years after the American Revolution, and nearly three quarters of a century after the adoption of the Universal Declaration of Human Rights by the "international community," human societies must have articulated and learned enough about democratic forms of governments to be able to formulate and implement a broadly accepted consensus on what the fundamental principles and modus operandi are. One would have expected that philosophers, political theorists, and other social scientists would have offered by now a robust framework for comparative analyses of the levels and effectiveness of democratization processes around the world.

Yet the world is far from it, as shown by the semi-chaotic transition between the presidencies of Donald Trump and Joe Biden in the United States in 2020–2021. Even the oldest "democracies" seem to function in ways that are reminiscent of regimes that are classified as autocracies, often with leaders at the highest levels of responsibility acting in ways that are considered unlawful and utterly immoral by their own peers. The traditional excuse that when such undemocratic and unethical patterns of behavior occur in countries with strong, independent, and credible legal systems, those systems are keeping even the most powerful politicians in check no longer holds: The judiciary has been politicized, instrumentalized, or circumvented in most "democracies" (Alexander 2010). In some advanced democracies, the prevailing laws and regulations grant more than enough space to political leaders to act in ways that would be viewed as autocratic, illegal, and immoral in developing countries with political and legal systems labeled "undemocratic."

Perhaps the most glaring recent illustration of this is the way the international community, self-proclaimed guardian of democratic values and models of good global governance, reacted to the medieval-style murder of the famous Saudi journalist Jamal Khashoggi in 2018. The US president, leader of the Free World, issued a statement (White House 2018) that read:

> The world is a very dangerous place! . . . The crime against Jamal Khashoggi was a terrible one, and one that our country does not condone. Indeed, we have taken strong action against those already known to have participated in the murder. After great independent research, we now know many details of this horrible crime. We have already sanctioned 17 Saudis known to have been involved in the murder of Mr. Khashoggi, and the disposal of his body. . . . This is an unacceptable and horrible crime. . . . That being said, we may *never* know all of the facts surrounding the murder of Mr. Jamal Khashoggi. In any case, our relationship is with the Kingdom of Saudi Arabia. They have been a great ally in our very important fight against Iran. The United States intends to remain a steadfast partner of Saudi Arabia to ensure the interests of our country, Israel and all other partners in the region. . . . After my heavily negotiated trip to Saudi Arabia last year, the Kingdom agreed to spend and invest $450 billion in the United States. This is a record amount of money. It will create hundreds of thousands of jobs, tremendous economic development, and much additional wealth for the United States. Of the $450 billion, $110 billion will be spent on the purchase of military equipment from Boeing, Lockheed Martin, Raytheon and many other great U.S. defense contractors. If we foolishly cancel these contracts, Russia and China would be the enormous beneficiaries—and very happy to acquire all of this newfound business. It would be a wonderful gift to them directly from the United States!

If there was ever a public, "official" announcement of the death of democracy, whatever it meant, it is probably that self-explanatory statement by none other than the occupant of the White House. The dazzling candor from the leader of the most powerful democratic country in the world delegitimizes the notion that there is an ethical global order out there, and that people living in autocracies should aspire to. It also annihilates the romantic dream that advanced democratic countries carry and hold dear a set of values that make their political systems "better" and give credibility to the human collective quest for morality in governance.

As striking as it may have appeared, the White House statement of moral equivalence between the extraordinary killing and dismembering of the body of a journalist in plain sight, and the decision to ignore it (beyond even symbolic verbal criticism) so as to preserve some business transactions was nothing unusual. For centuries, the leaders of powerful "democratic" countries have behaved in a similar way and consistently shown willingness to overlook the crimes of allied countries and autocrats deemed strategically valuable to their interests. Strategic amnesia has often helped many world leaders lower the standards of global political governance and renege on their democratic duties by silently condoning brutal practices by authoritarian regimes identified as friendly.

Researchers have documented the brutality and negative externalities of military, active political interventions conducted by Western powers to overthrow democratically elected leaders in Iran (Mohammad Mosaddegh in 1953), Chile (Pinochet in 1973), and Congo (Patrice Lumumba in 1960). These Western powers have also freely selected and appointed political leaders inclined to support their mainly economic interests (Péan 1983, 2014; Smith and Glaser 1992, 1997). This problem is pervasive: Several UN secretaries general who have released their memoirs after their tenure at the helm of the world's multilateral political body have revealed the propensity of leaders in supposedly democratic countries to condone, if not organize, undemocratic practices around the world (Boutros-Ghali 1999; Annan 2013, 2014).

In the name of liberty and democracy, to be spread throughout the world, international law has also been instrumentalized to create new norms of global governance applied inconsistently, as they actually serve to identify and punish political leaders from non-Western countries viewed as undesirable. The International Criminal Court (ICC), created to judge individuals for genocide, war crimes, crimes against humanity, and aggression, has been the main tool for such calculated arbitrariness. Its jurisdiction and legal process have been crafted to grant broad leeway to the most powerful countries in the world, whose leaders can pick and choose their targets for referral to the ICC: Prosecutions are for crimes committed by a State Party national, or in the territory of a State Party, or in a State that has accepted the jurisdiction of the ICC; or the crimes must have been referred to the ICC prosecutor by the UN Security Council pursuant to a resolution adopted under chapter VII of the UN charter. These two conditions have allowed the world superpowers to basically decide who should be prosecuted by the ICC, which means arrested and imprisoned for many years while awaiting trial—even though in a number of high-profile cases, the ICC itself ended up dropping all charges and releasing political leaders whose life and careers had been ruined.[23] Moreover, the fact that powerful UN Security Council member countries, such as the United States, China, and Russia (some of whom are quite vocal on their defense of freedom and democracy in the world), have not even ratified the ICC's founding treaty (Rome Statute), has led to strong opposition in many parts of the world about its legitimacy.[24]

Finally, tactical repentance is also used by the "leaders of the Free World" (typically after leaving office) as a way of expressing remorse or to try to justify their inaction in the face of egregious violations of human rights, or their military interventions around the world in violation of international law. One would have expected that world leaders who engage in costly wars in foreign countries far away from their national boundaries would have learned from the Vietnam War mistakes, well acknowledged by former US Defense Secretary Robert McNamara, who led that war effort. Yet they still engage in wars not authorized by the UN Security Council, and they selectively and inconsistently overthrow authoritarian regimes (sometimes after supporting them for long periods of time). After classified documents released in 2004 revealed that the Clinton administration knew of a "final solution to eliminate all Tutsis" well in advance of the 1994 genocide, which left some 800,000 people dead in just a few weeks in Rwanda, the former US president admitted: "If we'd gone in sooner, I believe we could have saved at least a third of the lives that were lost . . . it had an enduring impact on me."[25] Likewise, after he left office, former US President Barack Obama said that failing to prepare for the aftermath of the 2011 ousting of Libyan leader Muammar Gaddafi was the "worst mistake" of his presidency. Libya became "a mess" (Obama's words quoted by Goldberg 2016) and fell into a long civil war that spread into neighboring countries.

If the "international community," self-identified as the custodian of liberty and democracy, is actually an evolving union of Western heads of state whose value scale depends much less on moral standards and ethical practices than on their random perceptions of their often-changing countries' interests, if the propensity of world leaders to speak out or to act in defense of their own conception of human rights and freedom is inversely proportional to the business deals available to their firms, then democracy has to be unmasked: It is an ineffectual concept, especially when used for comparative political analysis.

What conclusion can be drawn from all this? What should developing-country tyrants do to find acceptance as legitimate members of the club of world leaders committed to the virtues of "democracy" and the rule of law? The Machiavellian straightforward answer is that building or advertising the wealth of their nations and picking their allies from among the superpowers are the real criteria for being granted membership in the democracy club.

Recent global political developments have simply confirmed that the very idea of democracy is still mainly an abstract ideal for human societies struggling to come up with the most ethical and ambitious modes of self-government. Democracy does not lend itself easily to the big questions it was supposed to address at inception: Who should measure, assess, and judge the quality of freedom and democracy and political well-being in general, and what framework should be used to do it? From a comparative perspective, anchored in a set of constitutional and legal texts and widely accepted political and social norms, democratization has always carried an intrinsic contradiction.

On one hand, a prescriptive universalist approach based on strong (if not rigid) specific principles and modus operandi derived from international covenants and valid in all places and at all times would make democratization a totalitarian framework. Moreover, the postulate that founding documents (such as constitutions) should not be tampered with, except in exceptional circumstances requiring near unanimous consensus, negate the very basis of law and freedom, which is legitimacy. Why should American citizens in the twenty-first century be bound by political decisions and preferences expressed from 1776 and 1787 by a group of "Founding Fathers" (most of them slave owners) who successfully led the war for independence from Great Britain, wrote the Declaration of Independence, and inspired the US Constitution? Why should French citizens in 2019 be compelled to live their lives under a Constitution adopted in 1958? For how long should such adherence to political "traditions" go on?

On the other hand, a totally flexible approach to assessing democratization, allowing for particular features and preferences (or lack thereof) in various nations and regions at various times, would make it a more vulnerable political concept: It could be hijacked by cultural relativists and autocrats around the world to justify oppressive forms of government. Yet beyond these conflicting approaches, there is a need to organize the polity in ways that make it stable, legitimate, and also reflective of constantly evolving social preferences (Monga 2015).

Humans claim to be the most sophisticated and intelligent beings who have ever lived in the universe. This assertion is based on the presumably superior nature of the human brain and the many spectacular achievements of the species—from sending humans to the moon to building robots who may soon be able to "think." The breathtaking creativity of the human mind, the relentless passion for research, and the remarkable pace of innovation observed around the world over several millennia can indeed be viewed as preliminary evidence of the seemingly inexhaustible capabilities of one of the species of primate. Still, this intrinsically bright species has remained incapable of finding the appropriate institutions and laws for governing themselves democratically in a world where economic interests determine the ethics of governance and ultimately shape individual and collective behavior.

Notes

1. The entire process is carried out under the executive branch of the US government—with no role, no checks, and no oversight of any kind by the US Congress or by the judiciary. All decisions, the basis for making them, their implementation, and evaluation are secret.

2. In some ways, this new global chase fits into the long history of manhunts and resembles the great hunts of the past—tracking, cornering, controlling, and capturing (Dorlin 2017).

3. Interestingly, in the early 2000s, when then–US President George W. Bush invoked executive privileges to justify his refusal to disclose the memoranda from his Office of Legal Counsel (OLC) that legally authorized torture of presumed terrorists, rendition (the clandestine delivery of prisoners in US custody to other countries, where they can be subjected to harsh interrogation techniques), warrantless eavesdropping, and other bizarre practices, some well-known American lawyers, such as Dawn Johnsen (President Obama's first choice to lead the OLC), opposed it. They denounced the Bush practice as a grave threat to human rights, democracy, and freedom, warning that "the Bush Administration's excessive reliance on 'secret law' threatens the effective functioning of American democracy" and "the withholding from Congress and the public of legal interpretations by the [OLC] upsets the system of checks and balances between the executive and legislative branches of government" (Greenwald 2013). President Obama repeatedly refused to disclose the principal legal memoranda prepared by his own OLC lawyers that justified his "disposition matrix" and kill lists. He vigorously resisted lawsuits from institutions friendly to his administration (such as the *New York Times* and the American Civil Liberties Union) to obtain the OLC memorandum. Eventually, a "white paper" produced by the lawyers of the US Department of Justice was released, purporting to justify the US president's power to target even Americans for assassination without due process. It was presented as a summary of the still concealed confidential memorandum and titled: "Lawfulness of a Lethal Operation Directed against a US Citizen Who Is a Senior Operational Leader of Al-Qa'ida or an Associated Force." It basically equates any government *accusation* of terrorism with proof of guilt. In other words, a few people in the executive branch of the government simply have to assert without the burden of evidence or trial that any person anywhere on earth is a terrorist, to be believed at face value, and be granted the legal right to "dispose" of that person as they deem appropriate—with indefinite imprisonment or death.

4. The center of gravity of the world economy has moved from West to East, with China becoming the biggest contributor to global growth and soon to be the largest economy. Defying doomsday predictions, China's authoritarian political system has resisted shocks and crises, to the point of being viewed as an alternative model of governance to countries in various corners of the world (Bell 2015).

5. See Johnson and Clack (2015) on the consequences of military interventions.

6. In 2017, China adopted its National Intelligence Law that requires all its organizations and citizens to assist authorities with access to information. The Chinese law, which the United States claims is a tool for espionage, interference in national political matters, and possible manipulation of voters, has been cited by President Donald Trump's administration as a reason to avoid doing business with companies like Huawei Technologies Co. The following year, the United States enacted the Cloud Act (or the "Clarifying Lawful Overseas Use of Data Act"), requiring all US cloud service firms (Microsoft, Amazon,

IBM, etc.) to provide US authorities with data stored on their servers regardless of where it is housed (Fouquet and Mawad 2019).

7. "Humanity is on the verge of being reborn in a second form thanks to an intrinsic transformation of the horizon of calculation and an almost indefinite expansion of the apparatus of quantification" (Mbembe, 2019).

8. A good illustration of one of the rather naïve initiatives to revitalize the idea of democracy is the 2019 "Declaration of Principles for Freedom, Prosperity, and Peace" issued by a group of self-proclaimed "citizens, former officials, and representatives of governments and private entities, united by common values" (https://www.atlanticcouncil.org/wp-content /uploads/2019/02/Declaration_of_Principles.pdf). The declaration starts with the observation that many people, including citizens in "free" societies, have grown skeptical of democracy, open markets, and international institutions, and that nationalism, populism, and protectionism are ascendant, with "authoritarian" powers such as China and Russia seeking to weaken "Western solidarity and liberal values." This manifesto then claims that for seven decades, free nations have drawn on common principles to advance freedom, increase prosperity, and secure peace, and that "the resulting order, built on the foundation of democratic values and human dignity, has brought better lives for our citizens and billions of people around the world." Ironically, the manifesto ignores the fact that much of the increase in global prosperity observed in the world in the past four decades was due to China (which the authors of the manifesto consider to be a threat to freedom and Western values) and was also responsible for a large fraction of the reduction in poverty in the world.

9. The French Yellow Vest protest movement began in November 2018 as an act of defiance against the government's plan to raise fuel taxes, a decision presented as a measure to help France combat global climate change. It then became a rallying cry against President Emmanuel Macron (elected less than two years earlier), perceived by many as an out-of-touch "president of the rich." Crowds started protesting every Saturday throughout the country, demanding higher wages as well as greater social and fiscal justice. In some places, the protests turned into riots that rampaged against banks, businesses, and some iconic monuments.

10. See also Monga (2002) for a theory and empirics of democratic consolidation.

11. Gallup polls indicate that in August 2018, Americans' approval of the work the US Congress stood at only 17 percent, which was also about average for the previous 17 months. See https://news.gallup.com/poll/240896/congressional-approval-steady-low-august.aspx.

12. Extreme poverty is measured by World Bank researchers. It refers to people living on less than $1.90 per day. It takes into account nonmonetary forms of income, which are important for poor families relying on subsistence farming. The extreme poverty measure is also corrected for different price levels in different countries and adjusted for price changes over time. For a discussion of the pros and cons and the methodological challenges in this approach and the general issues with global poverty lines, see Basu (2015a,b) and Osberg and Xu (2008), and Deaton (2005).

13. *Washington Post* journalist O'Brien (2016) commented that it is "the most important chart for understanding politics today."

14. The Kharas-Seidel (Kharas and Seidel 2018) method, called a quasi-non-anonymous growth incidence curve, holds the country composition of each global decile or vigintile constant across time, which sheds light on the gains or losses of specific economic classes in specific countries over time. This study is based on household survey data only, which is typically weak in coverage of the bottom and top of the distribution.

15. The fact that a widely accepted founding rule of democracy is to refrain from changing the fundamental law governing it (even if it is several centuries old, like the US

Constitution) prevents or considerably limits the opportunity for experimentalism (Kyvig 1996).

16. This idea of taxes reflecting the consent of the governed already appeared in the 1215 Magna Carta and in the 1689 Bill of Rights of England. It culminated with the popular slogan "no taxation without representation," heard during the American War of Independence against Britain. The same idea is reflected in the French 1793 Declaration of Human and Civil Rights, Article 14. The flip side of the same argument could be viewed in France's 2018–2019 Yellow Vest movement and the Tea Party movement in the United States in the 2000s, for example.

17. Many countries around the world allow citizens living abroad to vote without being subject to tax back home, while resident aliens are subject to tax without the right to vote (Schön 2018).

18. Chinese political leaders have publicly expressed doubts about Western democracy. In 2017, China's Communist Party (CPC) issued a blueprint and guide to explain how their "meritocratic political system" mitigates the randomness effects of the type of democratic populism observed in the Western world. See http://www.idcpc.org.cn/english /picgroup/201605/t20160503_82487.html.

19. French newsmagazine *Le Point* (November 17, 2016) had as its headline: "Peut-on être élu sans raconter n'importe quoi?" ["Can one be elected to office without promising nonsense?"]

20. For instance, the war in Afghanistan has gone on for four decades and has been at a stalemate for a number of years. In 2018, the Armed Conflict Location & Event Data Project (ACLED) pronounced Afghanistan the most lethal conflict in the world in terms of battle-related deaths.

21. On empirical analyses of the welfare consequences of lobbying and special interests, see Blanes et al. (2012), Bertrand et al. (2014), De Figueiredo and Richter (2014), and Stratmann (2002, 2005).

22. Source: *Human Development Index Statistical Appendix 2018.* New York: United Nations Development Programme.

23. Perhaps the most notorious case is that of former President of Côte d'Ivoire Laurent Gbagbo, put on trial in 2011 on accusations of orchestrating "unspeakable violence" to hold on to power after losing an election in 2010. The trial was presented as a landmark in the history of the ICC. Fatou Bensouda, the ICC's chief prosecutor, vowed to "leave no stone unturned" in investigating alleged crimes by all sides in the conflict. Yet in January 2019, Gbagbo was acquitted by the ICC. While the prosecutor has appealed the decision, the initial ruling of acquittal has weakened the credibility and reputation of the court as a politically independent institution working for justice and democracy.

24. Skepticism about the impartiality of the ICC has been compounded by the fact that since its creation in 2002, most of the cases brought to its jurisdiction have targeted African political leaders, several of whom were acquitted after being put on trial for years. In the meantime, terrible tragedies, such as the Iraq and Syrian wars, have not yet triggered any prosecution. This has led many leaders of the African Union to consider quitting the ICC.

25. Interview with Tania Bryer on *CNBC Meets*, March 13, 2013.

References

Agamben, G. et al. 2009. *Démocratie, dans quel état?*, Paris: La Fabrique Editions.

Alexander, M. 2010. *The New Jim Crow: Mass Incarceration in the Age of Colorblindness.* New York: New Press.

Annan, K. A. 2013. *Interventions: A Life in War and Peace.* New York: Penguin Books.

Annan, K. A. 2014. *We the Peoples: A UN for the Twenty-First Century*. London: Routledge.

Basu, K. 2015a. "The Poverty Line's Battle Lines." *Project Syndicate*, November 11.

Basu, K. 2015b. "Measuring Poverty in a Rapidly Changing World." *Let's Talk Development*, http://blogs.worldbank.org/developmenttalk/measuring-poverty-rapidly-changing-world.

Bell, D. A. 2015. *The China Model: Political Meritocracy and the Limits of Democracy*, Princeton, NJ: Princeton University Press.

Bertrand, M., M. Bombardini, and F. Trebbi. 2014. "Is It Whom You Know or What You Know? An Empirical Assessment of the Lobbying Process." *American Economic Review* 105: 322–353.

Blanes, I., J. Vidal, M. Draca, and C. Fons-Rosen. 2012. "Revolving Door Lobbyists." *American Economic Review* 102: 3731–3748.

Bombardini, M., and F. Trebbi. 2019. "Empirical Models of Lobbying." NBER Working Paper 26287, National Bureau of Economic Research, Cambridge, MA.

Bourguignon, F. 2016. *Globalization and Inequality*. Princeton, NJ: Princeton University Press.

Bourguignon and Morrisson. 2002. https://ourworldindata.org/grapher/world-population-in-extreme-poverty-absolute?stackMode=relative.

Boutros-Ghali, B. 1999. *Unvanquished: A U.S.–U.N. Saga*. New York: Random House.

Bradatan, C. 2019. "Democracy Is for the Gods." *New York Times*, July 10, https://www.nytimes.com/2019/07/05/opinion/why-democracies-fail.html.

Canfora, L. 2006. *La démocratie: Histoire d'une idéologie*. Paris: Seuil.

Center for Systemic Peace. 2020. "The Polity Project: About Polity." http://www.systemicpeace.org/polityproject.html.

Chesterton, G. K. 1908. *Orthodoxy*. New York: John Lane Company.

Chotiner, I. 2019. "An Indian Political Theorist on the Triumph of Narendra Modi's Hindu Nationalism." *New Yorker*, May 24, https://www.newyorker.com/news/q-and-a/an-indian-political-theorist-on-the-triumph-of-narendra-modis-hindu-nationalism.

Corlet, A. 2016. *Examining an Elephant: Globalisation and the Lower Middle Class of the Rich World*. Resolution Foundation Report, https://www.resolutionfoundation.org/app/uploads/2016/09/Examining-an-elephant.pdf

Crawford, N. C. 2018. *Human Cost of the Post-9/11 Wars: Lethality and the Need for Transparency*. Providence, RI: Watson Institute, Brown University.

Crozier, M., S. P. Huntington, and J. Watanuki. 1975. *The Crisis of Democracy: Report on the Governability of Democracies to the Trilateral Commission*. New York: New York University Press.

Deaton, A. 2005. "Measuring Poverty in a Growing World (or Measuring Growth in a Poor World)." *Review of Economics and Statistics* 87(1): 1–19.

Deaton, A. 2017. "How Inequality Works." *Project Syndicate*, December 21, https://www.project-syndicate.org/onpoint/anatomy-of-inequality-2017-by-angus-deaton-2017-12.

Debray, R. 2007. *L'obscénité démocratique*. Paris: Flammarion.

De Figueiredo, J. M., and B. K. Richter. 2014. "Advancing the Empirical Research on Lobbying." *Annual Review of Political Science* 17: 163–185.

Diamond, L. 1994. "Rethinking Civil Society: Towards Democratic Consolidation," *Journal of Democracy* 5(3): 4–17.

Diamond, L. 1996. "Is the Third Wave Over?" *Journal of Democracy* 7(3): 20–37.

Diamond, L., 1997. *Is the Third Wave of Democratization Over? An Empirical Assessment*. Working Paper 236. Notre Dame, IN: Helen Kellogg Institute for International Studies, 2.

Diamond, L. 2015. "Facing Up to the Democratic Recession." *Journal of Democracy* 26(1): 141–155.

Dorlin, E. 2017. *Se Défendre: Une Philosophie de la Violence*. Paris: La Découverte.

Engerman, S. L., and K. L. Sokoloff. 2005. "The Evolution of Suffrage Institutions in the New World." *Journal of Economic History* 65(4): 891–921.

Fouquet, H., and M. Mawad. 2019. "Huawei Frightens Europe's Data Protectors. America Does, Too." *Bloomberg.com*, February 25, https://www.bloomberg.com/amp/news /articles/2019-02-24/huawei-frightens-europe-s-data-protectors-america-does -too?__twitter_impression=true.

Freund, C. 2016. *Deconstructing Branko Milanovic's "Elephant Chart": Does It Show What Everyone Thinks?* Washington, DC: PIIE. November 30, https://piie.com/blogs /realtime-economic-issues-watch/deconstructing-branko-milanovics-elephant -chart-does-it-show.

Friedman, D. 1996. *Hidden Order: The Economics of Everyday Life*. New York: Harper-Business.

Gauchet, M. 2002. *La démocratie contre elle-même*. Paris: Gallimard.

Goldberg, J. 2016. "The Obama Doctrine." *Atlantic*, April, https://www.theatlantic.com /magazine/archive/2016/04/the-obama-doctrine/471525./

Greenwald, G., 2013. "Chilling Legal Memo from Obama DOJ Justifies Assassination of US Citizens." *Guardian*, February 5, https://www.theguardian.com/commentisfree /2013/feb/05/obama-kill-list-doj-memo.

Guardian. 2015. "NSA Tapped German Chancellery for Decades, WikiLeaks Claims," July 8, https://www.theguardian.com/us-news/2015/jul/08/nsa-tapped-german-chancel lery-decades-wikileaks-claims-merkel.

Guvenen, F., G. Kaplan, J. Song, and J. Weidner. 2017. "Lifetime Incomes in the United States over Six Decades." NBER Working Paper 23371, National Bureau of Economic Research, Cambridge, MA.

Held, D. 1987. *Models of Democracy*. Stanford, CA: Stanford University Press.

Hobbes, T. 1651 [1929]. *Hobbes's Leviathan: Reprinted from the Edition of 1651*. Oxford, Clarendon Press, 97.

Huntington, S.P. 1991. "Democracy's Third Wave," *Journal of Democracy* 2(2): 12–34.

Johnson, R., and T. Clack (eds.). 2015. *At the End of Military Intervention: Historical, Theoretical and Applied Approaches to Transition, Handover and Withdrawal*. New York: Oxford University Press.

Khan, M. 2010. *Political Settlements and the Governance of Growth-Enhancing Institutions*. Research Paper Series on Governance for Growth, School of Oriental and African Studies (SOAS). London: University of London.

Khan, M. 2018. "Political Settlements and the Analysis of Institutions." *African Affairs* 117(469): 636–655.

Kharas, H., and B. Seidel. 2018. "What's Happening to the World Income Distribution? The Elephant Chart Revisited." Working Paper 114, Brookings Institution, Washington, DC.

Kirman, A. P. 1992. "Whom or What Does the Representative Individual Represent?" *Journal of Economic Perspectives* 6(2): 117–136.

Krugman, P. 2016. "After the Elephant Curve." Keynote Lecture, PIIE, Washington, DC. https://piie.com/system/files/documents/krugman20161117ppt.pdf.

Kyvig, D. E. 1996. *Explicit and Authentic Acts: Amending the U.S. Constitution, 1776–1995*, Kansas, Kansas University Press.

Lakner, C., and B. Milanovic. 2013. "Global Income Distribution: From the Fall of the Berlin Wall to the Great Recession." (English) Policy Research Working Paper WPS 6719,

World Bank Group, Washington, DC. http://documents.worldbank.org/curated/en/914431468162277879/Global-income-distribution-from-the-fall-of-the-Berlin-Wall-to-the-great-recession.

Lefort, C. 1994. *L'invention démocratique*. Paris: Fayard.

Levitsky, S., and D. Ziblatt. 2018. *How Democracies Die*. New York: Crown.

Lorenz, K. 1966. *On Aggression*. London: Routledge.

Maliar, S. 1999. "Heterogeneity and the Representative Agent in Macroeconomics." PhD dissertation, Universitat Pompeu Fabra, Barcelona.

Maskin, E. S., and A. Sen. 2017a. "The Rules of the Game: A New Electoral System." *New York Review of Books*, January.

Maskin, E. S., and A. Sen. 2017b. "A Better Way to Choose Presidents." *New York Review of Books*, June.

Mbembe, A. 2019. "Deglobalization." *Eurozine*, February 18, https://www.eurozine.com/deglobalization/.

Milanovic, B. 2017. "How I Lost My Past." Global Inequality Blog, September 16, http://glineq.blogspot.com/2017/09/how-i-lost-my-past.html.

Monga, C. 1996. *The Anthropology of Anger: Civil Society and Democracy in Africa*. Boulder: Lynne Rienner Publishers.

Monga, C. 2002. "A Theory of Democratic Consolidation." *Democracy & Development: Journal of West African Affairs*, Rains Edition 3(1): 5–25.

Monga, C. 2009. "Uncivil Societies: A Theory of Sociopolitical Change." World Bank Policy Research Working Paper 4942, Washington, DC.

Monga, C. 2015. "Measuring Democracy: An Economic Approach." In C. Monga and J. Y. Lin (eds.), *The Oxford Handbook of Africa and Economics*, Vol. 1: *Context and Concepts*, 427–452. New York: Oxford University Press.

Monga, C. 2017. "The Economy of Tastes, Feelings, and Opinions." Working Paper 270, African Development Bank, Abidjan, Côte d'Ivoire, https://www.afdb.org/fileadmin/uploads/afdb/Documents/Publications/WPS-270_The_Economy_of_Tastes__Feelings__and_Opinions.pdf.

O'Brien, M. 2016. "This May Be the Most Important Chart for Understanding Politics Today." *Washington Post*, January 13, https://www.washingtonpost.com/news/wonk/wp/2016/01/13/this-may-be-the-most-important-chart-for-understanding-politics-today/.

Osberg, L. S., and K. Xu. 2008. "How Should We Measure Poverty in a Changing World? Methodological Issues and Chinese Case Study." *Review of Development Economics* 12(2): 419–441.

Paller, J. 2013. "Political Struggle to Political Sting: A Theory of Democratic Disillusionment," *Polity*, 45(4), October.

Péan, P. 1983. *Affaires africaines*. Paris: Fayard.

Péan, P. 2014. *Nouvelles affaires africaines: Mensonges et pillages au Gabon*. Paris: Fayard.

Pinker, S. 2011. *The Better Angels of Our Nature: Why Violence Has Declined*. New York: Viking Books.

Pinker, S., and R. Muggah. 2018. "Is Liberal Democracy in Retreat?" *Project Syndicate*, March 30, https://www.project-syndicate.org/onpoint/is-liberal-democracy-in-retreat-by-steven-pinker-and-robert-muggah-2018-03.

Ravallion, M. 2016. *The Economics of Poverty: History, Measurement, Policy*. New York: Oxford University Press.

Ravallion, M. 2020. "On Measuring Global Poverty," *Annual Review of Economics* 12: 167–188, https://www.annualreviews.org/doi/pdf/10.1146/annurev-economics-081919-022924.

Reilly, K. 2016. "Rick Perry Infamously Forgot About the Department of Energy. Now He Might Lead It." *Time*, December 13, https://time.com/4598910/rick-perry-department-energy-oops-gaffe/.

Rodrik, D. 2011. *The Globalization Paradox: Democracy and the Future of the World Economy*. New York: W. W. Norton & Company.

Roser, M. C. 2017. "The Short History of Global Living Conditions and Why It Matters That We Know It." https://ourworldindata.org/a-history-of-global-living-conditions-in-5-charts.

Rothman, J. 2018. "Are Things Getting Better or Worse?" *New Yorker*, July 23, https://www.newyorker.com/magazine/2018/07/23/are-things-getting-better-or-worse.

Sarkozy, N. 2014. "Ce que je veux dire aux Français." *Le Figaro*, March 21.

Schön, W. 2018. "Taxation and Democracy." Unprocessed paper, New York School of Law, April 24.

Sen, A. 1999. "Democracy as a Universal Value." *Journal of Democracy* 10(3): 3–17.

Sharma, M.S. 2019. "Don't Blame RG: He Is Not Why Modi Has Crushed Congress." *NDTV.com*, May 23, https://www.ndtv.com/opinion/dont-blame-rg-he-is-not-why-modi-has-crushed-congress-2041123.

Sigmund, P. E. (ed.). 2005. *The Selected Political Writings of John Locke*. New York: W. W. Norton & Company.

Smith, S., and A. Glaser. 1992. *Ces messieurs Afrique*. Paris: Calmann-Lévy.

Smith, S., and A. Glaser. 1997. *Ces messieurs Afrique. Des réseaux aux lobbies*, Vol. 2. Paris: Calmann-Lévy.

Sterling, R. W., and W. C. Scott. 1985. *Plato: The Republic*. New York: W. W. Norton & Company.

Stratmann, T. 2002. "Can Special Interests Buy Congressional Votes? Evidence from Financial Services Legislation." *Journal of Law and Economics* 45(2): 345–374.

Stratmann, T. 2005. "Some Talk: Money in Politics. A (Partial) Review of the Literature." *Public Choice* 124: 135–156.

Stuart Mill, J. 1873 [1861]. *Considerations on Representative Government*. New York: Henry Holt & Company.

Tocqueville, A. de. 2004 [1835]. *Democracy in America*. New York: Library of America.

US National Institute for Lobbying and Ethic. (n.d.). Mission statement, https://www.lobbyinginstitute.com/about.

The White House. 2018. "America First!," *Statement*, November 20.

Wootson, Jr., C. R. 2017. "Listen to Russian Pranksters Trick Rick Perry into a Conversation about Pig Manure." *Washington Post*, July 26.

Zakaria, F., 2007. *The Future of Freedom: Illiberal Democracy at Home and Abroad*. New York: W. W. Norton & Company.

Zakaria, F., 2019. "In Defense of the Elites." *Washington Post*, February 2, https://www.washingtonpost.com/opinions/we-have-a-bleak-view-of-modern-life-but-the-world-is-making-real-progress/2019/01/31/6ee30432-25a8-11e9-ad53-824486280311_story.html.

THE THIRD FUNCTION OF LAW
Its Power to Change Cultural Categories

Karla Hoff and James Walsh

To categorize is to render discriminably different things equivalent, to group objects and events and people around us into classes, and to respond to them in terms of their class membership rather than their uniqueness.

—Jerome Bruner et al. (1956)

How does law change society? In the rational actor model, law affects society only by changing individuals' incentives and information—the *command and coordination* function of law. In the view that individuals are social animals with an innate desire to follow social norms and punish norm violators, law is also a guidepost for social norms (the *expressive* function of law) (Sunstein 1996). We propose a third function of law using the insight from cognitive science and social psychology that individuals are boundedly rational and cannot think without categories and other schemas, many of which are cultural.[1] The categories mediate individuals' experience of the world. By making possible new kinds of social interactions, prototypes, and role models, law can transform cultural categories. The categories have framing effects that influence behavior by enabling or constraining perception, associations, and interpretations. We call this the *schematizing* function of law.

The evolution of beliefs about how people make decisions is evident in the US judicial history of racial segregation.[2] In *Plessy v. Ferguson* (1896), racial hostility was treated as based on nature. Justice Brown argued that "[l]egislation is powerless to eradicate racial instincts." Fifty years later, in *Brown v. Board of Education* (1954), Chief Justice Warren argued that segregation shapes individuals' self-schemas:

To separate [Black children] from others of similar age or qualification solely because of their race generates a feeling of inferiority as to their status in the community that may affect their hearts and minds in a way unlikely ever to be undone.

Another fifty years later, Justice Breyer argued in a dissent to Chief Justice Roberts that segregation "perpetuated" racism:

> The context here is one of racial limits that seek, not to keep the races apart, but to bring them together . . . segregation policies did not simply tell schoolchildren "where they could and could not go to school" . . . they perpetuated a caste system rooted in the institutions of slavery and 80 years of legalized subordination.[3]

Considerable research in the behavioral sciences supports the views of Chief Justice Warren and Justice Breyer. Experience creates cultural categories; salient cultural categories influence how people think of themselves and others. At the stroke of a pen, law can issue a command but cannot change how people think, and yet, law can make possible experiences and exposure that over time do exactly that.

This essay has two main arguments, an analytical one and a policy one.

The Analytical Argument

The analytical argument is informed by research in many fields, particularly the social-psychological and philosophical literatures on schemas (or, equivalently, mental models). The main points are these:

1. *By exposing individuals to new kinds of social situations, prototypes, and potential role models, law may, in a time frame relevant to policymakers, change cultural categories and the contexts that activate particular categories in ways that change social norms and legitimize changes in legal rights.* Categories are largely defined by prototypes (Rey 1999; Smith and Medlin 1999). Exposure to new prototypes may change the meaning of a category and the self-image of its members. Law has a *schematizing* function.[4]

2. *We cannot think without categories.*[5] The categories we use influence perception and construal. Categories are often essentialized (Rothbart and Taylor 1992; Haslam et al. 2000; Mahalingam 2003). They influence beliefs about how it is natural and appropriate for members of particular groups to behave (Goffman 1963) and suggest implicit theories about how the world works.

3. *The cultural categories learned in a society in which ascriptive groups have unequal legal rights promote behaviors that make group inequality persist long after the abolition of inequality in formal rights.* Cultural categories

are conditioned by historically relevant forms of thought (Berger and Luckmann 1967; Boyd and Richerson 1988; Bruner 1990; Sen 1992; Nisbett and Cohen 1996; DiMaggio 1997; Nunn 2012; Hoff and Stiglitz 2010 and 2016; Demeritt and Hoff 2018) and by the accessible exemplars (Kahneman and Tversky 1973; Tversky and Kahneman 1973).

Institutional practices constitute categories with particular meanings, and the categories influence how people see themselves, how they behave, and how they are treated. So pernicious and stigmatizing are some group stereotypes that they "get inside the head" of members of the stigmatized groups and undermine their performance and their efforts to improve their lives (see the survey by Hoff and Walsh 2018). Negative stereotypes impair performance in school settings (Steele and Aronson 1995; Hoff and Pandey 2006, 2014), the job application process (Linos et al. 2017), and the workplace (Davies et al. 2005). Some discrimination against groups is based on a rational calculation (statistical discrimination; see List 2004), but there is evidence that does not fit well with this account and is explained better by the effect of cultural categories on attention, interpretation, and preferences (Goldin and Rouse 2000; Bertrand and Mullainathan 2004; Shayo and Zussman 2011; Alesina and La Ferrara 2014; Bartoš et al. 2016).

Beyond the instrumental harms that a stigmatized group identity may cause, it matters for intrinsic reasons (Anderson 1999; Wolff and De-Shalit 2007; Wolff 2015): "Lack of respect, though less aggressive than an outright insult, can take an equally wounding form. No insult is offered another person, but neither is recognition extended; he or she is not seen as a full human being whose presence matters" (Sennet 2003, 3).

Laws that mandate behavior that deviates sharply from popular views of appropriate behavior can be ineffective, or worse. Kaushik Basu (2018, 57) uses game theory to argue that if a law is enacted to direct a society to an outcome that could not have been an equilibrium in the absence of the law, it "is doomed to not be implemented." Two dramatic examples are laws in India that were intended to help wives and daughters but caused many to be killed. In colonial India, enforcement of the right of widows to inherit property from their husbands strengthened the norm of widow immolation (*sati*; Kulkarni 2017). In the period for which data are available, 1815–1821, the enforcement of inheritance rights for widows led to an average increase per district of between 115 and 437 widow immolations (the mean number of immolations in a district was 153 where the districts gave widows inheritance rights, and 25 where they did not). The group most strongly opposed to inheritance rights for widows were the Brahmins. An increase in the proportion of Brahmins in a district of one percentage point led to an average increase of between 56 and 102 burned on the funeral pyre of their husbands.

In modern India, legislation of equal inheritance rights for daughters and sons has increased female feticide, excess female infant mortality, and son-biased fertility stopping (Bhalotra et al. 2017; see also Rosenblum 2015). Kulkarni (2017, 479) concluded from his work on colonial India that "egalitarianism requires egalitarians."

The Policy Argument

Starting from a stable system with "matched" institutions and ideational patterns (Lieberman 2002), to use law to change society requires a kind of one-two punch. A one-two punch is defined as "two forces combining to produce a marked effect."[6] The two forces we focus on here are a change in rights (the *command and coordination* function of law) and a change in experience or exposure that creates cognitive foundations for the change in rights (the *schematizing* function). Like the one-two punch in a boxing match, the two forces independently might have little impact and yet, together, they have a large effect.

In general, the one-two punch requires the enactment of multiple laws, but there are exceptions. One exception is the 1993 Norwegian law that reserved four weeks of parental leave for fathers. Fathers who took the paternity leave usually did this when the child was about ten months old, an age when a child forms attachments. The leave affected the evolution of household roles: it increased paternal care for the children fifteen years later (Cools et al. 2015). This one Norwegian law exercised all three functions of law: (1) the *command* function—the law required firms to offer paternity leave, (2) the *expressive* function—the law expressed as a social value that a father should bear some child care responsibility, and (3) the *schematizing* function—the law ensured that more fathers would have the experience of paternity leave, which durably changed beliefs about what a "good father" does.

Part I: The Mechanics of Mental Models

Boundedly rational people (that is, all of us) have schematic structures that are both representations and information-processing mechanisms. These structures are called *mental models* or, equivalently, *schemas* (Axelrod 1973; Brewer and Treyens 1981; Brewer and Nakamura 1984; DiMaggio 1997). Bartlett (1932, 201) provides one of the earliest accounts of a mental model: It is "*an active organization of past reactions, or of past experiences, which must always be supposed to be operating in any well-adapted organic response*" (emphasis added). Mental models include categories, identities, stereotypes, and causal narratives that animate our mental lives (Carey 2009). They give us presuppositions and default assumptions about how the world is and how it works. In many cases, our use of mental models to process information is automatic and subconscious (Bargh and Pratto 1986).

Mental models influence how we allocate our attention and retrieve information. *Whereas society plays no part in how the rational actor thinks, it plays a key part in how humans think*: "The schematic mental structures that help us make sense of what we perceive . . . are usually based on intersubjective, conventionalized typifications"; they cause us to "'see' [the world through] *socio*mental lenses grounded in particular social environments" (Zerubavel 2009, 31; emphasis in original). Individuals are, thus, more likely to perceive and to recall information that is germane to their mental models and to resist disconfirming evidence (DiMaggio 1997 reviews many examples). Since cultural mental models are transmitted across generations, the social environments of long-distant ancestors may influence how individuals perceive the world.

Suppose that institutions arbitrarily forced a group of persons (call them a "race" or "caste") into the bottom rungs of society, making it customary for them to be treated in certain ways. Many years later, suppose that the legal basis of the institutions was abolished. Nonetheless, the mental models that underlie the customs might persist indefinitely. North (2005, 52) argues that the "interaction of beliefs, institutions, and organizations in the total artefactual structure makes path dependence a fundamental factor in the continuity of a society." The basic idea is not new. Tocqueville (1990 [1835], 357) wrote in *Democracy in America* that the real problem among the moderns is that of altering the customs, not the law.

Three sources of mental models operate over very different time spans. Over millions of years, evolutionary processes have embedded representational capacities in humans. Over generations, sociocultural processes have created repertoires of cultural mental models. And in our lifetimes, each of us creates idiosyncratic mental models (Carey 2009, 447–448; Zerubavel 2009). The focus of this chapter is on the sociocultural space, where *"the social order operat[es] on individuals' minds. . . .* Institutions have [a hold] on our processes of classifying and recognizing" (Douglas 1986, 3, emphasis added). Repertoires of categories and other mental models evolve in response to the social patterns and exemplars to which social groups are exposed (Smith and Medin 1999).

Recognition of the influence of cultural mental models on cognition sheds new light on the domain of choice. In standard economics, actions are a function (f) of incentives and endowments; preferences are treated as fixed, and beliefs in equilibrium are consistent with available information.

Equation 1: Actions = f (incentives, endowments).

Behavioral economics introduces two additional sets of variables: the context of decision making (which does not affect material payoffs but does influence what is salient to the decision maker) and mental models (which are both representations and information-processing mechanisms). Boundedly rational individuals do not perceive their full set of opportunities and cannot imagine their full set of possible lives. The subset of things they perceive and consider depends on context and the mental models that are activated. Taking into account the additional variables that influence the choices people make extends the function:

Equation 2: Actions = g (incentives, endowments, *context, mental models*).

Laboratory experiments that manipulate the labels of a game illustrate the impact of context on behavior. In the prisoner's dilemma game, a player has a choice between generously cooperating or acting selfishly. In an experiment where US college students played this game, half the subjects were told that they were playing the "Wall Street Game," and the other half were told that they were playing the "Community Game" (Liberman et al. 2004). Sixty-seven percent of the subjects cooperated when they were told they were playing the "Community Game," but only 33 percent cooperated when they were told they were playing the "Wall Street Game." The mental model elicited by the context (the label) had a large effect on behavior.

A field experiment in Germany shows that experience can have a substantial effect on prosociality (Kosse et al., 2020). The participants were disadvantaged children. The study provided a randomly selected set of the children with a volunteer mentor for one year to give the child the experience of "an unrelated and highly prosocial attachment figure taking responsibility and devoting effort and time with him/her." The children who had this one-year experience are the treatment group, and the other children (who did not have this one-year experience) are the control group. Two years after the program ended, a set of standard laboratory experiments that reveal prosociality (including the dictator game) showed a significant increase in prosociality in the treatment group relative to the control group. This suggests that the experience changed the preferences of the treatment group durably. Contrary to the assumption of traditional economics, experience may change preferences in ways that matter for economic outcomes.

Although we include mental models as the independent variable in equation 2, policy can only indirectly influence the repertoire of mental models by guiding experience and exposure. A randomly assigned roommate in college (Boisjoly et al. 2006), success in the application of a citizen of Pakistan for a visa to travel to the Hajj (Clingingsmith et al. 2009), and broadcasts of Globo soap operas in a municipality in Brazil (La Ferrara et al. 2012) all expose individuals or communities to new people or new stories and thereby change their judgments of what is acceptable and desirable. But policy does not control the mental models that mediate an individual's experience of the world.

Recognizing that perception and preferences are influenced by the cultural categories and stories in people's heads greatly expands the set of economic equilibria. As the sociologist Paul DiMaggio (1997, 280) writes, it implies that "large-scale social change may be caused by large-scale, more-or-less simultaneous frame switches by many interdependent actors." The remainder of the first part of this chapter presents two examples to illustrate the power of mental models to explain economic outcomes. Part II illustrates the ability of law and policy to change mental models.

Example 1. Mental Models of Gender That Produce Inequality in a Laboratory Game

In industry and academia, there is a low proportion of women in the top ranks, and a high proportion of women in the lower ranks. A factor contributing to this polarization is the way women and men allocate their on-the-job time between tasks that affect career advancement and tasks that do not. For example, in for-profit firms, high-promotability tasks are revenue-generating; low-promotability tasks include orienting new employees and organizing a Christmas party. In universities that emphasize research, high-promotability tasks are research-related, and low-promotability tasks include advising undergraduates. Many people feel a sense of obligation to spend some time on tasks that help their organization at the cost of advancing their careers. But Babcock et al. (2017, 715) show that in US industry and academia, it is women who disproportionately do the tasks with low promotability.

Why? To investigate this, the researchers invented a very simple game and played it with US college students. The participants in each experimental session are seated in one large room, each with his or her own computer. They play the game for ten rounds. At the start of each of the ten rounds, the players are randomly divided into new three-person groups. Interactions are anonymous and one-shot. A player makes a decision in each round whether or not to volunteer to "invest." As soon as a group member volunteers, or two minutes have elapsed (whichever comes first), the round ends. Table 2.1 shows the payoffs.

A decision to invest increases the payoff of each member of the group, but by a lesser amount to the investor ($1.25) than to the non-investors ($2.00). If nobody in the group invests, the payoff to each player is $1.00. Thus, a player has a

TABLE 2.1.   Payoffs per round in the volunteer-to-invest game

	IF NO ONE VOLUNTEERS TO INVEST	IF SOMEONE, FOR EXAMPLE, PERSON A, VOLUNTEERS TO INVEST
Person A	$1	$1.25
Person B	$1	$2
Person C	$1	$2

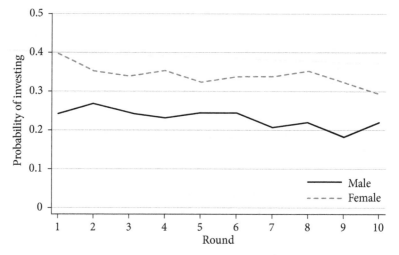

FIGURE 2.1.   In mixed-gender sessions, females volunteer more than males for the low-rewarded task.

Source: Babcock et al. (2017).

material self-interest to volunteer only under the belief that the other two players in the group will not volunteer.

In every round, nearly every player waited to see whether someone else in the group would volunteer to be the investor. Most investments were made in the last two seconds of a round. In mixed-gender sessions (which were about half men and half women), the women volunteered almost 50 percent more often than the men. The line graph in Figure 2.1 shows that in every round, the probability among women that someone invested was always substantially greater than the probability among men. The line representing women's behavior fluctuates from a probability of 0.4 to 0.3 from rounds one to ten, while the line for the men hovers around a probability of 0.25, decreasing in the later rounds.

Does the gender difference in behavior reflect differences in traits? Should one conclude from these results that women are nicer than men? No. When the experi-

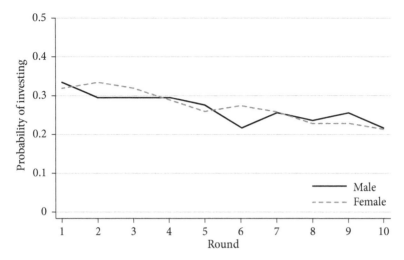

FIGURE 2.2.   In single-gender sessions, there are no gender differences in the probability of volunteering for the low-rewarded task.

Source: Babcock et al. (2017).

ment was run in single-gender sessions, so that participants knew that they were grouped only with members of their own sex, men and women were equally likely to volunteer to invest. This is shown by the line graph in figure 2.2, in which the lines for both men and women follow a similar downward trajectory, starting at a probability of just above 0.3 in round one and decreasing to just above 0.2 in round ten.

Because the gender gap did not emerge in single-gender groups, the gap in the mixed-gender sessions cannot be driven by gender differences in generosity. Neither can expectations of social sanctions explain the result, since the game is one-shot and anonymous.[7] But cultural categories and the social norms embedded in cultural categories can explain the outcomes. One explanation is that men and women expect women to volunteer for the low payoff. The convergence of expectations leads them to coordinate on an outcome that reproduces traditional gender inequality. Another explanation is that women want to conform to gender norms by taking the low-reward task. As Sunstein (1996, 2043) notes in the context of the gender division of domestic work, "[t]he social meaning of a woman's refusal may be a refusal to engage in her appropriate gender role. . . . [P]revailing norms help constitute inequality."

In summary, the experiment illustrates a situation that likely prevails throughout industry and academia in which gender-equal rules are not sufficient to provide gender equality of opportunity. Cultural mental models of gender bound the choice sets that women and men believe are available to them.

Example 2. Narratives of Race as a Weapon of the Southern Elite after the US Civil War

If a law is enacted that gives rights to one group at the expense of another group, the latter may not be passive. If it is well organized, it can fight back by transforming cultural representations and putting them to strategic use. The history of racism after the US Civil War provides a harsh example.

Until the beginning of the nineteenth century, the institution of slavery was the law of the land in the United States. Most slaves and most slaveholding families were in the South. Slaves provided the agricultural labor that produced much of the wealth of the Southern economy. In the mid-nineteenth century, the US government sought to prohibit slavery in the territories that had not yet become states. This led some states in the deep South to secede, which provoked the Civil War. After the US government won the war, the thirteenth, fourteenth, and fifteenth amendments to the US Constitution abolished slavery, guaranteed "equal protection under the law" to Black people, and gave Black men the right to vote.

The economic and political interests of the Southern White elite led them to staunchly oppose the extension of rights. Despite having lost the war, the elite were sufficiently well organized to pursue a strategy that made it very difficult for Black people to exercise their new rights. The Southern elite fostered hatred of Black men with "a 'daily barrage of Negro atrocity stories,' [and so] the familiar image of an inferior but not malign Black was replaced by the image of a lustful, violent, aggressive Black who had been guilty of crimes against Whites (and would commit them again, given the chance)" (Glaeser 2005, 67; see also Faust 1981). Glaeser (2005, 68) shows the time series of expressions of anti-Black hatred in the American South: "Hatred was low before the Civil War, rose in the Jim Crow period, and muted after World War I." The Southern elite represented as simple justice acts of terrorism against Black men who tried to exercise their right to vote, hold office, and work for themselves (Budiansky 2008).

We draw on game theory to illustrate in a very simple way some of the factors at play after the Civil War. Table 2.2 shows the strategy sets of two actors—the US government and the Southern elite—beside the rows and above the columns. It shows the utility of each player inside the cells (with the US government's payoff, incorporating the payoff to African Americans, coming first).

Each player chooses a strategy to maximize its utility. Whatever the Southern elite's strategy, the US government's best choice after the Civil War was to give equal rights to Black men. That reflected the evolution of attitudes in the North during the course of the war and the large contribution that slaves had made in fighting the war. Table 2.2 shows how US policy triggered a change in the strategy of the Southern White elite. Since it could not eliminate the possibility of equal rights, creating

TABLE 2.2. Game depicting interaction of US government and Southern White elite during Reconstruction

		SOUTHERN WHITE ELITE		
		PROMOTE THE IDEOLOGY OF RACIAL HIERARCHY	PROMOTE HATRED AND DISTRUST OF BLACK PEOPLE	PROMOTE THE IDEOLOGY OF RACIAL EQUALITY
US government during Reconstruction	Do not give equal political rights to Blacks and Whites	0, 10	–1, 3	5, 0
	Give equal political rights to Blacks and Whites	5, 5	1, 8	10, 2

an ideology of racial hostility based on the representation of Black men as evil and untrustworthy yielded the Southern elite its highest payoff in this game. Comparison of the elite's payoffs in row 2 shows that promoting hatred of Black people was the elite's preferred option. The game predicts a change in the stereotypes of Black people, a steep reduction in their payoffs compared to the outcome of equal rights and an ideology of racial equality, and low aggregate utility.

Achieving the US goal in Reconstruction of political equality for Black and White people would have required two kinds of intervention: the provision of equal legal rights and also measures to give racial equality a cognitive foundation that legitimized the equality of rights. A belief that oppression of Black people was morally repugnant might have overcome the Southern elite's economic self-interest.

The elite's ability to incite hatred of Black people can be understood as their ability to change the meaning of race. Even many poor Whites, who would have benefited from an increase in agricultural wages, came to hold racist views. It is often said that the North won the war, but the South won the peace (see Gates 2019). The outcome might have been different if the US government had sustained Reconstruction and provided land and education to the Black population—"40 acres and a mule" was the policy until the assassination of President Lincoln. Education and land would have created new prototypes and new social patterns that might have legitimized the extension of economic and political rights to Black people.

Acharya et al. (2016) show the link between economic factors in the immediate postbellum period and racial ideology today. They show that the ideology of White hatred of Black people is strongest in the counties of the US South that had been most dependent on slave labor and thus had the greatest economic and political incentives to reinforce racist norms to maintain control over the former slaves. In the counties that in 1860 had a higher proportion of slaves (and, hence, higher dependence in 1860 on slave labor), White people are today more likely to express racial resentment and oppose affirmative action, compared to White people who live in otherwise similar areas that had lower population shares of slaves. Anti-Black attitudes faded earlier in areas with a low historical dependence on slave labor, as well as in areas that recovered swiftly, through agricultural mechanization, from the economic shock that accompanied emancipation. Counties with higher historical levels of slave ownership had higher rates of Black lynchings: a 10-percentage point increase in slave ownership is associated with an increase of two lynchings per 100,000 residents. The relationship is causal. Acharya et al. (2016) also show that across the counties of the US South, the suitability of the land for growing cotton predicts current levels of White racial hostility and opposition to affirmative action.

To summarize, powerful groups created new mental models in the postbellum period to incite Whites to block the exercise by Black people of their new rights. Limited efforts were made by the US government to change the racist beliefs that prevailed either antebellum or postbellum.

Part II: Four Examples in Which Law Has Transformed Cultural Categories

We now show that law can transform cultural categories by making possible new kinds of social interactions and exposing people to new prototypes and role models. The effect can be emancipatory.

To put this in context, consider first the expressive function of law. Lawrence Lessig (1995) and Cass Sunstein (1996) showed that by expressing social values, law influences social norms. One way that it does this is by influencing individuals' beliefs about the actions that others approve or disapprove of—that is, the individuals' second-order expectations. Even a rule whose violation triggers little legal penalty can have a substantial effect on behavior if it affects the normative order. Funk (2007) demonstrates the expressive power of the laws in Swiss cantons that made voting compulsory. Violators were typically fined only about one euro, yet repeal of the laws reduced voter turnout by 6–10 percentage points. The repeal had expressive value.

The expressive function of law operates primarily on the *external* normative order, whereas the schematizing function of law operates on the *internal* cognitive

Command and
coordinating
function

Expressive
function

Schematizing
function

FIGURE 2.3.   Three functions of law. (1) *Command and coordinating function*—To define rights, duties, and prohibitions. (2) *Expressive function*—To fortify or change social norms, the *exterior normative order*. (3) *Schematizing function*—To provide cognitive foundations of institutions and norms, *the interior cognitive order*.

order. It changes that order by making possible new experiences or exposure to new prototypes or role models. The expressive function is something that the state directly controls, but the schematizing function is indirect; the state does not control what beliefs an individual will absorb from new social patterns. Figure 2.3 illustrates the three functions of law.

Cultural mental models, as noted above, can persist indefinitely. The location of pogroms in the fourteenth century during the Black Death predicts anti-Semitism centuries later (Voigtlander and Voth 2012). To illustrate the relationship with one comparison, consider the two small German towns of Konigheim and Wertheim. They are six miles apart and both had Jewish settlements before the Black Death. Konigheim did not witness a pogrom during the plague, but Wertheim did. Six centuries later, in 1928, the Nazi Party received 1.6 percent of votes in Konigheim compared to 8.1 percent in Wertheim.

The impact of experience and exposure on mental models, and of mental models on behavior, creates opportunities for policymakers to use the law and policy to change how groups are perceived and how they perceive themselves. Below we present four examples.

Transforming Gender Representations by Political Reservations for Women

Philosophers once believed that individuals associated necessary and sufficient conditions with a concept: for example, for a square, the conditions would be plane figure, four equal sides, and four equal angles. This is the "classical view" in the philosophy of concepts. In contrast, the modern view in philosophy is that people use prototypes and exemplars to define concepts (Rey 1999: Smith and

Medin 1999). Kahneman and Tversky (1973) present many kinds of evidence that humans conceptualize in terms of prototypes and exemplars, since they are more accessible than abstract conditions.

The Constitution of India of 1950 gave men and women equal political rights, but in the following decades, few women ran for political office in local or state government. Far fewer were elected. In villages in India, it is commonly observed that "[w]omen are taught from childhood to confine themselves to household tasks and help men in the family occupation" (Dandekar 1986, 68). Villages had few exemplars of local female leaders, with the exception of wives of former village heads who were elected as village heads to permit their husbands to effectively extend their terms in office.

A 1993 amendment to the Constitution of India reserved the position of village head (*pradhan*) for a woman in a random selection of one-third of the villages in India. Through many measures of the impact in the state of West Bengal, Beaman et al. (2009, 2012) show that the law reduced prejudice against women leaders and led people to see women in new ways. To evaluate prejudice against women leaders, villagers were asked to listen to speeches involving village leaders and to rank them on a scale of effectiveness. The content of the speeches was always the same, but the gender of the speaker was randomized. (This test is an example of the Goldberg paradigm.) The speeches were adapted from actual village meetings. Respondents in the control villages (without reservations for women) ranked female leaders lower than male leaders in the speeches. So did respondents in villages with only five years of exposure to a woman as head of the village council. But after seven years' exposure, men's bias against women leaders vanished.

A second measure consisted of Implicit Association Tests. These tests ask respondents to categorize a series of terms. Scores depend on accuracy and speed. One test used the following categories: man, woman, leadership activities, and domestic tasks. Sometimes the categories would be grouped in a way congruent with gender stereotypes—

Woman   Man
Domestic tasks   Leadership activities

and sometimes incongruent:

Woman   Man
Leadership activities Domestic tasks

An individual would categorize each term into the left or right column on a computer monitor. The difference in accuracy and speed between the tests under the stereotype-congruent condition and under the stereotype-incongruent condition is a measure of the strength of the stereotype. Exposure to female leaders through reservations weakened the stereotype. That is, it increased the ability of men to associate women with leadership activities.

A third measure to evaluate the impact of political reservations for women was villagers' evaluation of the *pradhan* of their own villages. For villagers who were exposed for the first time to a woman *pradhan*, evaluations were less favorable than evaluations by villagers with a male *pradhan*. But for villagers exposed for the second time to a women *pradhan*, evaluations of the woman *pradhan* were no less favorable than evaluations of a male *pradhan*. This finding is consistent with a change in villagers' perceptions of women leaders, but does not prove that a change had occurred, since the second-term women could have been more qualified than the first-term women.

The strongest evidence that exposure to women *pradhans* changed cultural categories and removed the barriers to women to exercise their right to hold political office is that in free elections following a period of political reservations, women were more likely to run for office and female candidates were more likely to win. The rational actor model can explain this, but it cannot explain the results of the Implicit Association Test (since for the rational actor, thinking entails no costs). An alternative theory that can explain both sets of results is that individuals think with cultural categories, and exposure to women leaders changed individuals' cultural understandings of what a good leader and a woman are. People have vivid pictures of what a category of person is like, and the pictures organize their understandings (Swidler 2001, 36 and note 10).

The philosopher Georges Rey argues that "what competent users of a concept know are typicalities. . . . The necessary and sufficient conditions of the Classical View simply do not appear to play a role in people's actual acts of categorization" (Rey 1999, 281). Individuals rely heavily on stereotypical information. Stereotypes tend to exaggerate small differences between groups.[8] In India, two rounds of political reservations appear to have given villagers sufficient exposure to local women leaders to change the concepts of good leader and woman: it became ordinary to accept that a woman could be a good leader.

Concepts influence preferences. If cultural categories of women change, preferences of females and attitudes toward them are also likely to change. Beaman et al. (2012) show that they did. Compared to villages without a politically reserved woman leader, seven years' exposure to reserved women leaders caused teenage girls to be less likely to want to become housewives, less likely to want their in-laws to determine their occupation, more likely to want to marry after the age of 18, and more likely to want a job that required more education. Similar changes in parents' aspirations appear to have changed the way that parents treated their children. It reduced slightly the gender gap in the amount of time that teenagers spent on housework.

The changes in behavior and aspirations described here occurred despite the absence of any change in the educational and labor market opportunities for females.

Another change made by the 1993 amendment to the Constitution of India was to reserve for women in all villages one-third of the seats of the village council. Different states of India began applying the law in different years. The introduction of the law over time facilitates identification of the causal impact. Iyer et al. (2012) find a large upward trend in registered crimes against women after a state applied the new law, and yet no evidence of an increase in actual crimes against women. Evidence from many sources support the conclusion that the increase in registered crimes against women was largely due to more women who were victims of crimes being willing to report the crimes to the police, and police officers being more willing to record the crimes. In the long run, the increase in reported crime should provide equal deterrence to crimes against men and women through legal action.

In summary, the evidence on the impact of political reservations in India for women suggests that it changed village culture. This kind of effect is not automatic. The same constitutional amendment that created political reservations for women in India also created political reservations for Scheduled Castes (the former Untouchables). There is not—at least not yet—any evidence that this affected the cultures of villages. Instead, the evidence so far available shows that the presence of a reserved Scheduled Caste (SC) *pradhan* spurred high-caste teachers to harass SC students more. Priyanka Pandey (2005) conducted a study in which she visited public schools in North India at random times. In villages with SC-reserved *pradhans*, she found that high-caste public school teachers stole more of the scholarship money from SC students, were more often absent from work, and improved student achievement by less. An interpretation is that the law triggered a backlash in the high caste to try to put SCs in "in their place."

Victoire Girard (2018) studied the impact of five years of SC reservations on discrimination as measured by one question on India's Rural Economic and Development Survey of 2006: "Have you, or any member of your family, been prevented from entering any street within the village because of your caste now?" In 2006, 45 percent of SC households said yes. The survey results show that during the tenure of SC village leaders, SC reservations reduced caste-based discrimination against SCs by 10 percentage points, but that the effect did not persist after the SC reservation ended. SCs are deeply stigmatized. For many centuries and even in many villages today, the isolation between SCs and upper castes is extreme.

We have argued that starting from a stable social equilibrium, two kinds of measures (a one-two punch) may be needed for law to bring about social change—a change in incentives and a change in cultural mental models. Unfortunately, there is no assurance that a second punch—providing new exemplars of a cultural category—will transform it.

Reducing Discrimination by a Legal Ruling That Desegregated Some Elite Schools by Income Class

If a law increases engaging experiences with an out-group, it may reduce the limited understanding of the out-group that often drives discrimination (Allport et al. 1954; Pettigrew and Tropp 2006; see Enos 2014 for a different finding). Gautam Rao (2019) shows that interactions in a context of cooperation between rich and poor students in New Delhi private schools, beginning at age four, reduced rich students' discrimination against poor children and also made the rich students more generous.[9]

The Delhi government leases land to many private schools in perpetuity at highly subsidized rates. In exchange, the law mandates that the schools serve "weaker sections" of society. The law was not enforced until a Delhi High Court ordered almost 400 private schools to reserve one-fifth of their seats for students from poor households (with partial compensation provided by the state). The decision required the schools to admit a random selection of applicants from poor households. It also required the schools to integrate the scholarship students into the classes of the non-scholarship students. As a result, beginning in 2007, rich students (typically from above the ninety-fifth percentile of the consumption distribution in Delhi) shared classes with students who were on average at the twenty-fifth percentile of the distribution.

In Delhi, most children enter school at age four and remain in the same school through the higher grades. The court order applied only to new admissions of children. Beginning in either 2007 or 2008, cohorts of students in the affected elite private schools were made up of 20 percent poor students. By using controls for fixed differences among the schools to which the court order applied, Rao identifies the impact of desegregation (the "treatment").

To study discrimination, Rao created a relay race with prize money. Before the experiment began, students watched each child run a series of one-on-one sprints, which revealed how fast all the children could run. Then the subjects who were not going to run themselves (we will call them "team leaders") chose the runners whom they wanted on their team. Among children whom they could recruit, if a poor child was a faster runner than a wealthy child, the leader faced a trade-off: If the leader chose the fast but poor child, the likelihood of winning the relay prize increased, but she might have less fun interacting with the poor child. If she chose the slow wealthy child, the likelihood of winning the prize declined, but she might have more fun interacting socially with someone who was in an income class similar to her own.

The treatment reduced discrimination. Exposure to poor students at school reduced by half the proportion of wealthy students who discriminated against poor children. Among wealthy students without poor classmates, 23 percent discriminated against poor children: they selected a wealthy teammate, even though a poor child had been faster in the sprint. Wealthy students with poor classmates discriminated less than those without poor classmates, and the effects were strongest for participants in the lowest-stakes race.

Rao also used a series of activities and games to compare the generosity of treated and untreated students. Students were invited to participate in weekend activities at the school to help fundraise for a charity serving disadvantaged children. Treated students were 10 percent more likely to volunteer than nontreated students. Rao also had the children play dictator games (the standard game, discussed above, to measure generosity toward anonymous others). Treated students shared 45 percent more of their endowment than did nontreated students.

Rao was able to pin down the mechanism that drove the changes in behavior. The schools form "study groups" of two to four students to work cooperatively to solve problems in math, reading, and crafts. In some schools, the groups are formed by clustering names that appear together in the alphabetical list of a class; that is, Aarav would be grouped with Aditay and Arjun. This makes the grouping of a rich child with a poor child a quasi-natural experiment; it depends on the accident of how closely their names appear on the alphabetically ordered list.[10] For schools that use this alphabetical method to form student groups, Rao contrasted the behavior of the treated rich students whose names are adjacent to only rich students' names with rich students whose names are adjacent to poor students' names. Figure 2.4 compares the level of discrimination of wealthy students with and without a name adjacent to poor students' names. The figure shows that it was the close interaction provided by being in a study group with a poor student that caused the large change in discrimination. Wealthy students in study groups made up of only wealthy students were more than twice as likely to discriminate as wealthy students in study groups with poor students.

The Sustained Effects on Investment in Children and on Aspirations of a Short-Term Transfer Program

Living in poverty affects the qualities that a person is assumed to have; and the experience of poverty affects how people perceive themselves (Fell and Hewstone 2015). The stereotype held by many Americans that the poor are low in compe-

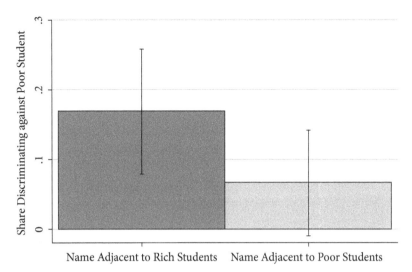

FIGURE 2.4. Interaction of wealthy students with poor students in study groups reduces discrimination against the poor.

Source: Rao (2019).

tence and warmth (Fiske et al. 2002) can lead people to treat them with contempt (Cuddy et al. 2007). The "self-schemas" of the poor can make them feel stigma and shame about their place in the world. In a global survey of people living in poverty, respondents emphasized the humiliations:

> One deeply felt deprivation is not being able to do what is customary in the society . . . not being able to entertain visitors or enjoy social life . . . shame from not having toilets for visitors, or money to buy a coffin for burying a relative. . . . Appearances and clothes . . . are mentioned as important for self-respect and, conversely, they can be an important source of shame. In Etropole, Bulgaria, "people who cannot afford warm clothes for the winter go to work. Then they come back and stay at home under a pile of blankets, shivering with cold. They don't go out. They are ashamed to meet other people. If they run into a friend and are invited for a drink, they must refuse. So they would rather not go out at all." (Narayan et al. 2000, 38–39)

Shame is associated with depleted self-efficacy (Baldwin et al. 2006). The psychological dimensions of poverty make it more challenging for the poor to improve their lot.

Exposure to high-achieving role models can sometimes help people develop self-efficacy (Bandura 1997) and increase their productivity (Henrich and

Broesch 2011). But poverty tends to put such role models out of reach: Residential neighborhoods and social networks are often income-segregated. As a result, people living in poverty may be guided to naturalize the situation they are in (Appadurai 2004; Ray 2006; Duflo 2012; Macours and Vakis 2014; Tanguy et al. 2014; Dalton et al. 2016).

Aspirations are conceptualized as both a preference and a *capacity* (Appadurai 2004; Duflo 2012). Aspirations depend on the social reference points that influence individuals' expectations (Dalton et al. 2016).[11] Vicariously experiencing upward mobility of social referents who are "mentally close" because of social interactions raises the capacity to aspire. Inequality that is so high that society is polarized by class—most people are either poor or well-off, and few are middle income—reduces the access of the poor to networks with slightly better-off peers. This can lower the aspirations of the poor and the effort they make to escape poverty, which can entrench the unequal income distribution (Genicot and Ray 2017).

A conditional cash transfer program (CCT) in Nicaragua reduced aspiration failure by bringing poor individuals into regular contact with upwardly mobile peers. In 2006, the Ministry of the Family in the government of Nicaragua implemented a one-year CCT to help poor people cope with financial strain and to promote upward mobility. It targeted six municipalities in a region that was plagued by drought. By lottery, it divided the 106 communities in the municipalities into a treatment and a control group (fifty-six treatment, fifty control). All poor households in the treatment communities were eligible to receive the cash transfer. To identify poor households, the government conducted a means test. Ninety percent of all households (about three thousand households) were eligible. The cash transfer was conditional on parents' investing in their children in three ways: (1) maintaining children's primary school attendance, (2) bringing children to health services, and (3) participating in local events on such topics as nutrition practices and job skills. Follow-up data were collected after nine months of program implementation and again two years after it had ended.[12]

In the treatment communities, the government held a public assembly to explain the logistics of the program. If there were more than thirty eligible households in a community, multiple assemblies were arranged. During the assemblies, women were asked to volunteer for the position of *promotora*—a leader role designed to improve information and compliance with the program. Volunteers to be *promotora* had to be approved by the assembly. Each *promotora* was assigned a group of roughly ten beneficiaries living close to her. At the end of each assembly, all the beneficiaries—including the *promotoras*—participated in a second lottery to determine who would get, in addition, a $200 lump-sum grant, provided that the individual wrote a business plan and invested the $200 in her own business (Macours et al. 2012).[13] The authors compared the pure control (the fifty control communities), the individuals who received the cash transfers but did not receive the productive investment grant, and the individuals who received the productive investment grant as well as the cash transfers.

The design of the study also enabled the researchers to experimentally assess second-order effects of the packages that the *promotoras* received (that is, the effect of the *promotora*'s treatment status on the non-*promotora* beneficiaries).[14] Just like the regular beneficiaries, the *promotoras* had a one-third chance of receiving the investment grant. Because a typical assembly had four leaders, the variation was substantial across assemblies in the share of leaders that received the largest package. (This was not the case for nonleaders, where approximately a third of the beneficiaries in all assemblies got the largest package.)

Understanding the second-order effects of the leaders' benefit packages is important, because the *promotoras* played a central role in the program. Interviews conducted during and after the program found that the *promotoras* took ownership of the goals and messages of the project, and they encouraged the other beneficiaries to invest in their children's nutrition and education. Leaders had on average five years of education; beneficiaries had only three. For the leaders who received the productive investment grant, the higher education levels were likely to help them manage their new, nonagricultural activities.

The impact evaluation of the program two years after it had ended gives evidence that the *promotoras* served not only as communicators during the one-year program but also as powerful role models for the other beneficiaries after it had ended (see table 2.3). Households exposed to the *promotoras* who received the investment grant invested more in their children and had higher expectations and aspirations for their children. In assemblies where all *promotoras* had received the investment grant, school expenditures increased by 49 percent, and school absences declined by 21 percent. Beneficiaries with one additional leader in their assembly who had received the investment grant had 0.4 days fewer school absences per month by their children, and 16 percent higher expenditures on their children's schooling. Considering the effect on school investment, the two-year impacts of interacting with leaders who had received the investment grant are the same as, or larger than, the impacts during the program implementation (Macours and Vakis 2016).

Why were the effects of the CCT persistent? Two years after the program ended, the former program participants were getting no financial support from the program, and it is likely that any special knowledge of the *promotoras* would already have been passed on to the group members. The authors provide evidence that *the leaders shifted the mental models of the program beneficiaries*: Exposure to leaders with the $200 investment grant raised parents' expectations that their children would move into a professional or skilled salary job. One additional such leader

TABLE 2.3.   Estimated social interaction effects on human capital investments and aspirations 2 years after the Nicaragua CCT program ended

	BENEFICIARIES		
	CONTROL	INTENT-TO-TREAT EFFECT	INTENT-TO-TREAT INTERACTED WITH PERCENTAGE OF PROMOTORAS WITH THE INVESTMENT GRANT
HUMAN CAPITAL INVESTMENTS			
Percent attending school (7–18-year-olds)	0.777	−0.008	0.045
Number of days absent from school (7–18-year-olds)	6.341	0.197	−1.506*
School expenditures (7–18-year-olds)	493.4	−68.8	310.9***
Share of food expenditures for vegetables and fruit	0.0581	0.001	0.022***
ASPIRATIONS AND EXPECTATIONS			
Desired years of education	13.29	−0.09	0.946**
Expected years of education	8.41	−0.132	0.805
Desired professional occupation	0.5	−0.015	0.115*
Expected professional occupation	0.023	0.002	0.035**

Note: This table is based on intent-to-treat estimators from tables 2 and 6 of Macours and Vakis (2016). The share of leaders measures the share of female leaders with the productive investment package over all female leaders in a beneficiary's registration assembly. The data for school attendance and school expenditures are individual-level data for all children of age 7–18 years in a household. The data for desired and expected occupation indicate the share of mothers who desired or expected a professional job for their child, i.e., a job for which university education was required. The data for food expenditures are household-level data. Excluded from the data are households with female leaders. Highest and lowest 0.5 percent of outliers in expenditures are trimmed.
*** $p < 0.01$, ** $p < 0.05$, * $p < 0.1$.

in the community increased parents' expectations that their children would become professionals by nearly 50 percent. An increase from no leaders in their neighborhood with the $200 grant, to all leaders in their neighborhood with that grant, increased aspirations by more than one-fifth of a standard deviation. This suggests that mental models are not just "an overlay" on basic psychological processes, but a dimension that constitutes a person's psychology (see DiMaggio and Markus 2010).

The Sustained Effect on Education and Aspirations of a National Math Competition

Brazil has a low overall education level. It is increasing at a very slow rate. At the current rate, it would take Brazil an estimated 260 years to attain the Organization for Economic Co-operation and Development member countries' average proficiency in reading and 75 years to do that in mathematics (World Bank 2018). Can the schematizing function of law help? A government program in Brazil shows that it can. Successful role models in a student's class increase aspirations and improve the educational and economic outcomes of high-ability students.

A government institute for research in mathematics runs a math competition, the Brazilian Math Olympiad. It is open to students in grades 6–12 in all public schools and is advertised on television and in the schools. About 18 million students take part in the competition each year. Around 800,000 advance to the second round, where they are nationally ranked. The top 2,300 performers win gold, silver, and bronze medals. The 30,000 students in the next tier receive Honorable Mentions.

The impact of the Honorable Mention is the focus of a study by Diana Moreira (2017). Two features of the award make it possible to identify the psychological effects on peers of recognizing students for their performance. First, the 4 percent of participants who receive an Honorable Mention receive no other benefit—no monetary prize, mentoring opportunities, or training. Second, the winners' names are listed on a publicly available website, and there is a strict cutoff. No information is publicly disclosed on the performance of those who do not win an award (although the researcher had this information). By comparing cases of a student was just above the cutoff for an Honorable Mention with cases in which a student was just under the cutoff, one can assess the causal impact of the receipt of an award on the recipient and on his/her classmates as a quasi-experiment. The small differences in the scores of classmates can be attributed to random luck.

Comparing classrooms with narrow winners and losers—that is, people who were just above or just below the cutoff and therefore who were in essence of the same caliber—Moreira investigates the effect of the award on the subsequent performance of the award winners and of their classmates. Not surprisingly, winning the award boosted the performance of the winners. The surprising finding is that the award had meaningful spillover effects. The average effect on subsequent Math Olympiad performance of being in a class with a student who received an Honorable Mention is one-fifth as large as the effects on the winner. The effect on economic outcomes was also large: The enrolment rate of classmates of a narrow award winner in selective colleges increased by 10 percent, increasing the yearly earnings of the average classmate by about 0.5 percent per capita income in Brazil. The award also affected students' performance in the following year on exams, grades, and dropout rates.

Proximity to the winner in two respects plays a critical role—proximity in that a student is physically in the same classroom as the winner, and proximity in ability.

Only those students in the top quartile of the test score distribution were affected by having a classmate win an Honorable Mention.

Moreira finds no support for some alternative explanations for the impact on classmates of a narrow winner compared to a narrow loser. For example, the award did not affect how students were tracked in classes; stronger classmates were not more likely to be put into classes with the winner.

Moreira views self-perception as the core mechanism for the performance effects on peers. Daily exposure to the Honorable Mention winner in one's classroom makes salient a new self-schema. It changes the high-ability classmates' belief in their own abilities and the goals that are within reach, which promotes their educational efforts and their selection of good colleges.

This chapter has proposed that a third function of law—besides command and coordination and the expression of social values—is to transform the mental models that mediate individuals' experience of the world. Law can sometimes do this by making possible new kinds of social interactions and the emergence of new prototypes, exemplars, and role models.

The economist Deirdre McCloskey (2005, 29) imagines a heckler defending the assumption in standard economics of the decision maker as the rational actor: "Give me a break: I'm not in the business of explaining all behavior. I propose merely to explain some portion, and in many cases a large portion." This would be a fair objection to adopting a more realistic model of human decision making if changes in the sociocultural environment did not affect individuals' judgments and preferences or if, in the problems under consideration, judgments and preferences were more stable than material constraints. But much evidence suggests that laws that change people's experiences, or that expose them to new social patterns, may have persistent effects on how they think and what they want. The human actor is not, as assumed in standard economics, the autonomous thinker with unbounded rationality and stable preferences. The human actor, unlike the rational actor, cannot imagine all possible states of the world and make the best choice among all available opportunities. For boundedly rational individuals, the social patterns that laws create shape their socio-mental lenses.

In a society where widely shared mental models and institutions match—that is, the former provide the cognitive foundations for the latter, a change in the legal superstructure is generally insufficient to induce long-run societal change. In such a case, a critical use of law and policy is to transform the cultural mental models. We have called this the *schematizing* function of law. We presented examples where law served this function. We also presented examples where changes in the legal superstructure without interventions to promote change in its cognitive foundations generated a backlash that hardened the cultural mental models, making social progress more difficult to achieve.

Notes

We thank Cass Sunstein, Vafa Ghazavi, and especially Nancy Folbre for comments.
1. A seminal paper is Markus (1977).
2. This history is reviewed in Turner (2015).
3. Parents Involved in Community Schools v. Seattle School District No. 1 (2007).
4. The schematizing power of institutions has been discussed by the anthropologists Berger and Luckmann (1967) and Mary Douglas (1973, 1986); the psychologists Bruner (1990, 58), Nisbett and Cohen (1996), and Markus and Kitayama (2010); and the sociologists Friedland and Alford (1991) and DiMaggio (1997). These scholars showed that institutions influence cognition. A closely related argument is that a strategy of "debiasing through law" may be accomplished by affirmative action (Jolls and Sunstein 2006). We are indebted to the work of all these scholars.
5. The world presents the person with an infinite array of discriminable objects. Experts estimate, for example, that we can distinguish between more than 100,000 colors—and perhaps as many as 7 million (Myers 1995). Yet were we to treat each distinguishable color or object as unique, we would soon be overwhelmed. As Bruner et al. (1956, 1) put it, "the resolution of this seeming paradox—the existence of discrimination capacities which, if fully used, would make us slaves to the particular—is achieved by man's capacity to categorize."
6. Online *Merriam-Webster Unabridged*.
7. If a game is not one-shot and anonymous, impartial formal rules are no guarantee of gender equality, since individuals may impose sanctions in later interactions. A case study in Mali by Gottlieb (2014) is illustrative. Provision of a civics course to the population in some localities in Mali was designed to increase participation in civic life, particularly by women. In fact, it increased the participation of men in civic life but decreased that of women, because male relatives and village elders sanctioned women who engaged in civic activity. The civics course increased awareness of the importance of civic participation, which transformed it into "a man's job."
8. Bordalo et al. (2016) demonstrate this experimentally.
9. Rao also evaluates the impact on academic achievement by the rich students. He conducted tests of learning in English, Hindi, and math, and he collected reports on student behavior. He finds marginally significant decreases in rich students' English language scores, but no effect on their scores in Hindi, math, or a combined index over all subjects. This indicates that the increase in rich students' understanding and empathy for poor people came at a very low cost in terms of academic achievement.
10. Except if wealthy and poor people with different traits give their children names with systematically different starting letters, with the result that some fair-minded and generous wealthy children are more likely to have the same initial letter in their first name as the initial letter of a poor child. This is improbable.
11. The reference points drawn from the values, behaviors, and accomplishments of an individual's cognitive world will form an individual's *aspirations window* (Ray 2006). A very low window leads to inertia, and a very high window to frustration. Aspirations and effort are jointly determined, and low aspirations and low effort can reinforce each other in a community.
12. The data are unusually extensive, because the program was a pilot. The research team is engaged in a project to understand the long-run impact of the program.

13. For instance, an investment for a seamstress might be a sewing machine. The financial support was substantial: The total of the transfers under the CCT was almost one-fifth of average household income; the investment grant was more than one-third of average annual household income.

14. In defining leaders, the authors considered both the women in leadership positions created by the program (the *promotoras*) and women who held leadership positions in the community. The two groups are not mutually exclusive: Many health coordinators and teachers volunteered to be *promotoras*.

References

Acharya, Avidit, Matthew Blackwell, and Maya Sen. 2016. "The Political Legacy of American Slavery." *Journal of Politics* 78(3): 621–641.

Alesina, Alberto, and Eliana La Ferrara. 2014. "A Test of Racial Bias in Capital Sentencing." *American Economic Review* 104(11): 3397–3433.

Allport, Gordon W., Kenneth Clark, and Thomas Pettigrew. 1954. *The Nature of Prejudice*. Boston: Addison-Wesley.

Anderson, Elizabeth S. 1999. "What Is the Point of Equality?" *Ethics* 109(2): 287–337.

Appadurai, Arjun. 2004. "The Capacity to Aspire: Culture and the Terms of Recognition." In Vijayendra Rao and Michael Walton (eds.), *Culture and Public Action*. Stanford, CA: Stanford University Press, 59–84.

Axelrod, Robert. 1973. "Schema Theory: An Information Processing Model of Perception and Cognition." *American Political Science Review* 67(4): 1248–1266.

Babcock, Linda, Maria P. Recalde, Lise Vesterlund, and Laurie Weingart. 2017. "Gender Differences in Accepting and Receiving Requests for Tasks with Low Promotability." *American Economic Review* 107(3): 714–747.

Baldwin, Kim M., John R. Baldwin, and Thomas Ewald. 2006. "The Relationship among Shame, Guilt, and Self-Efficacy." *American Journal of Psychotherapy* 60(1): 1–21.

Bandura, Albert. 1997. *Self-Efficacy*. New York: W. H. Freeman & Company.

Bargh, John A., and Felicia Pratto. 1986. "Individual Construct Accessibility and Perceptual Selection." *Journal of Experimental Social Psychology* 22(4): 293–311.

Bartlett, Frederic Charles. 1932. *Remembering: A Study in Experimental and Social Psychology*. Cambridge: Cambridge University Press.

Bartoš, Vojtěch, Michal Bauer, Julie Chytilová, and Filip Matějka. 2016. "Attention Discrimination: Theory and Field Experiments with Monitoring Information Acquisition." *American Economic Review* 106(6): 1437–1475.

Basu, Kaushik. 2018. *The Republic of Beliefs: A New Approach to Law and Economics*. Princeton, NJ: Princeton University Press.

Beaman, Lori, Raghabendra Chattopadhyay, Esther Duflo, Rohini Pande, and Petia Topalova. 2009. "Powerful Women: Does Exposure Reduce Bias?" *Quarterly Journal of Economics* 124(4): 1497–1540.

Beaman, Lori, Esther Duflo, Rohini Pande, and Petia Topalova. 2012. "Female Leadership Raises Aspirations and Educational Attainment for Girls: A Policy Experiment in India." *Science* 335: 582–586.

Berger, Peter L., and Thomas Luckmann. 1967. *The Social Construction of Reality: A Treatise in the Sociology of Knowledge*. London: Penguin Books.

Bertrand, Marianne, and Sendhil Mullainathan. 2004. "Are Emily and Greg More Employable than Lakisha and Jamal? A Field Experiment on Labor Market Discrimination." *American Economic Review* 94(4): 991–1013.

Bhalotra, Sonia R., Rachel Brulé, and Sanchari Roy. 2017. "Women's Inheritance Rights Reform and the Preference for Sons in India." No. 11239. Bonn: Institute of Labor Economics IZA.

Boisjoly, Johanne, Greg J. Duncan, Michael Kremer, Dan M. Levy, and Jacque Eccles. 2006. "Empathy or Antipathy? The Impact of Diversity." *American Economic Review* 96(5): 1890–1905.

Bordalo, Pedro, Katherine Coffman, Nicola Gennaioli, and Andrei Shleifer. 2016. "Stereotypes." *Quarterly Journal of Economics* 131(4): 1753–1794.

Boyd, Robert, and Peter J. Richerson. 1988. *Culture and the Evolutionary Process.* Chicago: University of Chicago Press.

Brewer, William F., and Glenn V. Nakamura. 1984. "The Nature and Functions of Schemas." In Robert S. Wyer and Thomas K. Srull (eds.), *Handbook of Social Cognition,* Vol. 1: 119–160. Hillsdale, NJ: Erlbaum.

Brewer, William F., and James C. Treyens. 1981. "Role of Schemata in Memory for Places." *Cognitive Psychology* 13(2): 207–230.

Brown v. Board of Education (1954) 347 U.S. 483.

Bruner, Jerome. S. 1990. *Acts of Meaning.* Cambridge, MA: Harvard University Press.

Bruner, Jerome S., Jacqueline J. Goodnow, and A. George Austin. 1956. *A Study of Thinking.* New York: John Wiley & Sons.

Budiansky, Stephen. 2008. *The Bloody Shirt: Terror after Appomattox.* New York: Viking.

Carey, Susan. 2009. *The Origin of Concepts.* Oxford: Oxford University Press.

Clingingsmith, David, Asim Ijaz Khwaja, and Michael Kremer. 2009. "Estimating the Impact of the Hajj: Religion and Tolerance in Islam's Global Gathering." *Quarterly Journal of Economics* 124(3): 1133–1170.

Cools, Sara, Jon H. Fiva, and Lars J. Kirkeboen. 2015. "Causal Effects of Paternity Leave on Children and Parents." *Scandinavian Journal of Economics* 117(3): 801–828.

Cuddy, Amy J.C., Susan T. Fiske, and Peter Glick. 2007. "The BIAS Map: Behaviors from Intergroup Affect and Stereotypes." *Journal of Personality and Social Psychology* 92(4): 631–648.

Dalton, Patricio S., Sayantan Ghosal, and Anandi Mani. 2016. "Poverty and Aspirations Failure." *Economic Journal* 126(590): 165–188.

Dandekar, Hemalata C. 1986. *Men to Bombay, Women at Home.* Ann Arbor, MI: Center for South and Southeast Asian Studies, University of Michigan.

Davies, Paul G., Steven J. Spencer, and Claude M. Steele. 2005. "Clearing the Air: Identity Safety Moderates the Effects of Stereotype Threat on Women's Leadership Aspirations." *Journal of Personality and Social Psychology* 88(2): 276.

Demeritt, Allison and Karla Hoff. 2018. "The Making of Behavioral Development Economics." *History of Political Economy* 50 (annual supplement): 303–322.

DiMaggio, Paul. 1997. "Culture and Cognition." *Annual Review of Sociology* 23: 263–287.

DiMaggio, Paul, and Hazel Rose Markus. 2010. "Culture and Social Psychology: Converging Perspectives." *Social Psychology Quarterly* 73(4): 347–352.

Douglas, Mary. 1973. *Rules and Meanings: The Anthropology of Everyday Knowledge.* Oxford: Routledge.

Douglas, Mary. 1986. *How Institutions Think.* Syracuse, NY: Syracuse University Press.

Duflo, Esther. 2012. "Human Values and the Design of the Fight against Poverty." *Tanner Lectures* 1–55.

Enos, Ryan D. 2014. "Causal Effect of Intergroup Contact on Exclusionary Attitudes." *Proceedings of the National Academy of Sciences of the United States of America* 111(10): 3699–3704.

Faust, Drew Gilpin. 1981. *The Ideology of Slavery: Proslavery Thought in the Antebellum South: 1830–1860*. Library of Southern Civilization. Baton Rouge: Louisiana State University Press.

Fell, Ben, and Miles Hewstone. 2015. "Psychological Perspectives on Poverty: A Review of Psychological Research into the Causes and Consequences of Poverty." London: Joseph Rowntree Foundation, https://www.jrf.org.uk/report/psychological-perspectives-poverty.

Fiske, Susan T., Amy J. C. Cuddy, Peter Glick, and Jun Xu. 2002. "A Model of (Often Mixed) Stereotype Content: Competence and Warmth Respectively Follow from Perceived Status and Competition." *Journal of Personality and Social Psychology* 82: 878–902.

Friedland, Roger, and Robert R. Alford. 1991. "Bringing Society Back In: Symbols, Practices and Institutional Contradictions." In Walter W. Powell and Paul J. DiMaggio (eds.), *The New Institutionalism in Organizational Analysis*. Chicago: University of Chicago Press.

Funk, Patricia. 2007. "Is There an Expressive Function of Law? An Empirical Analysis of Voting Laws with Symbolic Fines." *American Law and Economics Review* 9(1): 135–159.

Gates, Henry Louis, Jr. 2019. *Stony the Road: Reconstruction, White Supremacy, and the Rise of Jim Crow*. New York: Penguin.

Genicot, Garance, and Debraj Ray. 2017. "Aspirations and Inequality." *Econometrica* 85(2): 489–519.

Girard, Victoire. 2018. "Don't Touch My Road. Evidence from India on Affirmative Action and Everyday Discrimination." *World Development* 103: 1–13.

Glaeser, Edward L. 2005. "The Political Economy of Hatred." *Quarterly Journal of Economics* 120(1): 45–86.

Goffman, Erving. 1963. *Stigma: Notes on the Management of Spoiled Identity*. New York: Simon & Schuster.

Goldin, Claudia, and Cecilia Rouse. 2000. "Orchestrating Impartiality: The Impact of 'Blind' Auditions on Female Musicians." *American Economic Review* 90(4): 715–741.

Gottlieb, Jessica. 2014. *Why Women Participate Less Than Men in Civic Activity: Evidence from Mali*. APSA 2014 Annual Meeting Paper.

Haslam, Nick, Louis Rothschild, and Donald Ernst. 2000. "Essentialist Beliefs about Social Categories." *British Journal of Social Psychology* 39(1): 113–127.

Henrich, Joseph, and James Broesch. 2011. "On the Nature of Cultural Transmission Networks: Evidence from Fijian Villages for Adaptive Learning Biases." *Philosophical Transactions of the Royal Society of London B: Biological Sciences* 366(1567): 1139–1148.

Hoff, Karla, and Priyanka Pandey. 2006. "Discrimination, Social Identity, and Durable Inequalities." *American Economic Review* 96(2): 206–211.

Hoff, Karla, and Priyanka Pandey. 2014. "Making Up People—The Effect of Identity on Performance in a Modernizing Society." *Journal of Development Economics* 106: 118–131.

Hoff, Karla, and Joseph E. Stiglitz. 2010. "Equilibrium Fictions: A Cognitive Approach to Societal Rigidity." *American Economic Review* 100: 141–146.

Hoff, Karla, and Joseph E. Stiglitz. 2016. "Striving for Balance in Economics: Towards a Theory of the Social Determination of Behavior." *Journal of Economic Behavior and Organization* 126(B): 25–57.

Hoff, Karla, and James Walsh. 2018. "The Whys of Social Exclusion: Perspectives from Behavioral Economics." *World Bank Research Observer* 33(1): 1–33.

Iyer, Lakshmi, Anandi Mani, Prachi Mishra, and Petia Topalova. 2012. "The Power of Political Voice: Women's Political Representation and Crime in India." *American Economic Journal: Applied Economics* 4(4): 165–193.

Jolls, Christine M., and Cass R. Sunstein. 2006. "The Law of Implicit Bias." *California Law Review* 94: 969.

Kahneman, Daniel, and Amos Tversky. 1973. "On the Psychology of Prediction." *Psychological Review* 80(4): 237–251.

Kosse, Fabian, Thomas Deckers, Pia Pinger, Hannah Schildberg-Horisch, and Armin Falk. 2020. "The Formation of Prosociality: Causal Evidence on the Role of Social Environment." *Journal of Political Economy* 128(2): 434–467.

Kulkarni, Parashar. 2017. "Can Cultural Norms Undermine Effective Property Rights? Evidence from Inheritance Rights of Widows in Colonial India." *British Journal of Political Science* 47: 479–499.

La Ferrara, Eliana, Alberto Chong, and Suzanne Duryea. 2012. "Soap Operas and Fertility: Evidence from Brazil." *American Economic Journal: Applied Economics* 4(4): 1–31.

Lessig, Lawrence. 1995. "The Regulation of Social Meaning." *University of Chicago Law Review* 62(3): 943–1045.

Liberman, Varda, Steven M. Samuels, and Lee Ross. 2004. "The Name of the Game: Predictive Power of Reputations versus Situational Labels in Determining Prisoner's Dilemma Game Moves." *Personality and Social Psychology Bulletin* 30(9): 1175–1185.

Lieberman, Robert C. 2002. "Ideas, Institutions, and Political Order: Explaining Political Change." *American Political Science Review* 90(4): 697–712.

Linos, Elizabeth, Joanne Reinhard, and Simon Ruda. 2017. "Levelling the Playing Field in Police Recruitment: Evidence from a Field Experiment on Test Performance." *Public Administration* 95(4): 943–956.

List, John A. 2004. "The Nature and Extent of Discrimination in the Marketplace: Evidence from the Field." *Quarterly Journal of Economics* 119(1): 49–89.

Macours, Karen, and Renos Vakis. 2014. "Changing Households' Investment Behaviour through Social Interactions with Local Leaders: Evidence from a Randomised Transfer Programme." *Economic Journal* 124(576): 607–633.

Macours, Karen, and Renos Vakis. 2016. "Sustaining Impacts When Transfers End: Women Leaders, Aspirations, and Investment in Children." NBER Paper 22871, National Bureau of Economic Research, Cambridge, MA.

Macours, Karen, Patrick Premand, and Renos Vakis. 2012. "Transfers, Diversification and Household Risk Strategies: Experimental Evidence with Lessons for Climate Change Adaptation." World Bank Policy Research Working Paper 6053, World Bank, Washington, DC.

Mahalingam, Ramaswami. 2003. "Essentialism, Culture, and Power: Representations of Social Class." *Journal of Social Issues* 59(4): 733–749.

Markus, Hazel. 1977. "Self-schemata and Processing Information about the Self." *Personality and Social Psychology* 35(2): 63–78.

Markus, Hazel Rose, and Shinobu Kitayama. 2010. "Cultures and Selves: A Cycle of Mutual Constitution." *Perspectives on Psychological Science* 5(4): 420–430.

McCloskey, Deidre. 2005. "The Demoralization of Economics: Can We Recover from Bentham and Return to Smith?" In Martha Fineman and Terence Dougherty (eds.), *Feminism Confronts Homo Economicus: Gender, Law, and Society*. Ithaca, NY: Cornell University Press, 20–31.

Moreira, Diana. 2017. "Recognizing Performance: How Awards Affect Winners' and Peers' Performance in Brazil." University of California at Davis. Manuscript, https://www.dropbox.com/s/7sh5p8u6olze32g/Moreira_JMP.pdf?dl=0.

Myers, David G. 1995. *Psychology*. New York: Worth Publishers.

Narayan, Deepa, Robert Chambers, Meera K. Shah, and Patt Petesch. 2000. *Voices of the Poor: Crying Out for Change*. New York: Oxford University Press for the World Bank.

Nisbett, Richard, and Dov E. Cohen. 1996. *Culture of Honor: The Psychology of Violence in the South*. Boulder, CO: Westview Press.

North, Douglass C. 2005. *Understanding the Process of Institutional Change*. Princeton, NJ: Princeton University Press.

Nunn, Nathan. 2012. "Culture and the Historical Process." *Economic History of Developing Regions* 27: S108–S126.

Pandey, Priyanka. 2005. "Service Delivery and Capture in Public Schools: How Does History Matter and Can Mandated Political Representation Reverse the Effects of History?" World Bank manuscript, Washington, DC.

Pettigrew, Thomas F., and Linda R. Tropp. 2006. "A Meta-analytic Test of Intergroup Contact Theory." *Journal of Personality and Social Psychology* 90(5): 751–783.

Plessy v. Ferguson. 163 U.S. 537 (1896).

Rao, Gautam. 2019. "Familiarity Does Not Breed Contempt: Generosity, Discrimination, and Diversity in Delhi Schools." *American Economic Review* 109(3): 774–809.

Ray, Debraj. 2006. "Aspirations, Poverty, and Economic Change." In Abhijit Vinayak Banerjee, Dilip Mookherjee, and Roland Benabou (eds.), *Understanding Poverty* 409–421.

Rey, Georges. 1999. "Concepts and Stereotypes." In Eric Margolis and Stephen Laurence (eds.), *Concepts: Core Readings*. Cambridge, MA: MIT Press, 279–299.

Rosenblum, Daniel. 2015. "Unintended Consequences of Women's Inheritance Rights on Female Mortality in India." *Economic Development and Cultural Change* 63(2): 223–248.

Rothbart, Myron, and Marjorie Taylor. 1992 "Category Labels and Social Reality: Do We View Social Categories as Natural Kinds?" In Gun R. Semin and Klaus Fielder (eds.), *Language, Interaction, and Social Cognition*. London: Sage, 11–36.

Sen, Amartya. 1992. *Inequality Reexamined*. London: Clarendon Press.

Sennett, Richard. 2003. *Respect in a World of Inequality*. New York: W. W. Norton & Company.

Shayo, Moses, and Asaf Zussman. 2011. "Judicial Ingroup Bias in the Shadow of Terrorism." *Quarterly Journal of Economics* 126(3): 1447–1484.

Smith, Edward, and Douglas Medin.1999. "The Exemplar View." In Eric Margolis and Stephen Laurence (eds.), *Concepts: Core Readings*. Cambridge, MA: MIT Press, 207–222.

Steele, Claude M., and Joshua Aronson. 1995. "Stereotype Threat and the Intellectual Test Performance of African Americans." *Journal of Personality and Social Psychology* 69(5): 797–811.

Sunstein, Cass R. 1996. "On the Expressive Function of Law." *University of Pennsylvania Law Review* 144: 2021–2053.

Swidler, Ann. 2001. *Talk of Love: How Culture Matters*. Chicago: University of Chicago Press.

Tanguy, Bernard, Stefan Dercon, Kate Orkin, and Alemayehu Taffesse. 2014. "The Future in Mind: Aspirations and Forward-Looking Behaviour in Rural Ethiopia." CEPR Discussion Paper 10224, Centre for Economic Policy, London.

Tocqueville, Alexis de. 1990. *Democracy in America*, Vol. 1. New York: Random House.

Turner, Ronald. 2015. "The Way to Stop Discrimination on the Basis of Race." *Stanford Journal of Civil Rights and Civil Liberties* 11: 45–86.

Tversky, Amos, and Daniel Kahneman. 1973. "Availability: A Heuristic for Judging Frequency and Probability." *Cognitive Psychology* 5: 207–232.

Voigtlander, Nico, and Hans-Joachim Voth. 2012. "Persecution Perpetuated: The Medieval Origins of Anti-Semitic Violence in Nazi Germany." *Quarterly Journal of Economics* 127(3): 1339–1392.

Wolff, Jonathan. 2015. *Social Equality and Social Inequality*. Oxford: Oxford University Press.

Wolff, Jonathan, and Avner De-Shalit. 2007. *Disadvantage*. Oxford University Press on Demand.

World Bank. 2018. *World Development Report 2018: Learning to Realize Education's Promise*. Washington, DC: World Bank.

Zerubavel, Eviatar. 2009. *Social Mindscapes: An Invitation to Cognitive Sociology*. Cambridge, MA: Harvard University Press.

FIGHTING CORRUPTION IN CHINA

The Roles of Formal and Informal Institutions

Cheryl Long

President Xi's anticorruption campaign has taken down more government offi-cials in the past four years than was accomplished in the previous four decades combined (Figure 3.1). Apart from the criticisms by his detractors for the cam-paign's political motivation and focused targeting of potential opponents and challengers, it is worth investigating whether the campaign has been effective in reducing corruption, especially for the years to come.

In fact, according to Transparency International's Corruption Perceptions In-dex 2017, although 100,000 officials have been arrested in the past six years, China has edged up just two places in the country rankings to seventy-seventh but has kept a low score of only 41.

Although there are measurement issues related to Transparency Internation-al's Corruption Perceptions Index, it is still worth asking why there has been so little progress in combating corruption in China. To address this question, I out-line a simple theoretical model to highlight the challenges faced by any typical corruption fighter in a country burdened with substantial government regulations and a long tradition of heavy reliance on social connections. In particular, firms operating in such an environment are shown to have a strong incentive to make relation-based investments in response to the important roles played by regula-tion and social connections. Although such investments are intrinsically linked to corruption and have a negative impact on economic growth in general, under certain conditions, corruption can help increase productivity, as it allows firms with higher productivity but fewer connections to obtain market access.[1]

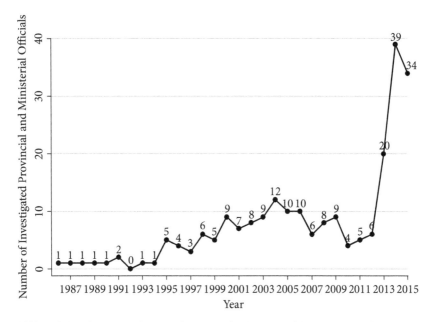

FIGURE 3.1. Number of corruption investigations involving provincial level officials. Data sources: The data before 2013 came from a news report by Yang (2014) in Oriental Morning Post, and data for later years are collected and calculated by authors based on investigation cases announced by the CCDI.

The model implies that it is extremely challenging to successfully combat corruption, which requires both fewer regulations and reduced reliance on social connections as alternative mechanisms for governing a market economy, whereas a higher penalty for detected corruption (which is the core of the ongoing anti-graft campaign) is only one of the crucial ingredients of an effective prescription. Another implication of the model is that a reduction in corruption without reduced regulation may slow down economic growth, because market access becomes more restricted for less well-connected firms, which cannot rely on corruption to grease the wheels of a cumbersome bureaucracy.

Empirical findings are also provided to support the two above-mentioned theoretical predictions. Both the amount of regulation and the degree of reliance on social connections significantly explain the level of public corruption in Chinese provinces, while the higher penalty introduced by the current anticorruption campaign has reduced investment growth at the prefectural city level in China.

The remainder of this chapter is structured as follows. Section 1 outlines a theoretical model that explains how corruption emerges as the rational choice of

TABLE 3.1.   Corruption rankings by country

	TRANSPARENCY SNAPSHOT		
COUNTRY	2017 RANK	2016 RANK	CHANGE
New Zealand	1	1	0
Denmark	2	1	−1
Finland	3	3	0
Norway	3	6	−3
Switzerland	3	5	+2
Singapore	6	7	+1
Sweden	6	4	−2
Canada	8	9	+1
Luxembourg	8	10	+2
Netherlands	8	8	0
Britain	8	10	+2
Hong Kong	13	15	+2
United States	16	18	+2
Japan	20	20	0
China	77	79	+2
Philippines	111	101	−10
North Korea	171	174	+3
Somalia	180	176	−4

Source: Transparency International (2017).

firms solving a maximization problem. Section 2 provides a theoretical discussion of the various factors that help determine the level of corruption as well as the potential effects of anticorruption measures. Section 3 describes empirical findings that are in support of the theoretical predictions linking corruption and various other factors. Section 4 concludes with a discussion and comments on how to evaluate the ongoing anticorruption campaign in China.

1. Explaining Corruption in Chinese Society—A Theoretical Model

While the definition of corruption as the abuse of public power for private gain suggests the importance of government regulation in creating a favorable environment for graft in an economy, the tendency to rely on personal connections in resource allocation also plays an important role in determining the level of corruption in the society. Most likely this explains why countries that have stronger familial ties and rely on social connections tend to register more corruption, including Asian countries influenced by Confucian teachings that respect seniority (such as China and Vietnam) as well as Catholic communities that cherish family connections (such as Italy and most Latin American countries).

To better illustrate the argument above, this section outlines a simple theoretical framework where a firm makes the decision regarding resource allocations in two kinds of investment: that in productive capital directly used to produce goods and services; and that in social capital used to obtain a scarce resource from the government, which is also required in the production process.[2]

To simplify the analysis, let us assume that the firms all produce the same goods. The production of the goods requires two inputs, one of which, the productive input, is purchased on the market, while the other one is controlled and allocated by a social planner (for instance, the government). For ease of exposition, let us refer to the productive factor as "human capital" and the scarce resource allocated by the government as "regulatory capital." Part of the regulatory capital is equally divided among all firms, while the remaining part is assigned to firms based on their level of social capital, with more allotted to those possessing more social capital.

Assume that the government reflects prevailing social preferences. The proportion of regulatory capital assigned according to firms' social capital level is thus a measure of the importance of social connections in the economy. For societies with a greater reliance on personal connections, more of the regulatory capital will be allocated based on the endowment of social capital; whereas for societies that employ fewer personal connections, a larger part of the regulatory capital will be distributed equally among firms.

Each firm is faced with a budget constraint, which limits the total amount of financial resources available to purchase human capital on the market and to obtain regulatory capital from the government. As the regulatory capital allocation relies on the firm's social capital level to some extent, the firm will have an incentive to invest in social capital, which is also costly but is assumed to be the same price for all firms. Under these conditions, the firm then strives to maximize its output.[3]

1.1. Similar Firms

To derive the implications from the model, let us begin with the case of only one type of firm, so that all firms have similar initial characteristics, including their initial social capital endowment, budget constraint, and production function.

Clearly, if the government simply distributes all the regulatory capital equally among the firms, none of the latter will have the incentive to invest in any social capital, allowing all the financial resources to be invested in human capital, which is then combined with the equally allotted regulatory capital to produce the desired output. But when the allocation rule has to do with one's level of social capital, the firms will devote a positive amount of financial resources to build social connections that will help secure regulatory capital from the government.

As all firms are similar, they will all end up choosing the same amount of investment in social capital in equilibrium, which implies equally distributed regulatory capital but reduces the amount of investment that could have been made to human capital. We can refer to the case with positive investment in social capital as the "corruption" outcome. Clearly, total output and thus efficiency is reduced because of corruption, as the competition among firms for obtaining social capital creates pure waste to the economy. Thus, we have arrived at the widely held belief that *corruption lowers output and efficiency* (Murphy, Shleifer, and Vishny 1991, 1993; Shleifer and Vishny 1993).

1.2. Differentiated Firms

Now consider the possibility of differentiated firms. In particular, assume that there are two groups of firms with similar characteristics, except for the following features. Firms in the first group have a high level of social capital endowment to begin with, whereas those in the second group have a low level of initial social capital endowment. In the Chinese context, the first group refers to the state-owned enterprises (SOEs), and the second group consists of the private firms. But more generally, the first group consists of larger firms that are better established, while the second group consists of new start-up firms that lack access to market or other production factors. So the model is a fitting description of any economy where new firms experience discriminatory treatment.

It can be shown under fairly general settings that the second type of firms, which lack initial social capital, are driven to make more investment in social capital. This result is consistent with the common observation in China that *private firms engage in more corruption*.[4]

To have a more realistic depiction of reality, another difference between the two types of firms needs to be introduced: productivity. Without loss of generality, let us assume that the more established firms (for example, SOEs in China) have a low level of productivity (or low efficiency), whereas the new firms are more innovative and more productive. This is in line with both economic theory and empirical findings.

In the presence of differential productivity, investment in social capital (i.e., corruption) now has two implications. As discussed above, it still brings about social waste, because fewer resources are available to invest in human capital, the productive factor in creating output. But in addition, the higher social capital investment made by the second type of firms now gains access for them to precious regulatory capital, which is also required for the production process. Because these new firms are more productive, their investment in social capital and the consequent access to production allows the possibility for the total output and the efficiency of the whole economy to increase.

In contrast to the conclusion in Section 1.1 that corruption uniformly lowers output and efficiency due to the pure social waste caused by investment in social capital, in the case with differentiated firms, investment in social capital can help some firms gain access to production opportunities and thus increase output and efficiency, when market access is more limited for firms with higher productivity and less social capital endowment. In such cases, corruption may help the economy achieve both higher total output and higher efficiency, as long as the new firms' productivity is sufficiently high. This is essentially the "greasing-the-wheel" theory of corruption (Leff 1964, Krueger 1974, Lui 1985, Mauro 1995), which maintains that *corruption could enhance output and efficiency when it helps more productive firms gain more market access.*[5]

2. Corruption and Its Correlates in China

The framework outlined above helps us understand the many factors that cause corruption, as well as the potential effects of various anticorruption measures.

2.1. Causes of Corruption

As can be seen from the model described above, although it is firms that engage in corrupt behaviors (i.e., invest in social capital), the root of corruption lies in the economic reality that regulatory capital is required during the production process, and its allocation rule is based on the firm's social capital. Thus, the emergence of corruption relies on both the prevalence of regulation and the division rule of regulatory resources with a dependence on social connections. But the model outlined above implies that other factors also play a role in explaining corruption. We discuss the various causes of corruption below.

RELIANCE ON SOCIAL CONNECTIONS INCREASES CORRUPTION

If all production factors are purchased on the market, then firms compete for them guided by price signals, with no resources wasted in the rent-seeking behaviors. But as the rule of assignment is determined by the government for regulatory capital, additional costs may result. If the allocation of regulatory capital follows the equal division rule, which is strictly enforced, then the only additional cost will be the administrative cost due to bureaucratic process.

Assuming strict rule enforcement, rent-seeking behaviors of government officials who may be interested in using their delegated authority for private gains are nonexistant. But once this assumption is relaxed, the allocation of regulatory capital will depend on the extent of connections between the firm and the government bureaucrat in charge of distributing the regulatory capital. The greater the reliance placed on social connections when assigning regulatory capital, the more corruption will be expected, as more resources will be invested in building social capital. It is thus not surprising that one sees more graft in countries where close social ties and personal relationships are more cherished.

PREVALENCE OF REGULATION BREEDS CORRUPTION

Given the reality that strict equal division of regulatory capital is not possible, the existence of regulation necessarily leads to corruption, and greater prevalence of regulation in the economy is correlated with higher levels of corruption.

Firms choose to invest in social capital, which takes resources away from investment in productive human capital, because regulatory capital is required in the production process. So the less important regulatory capital is in the production process, the less need there is to spend resources on socially wasteful social capital. Conversely, if the production process involves more regulation, then profit-maximizing firms will choose to engage in more corruption. Along the same line, if more sectors in the economy are under heavy regulation, then more firms (from more sectors) will make investment in social capital, resulting in more corruption in the economy as a whole.

DISADVANTAGE IN INITIAL SOCIAL CAPITAL INTENSIFIES THE NEED FOR CORRUPTION

In cases involving different types of firms, the variation in their initial social capital endowment is also key in explaining how much firms engage in corruption. Those with less social capital to begin with are at a disadvantage in the allocation of regulatory capital; thus they will need to make up for the gap by investing more in connections, or resorting to more graft.

Social commentators often resort to moral judgments or ethical standards when comparing the amount of corruption by private firms versus SOEs in China. But one should take into account that private firms have been routinely discriminated against in almost all areas, making it an absolute necessity for them to rely on corruption to grease the wheels of business. In some sense, private business owners in China have been forced into the gray area of unethical behaviors by the burdensome regulatory requirements.[6]

ECONOMIC GROWTH ENGENDERS MORE CORRUPTION

With the Chinese economy experiencing unprecedented continuous growth over the past forty years, it is not surprising that this growth has been accompanied by ever-increasing corruption. China's growth has been achieved in an economic system laden with heavy governmental regulation, which often increases in volume and variety along with economic growth.

As discussed in the above sections, in such a context, a larger economy implies more firms in need of regulatory capital. In addition, as firms grow in size with economic expansion, each firm accumulates more financial resources that can be used to purchase inputs for future production, which further intensifies the competition for the scarce regulatory capital among firms, leading to more investment in social capital. The larger number of firms and the higher average investment in social capital by each firm thus results in more corruption as the economy grows in size.

PENALTY REDUCES CORRUPTION BUT HAS LIMITATIONS

Against the multiple factors contributing to an ever-rising level of corruption in China, there is the lone restraining force of punishment for graft. Realizing the damage to its reputation for providing equal income distribution and the potential danger to social stability caused by increasing corruption, the Chinese government has continuously battled corruption and implemented many specific measures over the years. All these efforts share the same strategy of increasing the expected penalty on those caught engaging in corruption.

In the analytical framework outlined above, a higher penalty for corruption is equivalent to increased price of social capital, thus implying fewer investment activities in it (Becker 1968). Yet there is uncertainty regarding the total amount of resources invested in social capital. In other words, whereas the quantity of grafting is reduced, we do not know for sure whether the total value of corruption will be lower. One can think of the quantity of corruption as the number of people engaged in corruption but the total value of corruption as the total amount of funds involved.

Of course, if the punishment becomes extremely harsh (for example, frequent applications of the death penalty), then the dampening effect on corruption will be fierce and swift. But the possibility of political motivation and wrongful conviction limits the long-term use of this approach, implying that any such campaign has to be short lived without the society descending into total tyranny.

2.2. Challenges in Fighting Corruption and Potential Effects of Anticorruption Measures

The discussion above implies that the primary causes of corruption are institutional ones. On one hand, formal institutions determine the degree of governmental intervention in the economy via regulation and the severity of penalties imposed on corrupted parties via the application of legal and executive measures. (The former increases the benefit from corruption, whereas the latter increases the cost of corruption). On the other hand, informal institutions, such as the importance of social connections in resource allocation, increase the benefit from corruption, which, combined with the regulatory requirements on production, result in more wasteful investment in social capital.

Two additional sets of factors are helpful in accounting for variations in the level of corruption. Technological factors play an important role in determining individual firms' decisions regarding how much investment to make in social capital. Thus firms whose production technology assigns greater importance to human capital are less involved in social capital investment and thus engage less in corruption. Initial endowment of social capital also helps explain the variation in corruption engagement among firms, where those with lower initial endowment compensate for their disadvantaged positions by investing more in social capital, which manifests as more involvement in corruption.

But as the root of corruption is institutional in nature, any long-term solution to the ills of graft will have to rely on fundamental institutional changes. For formal institutions, although the high intensity of a campaign-style fight on corruption could have immediate short-term success, the deterrence effect can only be long lasting if the inspection and punishment mechanisms can be installed as a set of impartial and transparent institutions that are insulated from executive or even personal interference. With the absence of meaningful independence of the judiciary system in China, it is hard to imagine how such institutional changes could come about.

Another channel through which corruption could be reduced in the long term is deregulation, so that the government would play a less important role in allocating resources required for the production process, thus leading to a reduced need for firms to compete for social capital with scarce resources. This solution is consistent with economic logic and is supported by the country's publicly pronounced goal of letting the market play the decisive role in allocating productive resources.[7] But the reality of China's gradualist approach to economic reforms implies that the areas in most need of structural reforms or deregulation lie exactly in the fields with the most entrenched vested interests, making the prospect of deregulation extremely challenging.

The even more challenging type of changes relate to informal institutions. As customs and social norms in a traditional society like China attach high value to personal relationships and the consequent preferential treatment, the individual bureaucrats in charge of resource allocation are bound to assign a positive weight to the amount of personal connection they have with the firms applying for regulatory capital from them, regardless of what the formal distribution rules stipulate. Accordingly, the firms operating in such an environment cannot escape the fate of trying to curry favor with the bureaucrats by investing in social capital with them. And as argued by North (1981) and Williamson (2000), informal institutions are the slowest to evolve, often taking centuries to manifest any visible changes. Given the long tradition of Chinese society relying on social connections as a governance mechanism, it would thus be extremely challenging to lessen the role played by social capital in any resource allocation mechanism that involves personal discretion.

It should be clear by now that combating corruption is very challenging in traditional societies such as China, and that any long-term effective cure to the social ill of corruption will require a combination of institutional changes, formal and informal, to be implemented with unrelenting effort over a long period of time. Among the various institutional changes required, increased pressure and penalties for corrupt behavior, albeit challenging, may be the easiest way to muster public support. The more important requirement to deregulate many economic sectors will undoubtedly face fierce opposition from vested interest groups, who benefit handsomely from the current regulatory arrangements that grant their monopolistic gains. Yet the most challenging task comes from the need to gradually transform the social norm of valuing personal connections in all economic and social activities, which may take centuries to achieve.

Because the phenomenon of corruption has deep economic roots, any measures aimed at combating corruption that are short of the complete prescription described above will have great economic consequences, many of which will be negative. Without the prescribed reduction in regulation and the required rule change in regulatory capital distribution (only equal division is allowed), firms that need regulatory capital in their production processes will only be able to rely on their initially endowed social capital to obtain it.

As a result, firms with less initial social capital but potentially higher productivity will have more limited market access, leading to lower investment and output; while firms with lower productivity but better social connections will occupy a larger share of the market. Thus we would expect to observe lower output and less investment in human capital by high-productivity firms, which also implies lower investment, output, and productivity for the whole economy.

3. Causes and Effects of Corruption in China: Empirical Evidence

The model discussed in the previous section has two straightforward implications. First, multiple factors determine the level of corruption, many of which are difficult to changes, making corruption an extremely challenging phenomenon to combat. Second, the economic fundamentals that account for the emergence and existence of corruption imply that any piecemeal anticorruption measure(s) short of the whole prescription package (which requires crucial institutional reforms) will have important negative short-term impacts on the economy. Let us now discuss some empirical findings that provide support for these theoretical predictions.

3.1. Factors Determining the Level of Corruption

The various factors outlined in section 2.1 that determine the level of corruption can be tested empirically. A recent study by Li et al. (2018) provides findings that are in support of the theoretical predictions.

In particular, the authors make use of Chinese provincial level data for the period of 1999–2012 to explore the potential determinants of corruption levels. The number of local cadres who were prosecuted for corruption is used as the measure of corruption in each province, for which the variables that can potentially explain include the National Economic Research Institute (NERI) index of marketization for the region, an index of the importance of *guanxi* (the number of lawyers in a region divided by its population), as well as the region's GDP (adjusted by its consumer price index [CPI]) and its number of industrial firms.

The NERI index is a proxy for the amount of regulation in the region, and in some specifications, the two NERI subindices are used as alternative measures that evaluate the relationship between market and government and the degree of government intervention over firms in the region, respectively. The *guanxi* index is meant to explore the impact of informal institutions (such as social connections in determining corruption levels), the presence of lawyers is a measure of the expected amount of penalty for corruption, and the regional GDP and the number of firms control the effects of economic growth on corruption.

The empirical findings are consistent with the theoretical predictions. In particular, government regulation and reliance on *guanxi* are both positively correlated with corruption, as are regional GDP and the number of firms. In contrast, the per capita number of lawyers has a negative correlation with regional corruption. These results are robust to several alternative specifications.

3.2. Effects of the Anticorruption Campaign

The damaging effects on economic growth, as predicted by the economic model outlined in section 1 and discussed in section 2.2, have also been corroborated by empirical evidence. Using monthly data at the prefectural level in China for January 2013 to December 2015, Huang and Long (2018) have documented the following pattern. The prefectural fixed-asset investment growth rate slowed down significantly a month after the announcement of a corruption investigation involving government officials from the same prefectural city (see Figure 3.2). This scatterplot shows that, compared to the other regions, the average growth rate of fixed-asset investment in the impacted regions hovered at around zero in the months leading up to an investigation, but then the data points for relative growth rate drop to the negative values for the first four months following an investigation.

The finding suggests that the higher penalty introduced by the anticorruption campaign has caused a reduction in investment growth in the impacted region. In addition, the empirical results show that the negative impact of corruption is mitigated in regions with less government intervention in the economy.

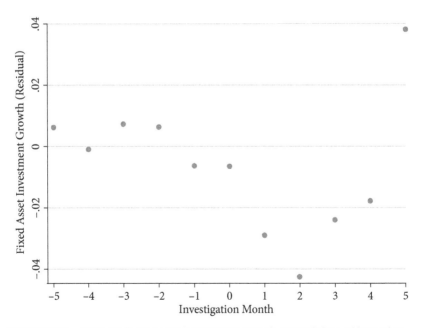

FIGURE 3.2.   Average fixed asset investment growth around time of investigation (January 2013–December 2015).

Note: Investigation month = 0 denotes the month when an investigation is announced by CCDI.

Several robustness checks have been conducted, giving essentially the same results. And tests for alternative explanations also lend more support to the "greasing-the-wheel" theory of corruption, highlighting the potential short-term damage to the economy of the anticorruption campaign, which has not been accompanied by the appropriate deregulation reforms.[8]

4. Challenges in Fighting Corruption in Transition Economies

It is now time to summarize what we have learned about corruption fighting from China's recent experiences. The theoretical analysis and the empirical findings have shown that by imposing a higher penalty, the ongoing anticorruption campaign may have succeeded in curbing much of the detectable corrupt behaviors, but the campaign has also had a negative impact on the Chinese economy, as far as investment growth is concerned.

Some observers may shrug this result off as merely a temporary cost to pay for long-term gains from graft cutting, but the complexities of corruption fighting makes us think otherwise. Any effort to effectively solve the problem of corruption in the long run needs to implement fundamental institutional changes to root out the fundamental causes of corruption. As a consequence, a campaign-style fight against corruption that relies on short-term expediencies or strong-man work styles will eventually fail, unless a society gives up opportunities for economic growth or adopts the planned economy mode for development. In addition, the long tradition of reliance on personal relationship dies hard in a traditional society, adding even more challenge to the task of corruption fighting. Consequently, one has to be cautious about the prospect of long-term success for President's Xi ongoing anticorruption campaign, which has not integrated many institutional changes called for by theoretical analysis, formal or informal.

Notes

1. For earlier review studies on corruption, see Bardhan (1997), Rose-Ackerman (1997), Treisman (2000), and Aidt (2003, 2009).
2. For a formal mathematical model and the related proofs, see Li et al. (2018).
3. As long as the price of the final good is not too high in comparison to those of the inputs, revenue maximization is equivalent to profit maximization for firms whose production function has constant returns to scale (Li et al. 2018).
4. See Wedeman (2012) for detailed discussion on corruption in China.
5. For empirical tests of the greasing wheel theory, see Mo (2001) and Méon and Weill (2010), among others.

6. A Chinese idiom refers to this phenomenon colorfully as "forced prostitution" (*biliangweichang*).

7. See Communist Party of China: "We must deepen economic system reform by centering on the decisive role of the market in allocating resources, adhere to and improve the basic economic system, accelerate the improvement of the modern market system, macro-control system and open economic system."

8. Long, Zhang, and Yang (2016) provide firm level evidence for the negative effects of anti-corruption measures on Chinese listed companies.

References

Aidt, T. S. 2003. "Economic Analysis of Corruption: A Survey." *Economic Journal* 113: 632–652.

Aidt, T. S. 2009. "Corruption, Institutions, and Economic Development." *Oxford Review of Economic Policy* 25: 271–291.

Bardhan, P. 1997. "Corruption and Development: A Review of Issues." *Journal of Economic Literature* 35: 1320–1346.

Becker, G. S. 1968. "Crime and Punishment: An Economic Approach." *Journal of Political Economy* 76: 169–217.

Communist Party of China. 2013. Communiqué of the Third Plenary Session of the 18th Central Committee of the CPC. http://www.china.org.cn/chinese/2014-01/16/content_31213800.htm.

Huang, X., and C. X. Long. 2018. "Anti-corruption Campaign and Investment Growth in China." Xiamen University Working Paper, Xiamen, China.

Krueger, A. O. 1974. "The Political Economy of the Rent-Seeking Society." *American Economic Review* 64: 291–303.

Leff, N. H. 1964. "Economic Development through Bureaucratic Corruption." *American Behavioral Scientist* 8: 8–14.

Li, M., C. X. Long, and J. Yang. 2018. "Corruption and Social Connection in China: Theory and Empirics." Xiamen University Working Paper, Xiamen, China.

Long, C. X., X. Zhang, and J. Yang. 2016. "Economic Effects of Dual Employment Regulation during Economic Transition." *China Industrial Economics* (in Chinese) 7: 40–56.

Lui, F. T. 1985. "An Equilibrium Queuing Model of Bribery", *Journal of Political Economy*, Vol. 93, 760–781.

Mauro, P. 1995. "Corruption and Growth." *The Quarterly Journal of Economics*, Vol. 110, 681–712.

Méon, P. H., and L. Weill. 2010. "Is Corruption an Efficient Grease?" *World Development*, Vol. 38, 244–259.

Mo, P. H. 2001. "Corruption and Economic Growth." *Journal of Comparative Economics* 29: 66–79.

Murphy, K. M., A. Shleifer, and R. W. Vishny. 1991. "The Allocation of Talent: Implications for Growth." *Quarterly Journal of Economics* 106: 503–530.

Murphy, K. M., A. Shleifer, and R. W. Vishny. 1993. "Why Is Rent-Seeking So Costly to Growth?" *American Economic Review* 83: 409–414.

North, Douglass C. 1981. *Structure and Change in Economic History*. Cambridge: Cambridge University Press.

Rose-Ackerman, R. 1997. "The Political Economy of Corruption." In K. A. Elliott (ed.), *Corruption and the Global Economy*. Washington, DC: Institute for International Economics, 31–60.

Shleifer, A., and R. W. Vishny. 1993. "Corruption." *Quarterly Journal of Economics* 108: 599–617.

Transparency International. 2017.

Treisman, D. 2000. "The Causes of Corruption: A Cross-National Study." *Journal of Public Economics* 76: 399–457.

Wedeman, A. 2012. *Double Paradox: Rapid Growth and Rising Corruption in China.* Ithaca, NY: Cornell University Press.

Williamson, O. 2000. "The New Institutional Economics: Taking Stock, Looking Ahead." *Journal of Economic Literature* 38: 595–613.

OVERRELIANCE ON LAW

Rural Credit in India, 1875–2010

Anand V. Swamy

> **In England we consider the agricultural seasons a failure which do
> not give 80% of the normal crop. In parts of the Bombay Deccan,
> I calculated some years ago that, in 1918 there was only 9% of a
> normal crop, and in 1920 very little more. No normal banking system,
> as usually understood, can face such a situation.**

—Harold Mann (1957, 78)

In the 1860s, the American Civil War cut off supplies of cotton to Britain. There
were huge profits to be made by growing cotton, and farmers in the Bombay Deccan, in western India, did precisely this. Lenders flocked to finance the costs of
cultivation, and a bubble emerged. Borrowers took loans from multiple lenders.
The bubble burst after the price of cotton fell. Lenders were no longer willing to
provide credit to overleveraged borrowers. In response, Deccan peasants "rioted"
in 1875, attacking moneylenders and seizing the documents that recorded their
loans. The hypercautious British Raj, already alarmed by claims of large-scale
default-related transfer of land from peasants to moneylenders, responded with
the Deccan Agriculturists' Relief Act (DARA) of 1879. Its goal was to protect the
borrower from lenders, who were viewed as unscrupulous and needing strict su-
pervision. Special courts were set up, and judges were given enormous discretion
to go "behind the bond" (i.e., look for bad faith on the part of the lender). DARA
also incorporated interest-rate ceilings and limited loan repayment to a maximum
of twice the original principal, an Indian credit rule known as *damdupat*.[1]

The Deccan crisis represented the failure of the private moneylenders to provide protection against an aggregate shock—the fall in the price of cotton. This
failure should not have been surprising, because these moneylenders did not have
deep pockets. But the Raj identified the problem as primarily one of lender malfeasance. Over the next 75 years, it passed a series of legislations to curb the private lender via usury laws, debt relief, and outright restrictions on land transfer
as a consequence of default. After independence, the Indian government, appropriately, took on the task of providing cheap rural credit and relief in the face of

aggregate shocks. Its action has helped alleviate poverty, but at a high cost, some of which is due to rent seeking. But the Indian government also doubled down on legislation to suppress the private lender, which has proved ineffectual. Moneylenders have not been eliminated, because only they have sufficiently good information to insure the rural poor against idiosyncratic shocks.

In the past three decades, the new kid on the block is microfinance. Again, it comes in two incarnations, the state-subsidized self-help group and the for-profit Microfinance Institution (MFI). The former has received good press, and there is credible research showing its benefits. The latter has been stigmatized via explicit comparison to the moneylenders. Former Reserve Bank of India Governor Y. Venugopal Reddy has said regarding the MFI that "if it is for profit and there is aggressive lending, it's just moneylending." He points out that while moneylenders lend their own money, MFIs often lend their members' deposits—thus the MFI is therefore just a "leveraged moneylender" and should be subject to the same type of regulation. The newspaper headline accompanying his remarks may have oversimplified his views: "For-profit MFI is worse than moneylenders."[2] Reddy's comments came in in 2010 after the MFI industry went through a crisis remarkably similar to that of the Bombay Deccan of the 1870s and ended with an even more draconian regulatory response. We seemed to have come full circle. Cooler heads have now prevailed, and MFI regulation is more sensible.[3] But the risk remains that the crises caused by low and variable incomes will again be overattributed to lender malfeasance and that counterproductive regulation will follow.[4]

I flesh out this argument in the remainder of this chapter. Section 1 discusses the late colonial period and describes the legal and policy regime that tried to suppress the private moneylender and, to a limited extent, encourage the emergence of credit cooperatives. Section 2 describes the first two decades after independence, when private moneylenders faced even more legal restrictions, and state-subsidized finance was primarily provided by credit cooperatives, which suffered from rent-seeking. Section 3 describes the era of state-subsidized public sector bank expansion, roughly 1975–1991. Bank expansion may have reduced rural poverty, but again, rent-seeking was common. Section 4 discusses the period of India's economic liberalization, starting in 1991: Policies have oscillated, with periods of rural banking decline, rural banking expansion, and the growth of microfinance. Throughout this narrative, the central argument discussed here is relevant. The core problem is that of low and uncertain incomes. In this environment, lenders must either be state subsidized and exposed to rent-seeking or, to remain financially viable, they will charge high interest rates and adopt recovery practices that will be perceived as cruel. As of now, we have to choose between these two evils, and no regulation can change this.

1. The Colonial Period

In early colonial India (1765–1857), legislation regarding land and credit had modest objectives. The state's overwhelming interest was in collecting taxes. It did not particularly matter who paid them. The transfer of land from one social group to another, whether by sale or via default on debt, was welcome, especially if the new owner had more capital. However, after the Mutiny of 1857, there was a complete change of attitude, and laissez-faire was abandoned in relation to land and credit. The goal became to maintain social stability by protecting the traditional landowner from the moneylender. In the early twentieth century, when the Indian national movement mobilized against colonial rule, it embraced these attitudes. Independent India then inherited them. This section tells this story.

Though land was transferable even in precolonial India, the early British Raj clarified ownership titles, so that lenders gained confidence in its value as collateral. The colonial state also played a much larger role in the enforcement of contracts than had previous regimes had. A lender in precolonial times may have had to rely on personal resources or the village council to recover money from a debtor. Lending relied heavily on personal connections within a small geographical area. Under the British, the lender could approach a District Court to recover money. Lenders could migrate to regions where the demand for credit was high, relying on the state to enforce contracts.

Dramatic changes occurred on the demand side as well. The East India Company wanted Indian agricultural produce—cotton, opium, indigo, tea—to be exported. This was facilitated by improvements in transportation, especially by the introduction of railways in the second half of the century. It also necessarily involved greater peasant involvement in the cash economy. A millet farmer who formerly consumed much of his or her crop might now grow cotton, sell it, and buy food. Because cotton was more resource intensive than traditional crops, the farmer now needed to borrow money. Especially in the first half of the nineteenth century, land taxes, which were collected in cash, were high. This also forced the peasant to borrow, especially since compared to preceding regimes, the Raj was more ruthless and effective in collecting taxes. For all these reasons, the demand for credit increased. In relatively poor regions with uncertain rainfall and limited irrigation, the moneylender was often an "immigrant" from another part of British India.

The process described in the two preceding paragraphs is usually called "commercialization," and its impact on the fortunes of the peasantry has been the subject of considerable debate. Commercialization certainly led to an expansion of the area under cultivation, but it has also been argued that exposure to the vagaries of international prices was hazardous for the Indian peasant. The combination of market exposure, weather fluctuations, and high land taxation, it is said, forced peasants to borrow. Often, they were unable to repay and needed the lender's forbearance. They often received it, but when credit bubbles occurred, with too many lenders and too much lending (or the borrower had otherwise become unviable), the moneylender would foreclose and seize land or refuse to lend any further. This could lead to violence against moneylenders. A prominent example is the Deccan Riots of 1875, discussed at the start of this chapter.

For the British, these riots were a political problem. The Raj always consisted of a very small number of Europeans ruling over a subcontinent. They believed the peasantry to be the backbone of Indian society and saw agrarian unrest as threatening their rule. British officialdom also came to embrace an argument that is still highly influential. According to this view, Indian peasants were naïve about financial and legal matters, especially compared to professional moneylenders. By facilitating borrowing against land, the Raj had, as one official put it, conferred a "fatal boon" on the feckless Indian peasant. This boon had to be taken back. How could it be revoked?

As mentioned above, the British era had seen two innovations that made it easier to lend. One was the operation of a court system, which supported impersonal lending. The second was facilitating the transferability of land. In the Bombay Deccan, the Raj chose to alter the way in which courts enforced contracts via the DARA of 1879, discussed in the introduction. As mentioned above, two important elements of this law were interest rate ceilings and a ceiling on the total repayment, limiting it to twice the original principal. But if the borrower's income is low and variable, he will often default. Interest rate ceilings may make lending unprofitable. Moreover, even if the borrower eventually repays, if the total repayment is limited to twice the principal, the lender's return will be low. DARA probably drove out the professional, often immigrant, lenders, who needed to resort to courts, and forced the poor peasant to rely on the mercies of his richer neighbors, who had more "informal" ways of enforcing contracts. Thus, an Act meant to protect peasants may have increased their vulnerability in some ways.[5]

But DARA was by no means the most radical intervention by the Raj. Many British officials felt that this legislation was too feeble. It left too many loopholes that the ingenious moneylender could exploit. For instance, a loan could be disguised by a repurchase agreement: Party A could "sell" his land to party B for 100 rupees and "buy" it back for 120 rupees. Default on the loan would leave the land with the creditor/purchaser. British officials were especially worried about credit when it came to the dealings between moneylenders and tribal populations that were geographically remote and culturally somewhat distinct from the mainstream of Hindu society. The tribal farmer was considered no match for the far more sophisticated immigrant moneylender. The policy adopted in this instance was to ban land transfer by tribals altogether, or to limit the transfer to another member of the tribe. A similar policy was enacted in the Punjab, a politically sensitive border region. The British were particularly concerned about western Punjab, where the lenders were Hindus and the borrowers were Muslim, and there was potential for lender-borrower and Hindu-Muslim tensions to reinforce each other. The Raj passed the famous Punjab Land Alienation Act of 1901, which prohibited the transfer of land from "agricultural castes" to "nonagricultural castes." This legislation was highly complex, requiring, among other things, district-by-district definition of which castes were "agricultural" and which were not.

Historians have argued that the Punjab Act made life worse for the poor Punjabi peasant, for reasons similar to those discussed above. The professional "nonagriculturist" moneylender was not interested in owning land—it locked up capital. But now that they had been weakened, poorer farmers were forced to borrow from richer farmers. Richer farmers were more interested in owning land and more likely to foreclose on mortgages. The Punjab Land Alienation Act was also evaded in clever ways. The "nonagriculturist" who wanted to lend money to an "agriculturist" sought the help of another "agriculturist" friend, who would be the ostensible creditor and would seize the land if the debtor defaulted. Again, in the name of protecting the borrower, corruption was being built into the system. This device of transacting ownership of properties in another person's name is known as *benami* and is used to avoid governmental regulation to this day.

By the 1930s, another big player was in the picture: the movement for Indian independence. Under Mahatma Gandhi, the movement had drawn in the peasantry. After the Depression, when agrarian India went into crisis, farmers were unable to repay their debts. A slew of new legislation was passed, especially by provincial governments, which, following the Government of India Act of 1935, were run by Indians. One set, the moneylender acts, were in the spirit of the Deccan Agriculturists' Relief Act mentioned above—they imposed interest rate ceilings, required moneylenders to register, and so forth. The second set was more radical. Various provinces passed debt relief acts, which provided ex post insurance, requiring the peasant to repay the moneylender significantly less than the latter was owed. In Punjab, the Indian provincial government proposed legislation in 1938 that simply canceled mortgage debt acquired before 1900 and also extended some of the provisions of the Punjab Land Alienation Act to agriculturist lenders as well. This led to a dramatic decline in mortgage lending, as figure 4.1 shows. To reveal the impact of the legislations on mortgage lending, the figure includes land sales, which did not see any decline.

Over time in Punjab and elsewhere, it was becoming increasingly difficult for private lenders to operate. Who would replace them? The cash-strapped Raj was not inclined to do much. It provided some agricultural credit, via the Land

FIGURE 4.1. Mortgages and sales in Punjab, 1925–1943.

Source: Authors' computations using Punjab, Board of Economic Inquiry, Agricultural Statistics of British Punjab (Lahore: Board of Economic Inquiry, n.d.).

Improvement Loans Act of 1883 and the Agriculturists Loans Act of 1884, but the sums were very modest. However, the Raj was forced to be more proactive by terrible famines in the late nineteenth century. The commissions it set up to investigate the causes of these famines and potential solutions had to address the question of credit. It was natural for the commissions to look toward the European experience. Rural credit cooperatives had emerged in several European countries, most notably in Germany. The rationale for the credit cooperative provided by the Famine Commission of 1901 has a very contemporary flavor, resembling the rationale for microfinance and self-help groups:[6]

> The underlying idea of all Mutual Credit Associations, such as we recommend, is that a number of persons, by combining together, create a new and valuable security, which none of them previously possessed as individuals. . . . It is simpler for a creditor to deal with a group of 50 or a 100 associated cultivators than with the same number singly; it is simpler for him to obtain repayment from the group than from each of the members composing it; it is simpler for the group to make its own arrangements with each member than for the lender to try to do so.

The cooperative would also, in principle, allow members to insure one another against idiosyncratic risks by rescheduling payments or paying for one another. In

1904, the central government passed an act allowing the formation of rural cooperative credit societies. The model was the Raiffeisen Society, named after its German inventor. Members would deposit savings as well as borrow. The key feature was unlimited liability (i.e., each member was liable for all the debts of the society).

The credit cooperatives were a European transplant, with no clear indigenous precedent. Their introduction was therefore top-down, with the state rather than the village community taking the lead. So, while in principle the cooperative was expected to be driven by the initiative and resources of its members, in fact government officials played a very important role. External involvement went hand-in-hand with another key aspect of the functioning of the cooperatives: They depended heavily on state resources rather than on members' deposits.

Though the number of rural credit cooperatives grew rapidly in the colonial period, they did not function very well. The most obvious symptom of this was the high rate of defaults. Cooperatives worked well in some irrigated regions, but where agriculture was unproductive and risky, cooperatives floundered. Even though the Raj was sometimes willing to use extremely coercive methods to recover loans, after the Depression, many cooperative societies had a large percentages of overdue loans (see table 4.1). Two other factors were also relevant, besides productivity. In stratified Indian villages with substantial caste divisions and animosities, cooperation was difficult. Also, wealthier peasants, who had resources to offer, were reluctant to join because of unlimited liability.[7] At the end of the colonial era, the consensus was that the cooperative movement had failed.

The British Raj had also created another problem, which, though not politically explosive, was still of substantive importance for the functioning of credit markets: It was not clear to the state who had what rights on a particular piece of land. Rights to land were recorded in two distinct locations. On the one hand, the land taxation department kept track of who owed taxes on a particular piece

TABLE 4.1. Overdue loans in Indian cooperatives, 1939

PROVINCE	AMOUNT OF LOAN OUTSTANDING IN RUPEES (LAKHS)	PERCENTAGE OF OVERDUE LOANS TO OUTSTANDING LOANS
Madras	351.99	46.1
Bombay	247.36	51.8
Bengal	396.39	87.4
U.P.	75.91	47.7
Punjab	629.40	40.8
Bihar	104.18	92.5

Source: Quereishi (1947, 58).

of land. On the other hand, transactions in land, such as sales and mortgages, were recorded by the registration department. In principle, a transaction recorded by the registration department should have led to alteration in the records of the land taxation department. But this coordination often did not happen, so it was not clear who owned a piece of land. This remains true to the present day and increases costs of land transactions, whether mortgages or sales.[8]

To sum up, the colonial period left five important legacies. The first was a highly negative attitude toward moneylenders and legislation to suppress them. Second, debt relief legislation was now part of the policymaker's toolkit. Third, restrictions on land transfers were part of the policy apparatus. Fourth, transaction costs of even legal land transfers were high. The fifth was the legacy of the state-heavy cooperatives' structure. Given the bad experience with cooperatives in the colonial period, we might have expected policymakers in independent India to be wary of them. In fact, as explained below, they enthusiastically embraced credit cooperatives, while attacking the private lender even more strongly.

2. Replacing the Moneylender with the Credit Cooperative: 1950–1975

The Indian central bank, the Reserve Bank of India (RBI), had been set up in 1935. After independence, it conducted the All-India Rural Credit Survey, a large-scale and ambitious effort, to collect evidence on which future policy would be based. The committee produced a vast volume of documentation, and its report was hugely influential. The RBI concluded that there was really no alternative to the credit cooperative—cooperation had failed because it had not received adequate state support. The cooperative was up against an array of powerful and interconnected forces. The moneylender, the trader, the landlord, and the lower levels of administration were in cahoots, often on the strength of caste-based relationships. A cooperative consisting of poor peasants could hardly be expected to compete with them. The RBI argued that "the forces of transformation have to be at least as powerful as those which are sought to be counteracted. Such forces can be generated not by Cooperation alone but by Cooperation in conjunction with the State."[9]

The paternalistic attitude of the report can be best understood by an analogy it used, to explain why the state had to support the cooperative:[10]

> One may consider an institution for the rehabilitation of crippled children struck down by the malady of infantile paralysis. The little patients are studied, courses of treatment prescribed and carried out, muscles gradually strengthened and all efforts made to rehabilitate them

and send them back to normal life. No one has yet suggested that those children should depend on themselves as much as possible and form themselves into a mutual association for individual rehabilitation.

It is not clear why the RBI and the rest of the Indian government, including the Planning Commission, were so confident that, with increased state support, the cooperatives would succeed. Ideological considerations, rather than the history of the cooperative movement in India, seem to have played a role. The village community had been idealized by Mahatma Gandhi. After independence, Acharya Vinoba Bhave, a Gandhian leader, was touring the country to persuade wealthier farmers to donate land for the poor (*Bhoodan*), and there was even a program in which the village as a whole would be owned by the community (*gramdan*). In 1959, the lower house in the Parliament of India (*Lok Sabha*) went so far as to express the hope that cooperative farming (i.e., cultivation itself, not just marketing and credit) would emerge. The socialist countries of that day were probably the inspiration for this idea. In comparison, the credit cooperative was a less ambitious undertaking!

Given state involvement and subsidized credit, the more powerful members of rural society tried to capture the cooperatives. This effort was facilitated by a legal change. Recall that in British India, credit cooperatives had operated under unlimited liability, a factor that tended to keep out the rich farmers, who did not want to be saddled with the debts of their poorer neighbors. This practice began to be abandoned immediately after independence. In 1947–1948, The Bombay Cooperative Societies Act (1925) was amended to make unlimited liability optional. The RBI made the same recommendation, and over time, most Indian cooperatives operated under limited liability.

Between December 1958 and June 1959, Daniel Thorner, an American economist, visited 117 cooperatives across the country, asking officials to send him to the ones that were working the best. He writes: "In general, I found that the heads of cooperatives were the big people of the villages and that they had their fingers in many other pies as well as cooperatives." The RBI had hoped that the state-supported cooperatives would take on the moneylenders/traders/landlords. In fact, the latter seem to have often captured the cooperatives. The politician had an outsized role. Punning on the initialism "MLA" (Member of Legislative Assembly) Thorner noted that South India cooperatives were suffering from "emmalaitis."[11]

The number of credit cooperatives and their membership expanded rapidly (see table 4.2). But the system was working poorly. By 1971, official agencies ("Institutional Finance") provided only 29 percent of total credit. Cooperatives provided the bulk of this—20 percent of all rural credit (table 4.3). Deposits continued to be a small fraction of loans. Profits on working capital were very low (table 4.4). As mentioned, due to poverty, risk, and rent-seeking, default rates were high, as shown in table 4.4. Careful village-level surveys came to the same conclusions. Perhaps the most respected studies conducted in the 1970s and 1980s were by the International Crop Research Institute for the Semi Arid Tropics (ICRISAT), whose investigators resided in the village itself and hence had very good information. ICRISAT found that there was a "culture" of non-repayment of loans from cooperatives.[12]

As a legal matter, it was not easy for a cooperative (for credit or another purpose) to shake off the state and operate independently. This was put to legal test in *Daman Singh and Others versus the State of Punjab, 1985.* The petitioners had challenged the state's decision to amalgamate cooperatives, supposedly to make them more effective. The argument was that the Indian Constitution guaranteed

TABLE 4.2. Membership of primary agricultural credit cooperatives, India, 1950–1969

YEARS	NUMBER OF PRIMARY AGRICULTURAL CREDIT COOPERATIVES	AVERAGE MEMBERSHIP	PERCENTAGE OF RURAL POPULATION COVERED BY ACTIVE SOCIETIES	PERCENTAGE OF BORROWING MEMBERS TO TOTAL MEMBERS
1950–1951	115,462	16	N.A.	N.A.
1960–1961	212,129	34	24	53
1968–1969	167,760	57	33	38

Source: Ghatak (1976, 113).
Note: N.A., not available.

TABLE 4.3. Main sources of rural credit, 1951–2013, in percentages

SOURCE OF CREDIT	1951	1961	1971	1981	1991	2002	2013
Cooperative societies/banks, etc.	3.1	9.1	20.1	28.6	18.6	27.3	24.8
Commercial banks, including regional rural banks	0.8	0.4	2.2	28	29	24.5	25.1
Professional moneylenders	44.8	14.9	13.8	8.3	9.4	19.6	
Agricultural moneylenders (rich farmers)	24.9	45.9	23.1	8.6	6.3	10.0	
All moneylenders (sum of above two rows)	69.7	60.8	36.9	16.9	15.7	29.6	33.2

Note: The percentages don't add up to 100, because we have excluded minor sources. The first six columns are taken from Pradhan (2013) and the last from Hoda and Terway (2015). These sources relied on All India Debt and Investment Surveys and NSSO.

TABLE 4.4. Performance of primary agricultural credit cooperatives, India, 1950–1969

YEARS	PERCENTAGE OF DEPOSITS TO WORKING CAPITAL	PERCENTAGE OF OVERDUE LOANS TO OUTSTANDING LOAN	PERCENTAGE OF PROFIT TO WORKING CAPITAL
1950–1951	12.4	22.1	2.1
1960–1961	5.3	20.3	1.6
1968–1969	7.0	34.6	1.2

Source: Ghatak (1976, 113).

the right to form associations. This right was violated if the state could merge this association with another one, which the citizen had not chosen to join. However, the Supreme Court relied on a provision in Article 31 of the Indian Constitution, according to which amalgamation of two "corporations" in the "public interest" could not be challenged on the grounds that it violated a fundamental right. The court ruled that a cooperative is a corporation. The petition was dismissed.

As a result, there was clearly a case for more liberal legislation to allow the formation of cooperatives that were more independent of the government. The Brahm Prakash Committee proposed model legislation along these lines in 1991. Andhra Pradesh and a few other states passed similar legislation. Still, the 2009 High-Powered Committee on Cooperatives recommended the extraordinary step of a constitutional amendment to liberate the cooperative from the state. Article 19, which guarantees various freedoms, would be amended. It would now specifically mention the right to "form and run Cooperatives based on principles of voluntary, democratic member control, member economic participation and autonomous functioning."[13] The ninety-seventh amendment to the Indian Constitution was approved by the president in January 2012. It is a measure of the state-heavy nature of Indian cooperatives that a constitutional amendment was required to (try to) shake it off.

The jury is still out regarding the impact of these legal changes to allow the formation of more autonomous cooperatives. Credit cooperatives have also received fresh infusions of funds to address debt overhang, following the recommendations of the Vaidyanathan Committee (2005). Still, Nonperforming Assets (NPAs) remain high. In 2011–2012 they were 26.8 percent for short-term loans by village-level cooperative societies and 36.7 percent for long-term loans.[14]

In sum, the cooperative movement in India underperformed on two fronts—it has low rates of loan recovery, and cooperatives have been captured by the better off. We do not have statistical evidence on their impact on poverty, nor do we know if they played an insurance function, for instance, by rescheduling debt when the poor needed it. We will be able to consider these issues in the context of public sector banks in the next section.

Meanwhile, what of the professional moneylender? The Government of India might have succeeded in sidelining the professional moneylenders to some extent. The proportion of credit coming from them had fallen from about 45 percent to 14 percent between 1951 and 1971 (see table 4.2), though these figures have to be taken with a large grain of salt. In a compelling critique, Clive Bell (1990) has pointed out that taken at face value, the RBI's figures for the total volume of debt imply implausible levels of credit contraction, inconsistent with careful local studies. It is likely that, after the passing of anti-moneylender legislation (see below), much moneylending simply went underground.

Various Indian states either retained moneylender legislation from the colonial period or passed fresh legislation to protect borrowers from exploitation.[15] The moneylender was required to obtain a license and maintain accounts in a specific format, was prevented from "molesting" the borrower, and was limited to a mandated maximum rate of interest. Some states (such as Rajasthan, Tamil Nadu, Bombay, and Karnataka) applied the rule of *damdupat* (described earlier), according to which the court could not award the lender a sum that exceeded the outstanding principal. Courts had wide discretion to reopen and examine a transaction to assess its fairness. The *Gazetteer of Poona* (Bombay 1954) reported that the Bombay Moneylenders' Act of 1947 was unpopular with moneylenders. Many refused to acquire licenses.

> It is likely therefore that a large number of them have either given up their business or have been doing it illegally. In these circumstances, those to whom moneylenders were an important source of credit now experienced difficulty in obtaining it. In the rural areas there has recently been a marked increase in the number of applications for *tagai* [government] loans which seems to be, at least in part, a result of the contraction of the business of money-lenders.[16]

Fragmentary statistics are consistent with this impression. For instance, the number of licensed moneylenders in Kolhapur district fell from more than 8,000 in 1949–1950 to fewer than 3,000 in 1955–1956.[17]

Various states also passed debt-relief legislation similar to that of the late colonial period. These legislations allowed agricultural borrowers to repay moneylenders less than the amount officially contracted. For instance, the Mysore Agricultural Debtors Relief Act of 1966 allowed a 40 percent reduction of debts incurred before January 1, 1941, and a 30 percent reduction for debts incurred between January 1, 1941 and January 1, 1950. Other legislation included the Gujarat Agricultural Debtors Relief Act of 1972, the Punjab Agricultural Debtors (Relief) Act of 1975, the Andhra Pradesh Agricultural Indebtedness (Relief) Act of 1977, and a slew of similar regulations in other states.[18] Debt relief for farmers continues to be policy relevant in the present day.

The moneylender was viewed not just as an ordinary businessman but as fundamentally antisocial. This perception was made explicit in *Fatehchand Himmatlal and Others versus the State of Maharashtra* in 1977. This case is worth discussing at some length because of the frankness with which a Supreme Court judge explains and justifies his animosity toward the moneylender. The Maharashtra Debt Relief Act of 1975 reduced or liquidated debts to private moneylenders, but not debts to the government, banks, or banking companies. The Act was challenged on the grounds that it violated the right to trade. The counsel for the plaintiffs asked "How is it fair that, if the object of the legislation is to save the victims of rural indebtedness and working-class burdens, that credit institutions should be exempted while noninstitutionalized lenders should be picked out for hostile treatment?"

Rejecting the challenge, Justice Krishna Iyer noted that Article 301 of the Indian Constitution, which referred to "freedom of trade," also permitted restrictions in "public interest." He wrote:

> There is no merit in the plea. Liabilities due to Government or local authorities are not tainted with the exploitation of the debtor. Likewise, debts due to banking companies do not ordinarily suffer from overreaching, unscrupulousness or harsh treatment.

Clearly, the justice believed that moneylenders were "ordinarily" unscrupulous. He went on to argue that "some stray moneylenders may be good souls," but the legislature could not make "meticulous exceptions."

It is of course true that moneylenders can be bad actors, but if interest rate ceilings, *damdupat*, and debt relief make legal lending unviable, law-abiding lenders will abandon the profession and only the unscrupulous will remain. The Reserve Bank of India (2007, 44) itself has noted that "the existing ceilings prescribed under the [moneylending] legislations are out of sync with market reality." It has recommended that instead of specifying a specific maximum for the interest rate, the law should allow the state government to adjust the maximum according to market conditions. Still, an article in a leading newspaper reported in 2015 that in two districts in Karnataka, moneylenders were being arrested for, among other things, charging interest rates in excess of the legal maximum of 14 percent for secured loans and 16 percent for unsecured loans.[19] This is remarkable, because until 2014, the RBI's ceiling for interest rates charged by MFIs was 26 percent. Even the not-for-profit Grameen Bank has charged interest rates that amount to 24 percent per year.[20] Indeed, the credit cards in my wallet, which potentially provide unsecured loans, have often charged more than 16 percent per year, even in the low inflation environment in the United States. In Andhra Pradesh, moneylenders were allowed to charge only 2 percent more than the commercial banks.[21] A similar rule applied in Kerala.[22] When the RBI changed MFI interest rate ceilings in 2014, they were linked to commercial banks as well. But the MFI's rates were allowed to be either 2.75 times the base lending rate of the commercial banks or a margin of 10 percent above costs, whichever was lower. It is difficult to understand why moneylenders were treated so much more strictly. There is loan sharking, no doubt, but legislation should not be so strict as to make legal moneylending unprofitable. It is worth noting (see table 4.2) that moneylenders (professional as well as agricultural, that is, rich farmers) currently provide 33 percent of rural credit.

What has been the impact of restrictions on land transfer, inherited from the colonial period? The Indian Constitution identified areas with large tribal populations and specifically permitted legislation preventing alienation of their land. This restriction potentially reduces tribal access to credit, since their land cannot be used as collateral. But, as mentioned, supporters of this legislation, from the colonial period to the present day, have justified such legislation on the grounds that the poor and financially and legally unsophisticated tribals are vulnerable to predatory moneylenders. Land transfer by tribals has become a much larger issue embroiled in debates on Eminent Domain, as industry seeks possession of their lands, which are often in mineral- or forest-rich areas. A separate and large body of legislation has been passed pertaining to tribal land rights. This class of issues requires a full-length discussion of its own.

3. The Expansion of Rural Banking: 1975–1991

By the end of the 1960s, given the checkered history of rural credit cooperatives, it was inevitable that the government would look for other alternatives. Indeed, as mentioned above, many of the problems faced by cooperatives had been identified during the colonial period itself. Commentators like Anwar Qureishi[23] had suggested that only entities with deep pockets like government-supported banks could effectively operate in India's volatile and precarious rural areas. Beginning in the late 1960s, the bank, rather than the cooperative, began to be viewed as the spearhead of rural credit provision. This change was part of a broader shift in economic policy.

In 1969, Prime Minister Indira Gandhi came to power and began to govern with an agenda that came to be called *garibi hatao* ("abolish poverty"). The state

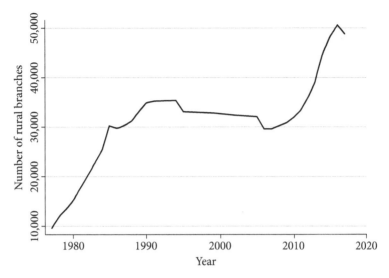

FIGURE 4.2.   Growth of rural branches of commercial banks.

Source: Reserve Bank of India (2017).

would now intervene even more intensively and aggressively than before. Indeed, in 1976, the Constitution of India itself was amended to include the word "socialist" in the description of the Republic of India. One of Indira Gandhi's first steps was to nationalize fourteen major commercial banks in 1969. Another six were nationalized in 1980. From 1976 on, a new set of Regional Rural Banks were opened to serve the rural poor. Banks were given rules for expansion. The focus was to be on opening branches in rural areas or in "unbanked" areas more generally. Figure 4.2 shows the expansion of rural branches of commercial banks. Banks were also given targets for lending. "Priority" sectors were identified, and they were to receive specified fractions of bank lending. As table 4.2 shows, the proportion of rural credit provided by banks increased from 2 percent to 28 percent between 1971 and 1981.

There are four important issues to consider here. First, did government-subsidized credit reach the poor, or was it captured by the better-off? Second, was it effective in reducing poverty? Third, were banks able to recover the money? Finally, did credit also perform an insurance function?

Significant evidence suggests that though the poor did receive subsidized credit, the better off captured a disproportionate share. This was demonstrated by numerous case studies as well as by careful statistical research[24] (see, for instance, table 4.5). There is also convincing statistical evidence that loans were distributed to influence elections, with little benefit to productivity.[25]

TABLE 4.5. Access to formal and informal credit by landownership, Western Orissa, 1981

FARM SIZE GROUP	FORMAL ONLY	INFORMAL ONLY	BOTH FORMAL AND INFORMAL	NOT BORROWING	TOTAL
Landless laborers	4.2	75.71	2.85	17.14	100
Marginal farmers	4.31	56.03	16.37	23.27	100
Small farmers	32.81	29.68	18.75	18.75	100
Medium farmers	42.5	10	27.5	20	100
Large farmers	60	13.34	10	16.66	100

Source: Sarap (1987).
Note: Each cell contains a percentage, which adds up to 100 across the row.

Legal and institutional factors were also in play. Banks usually require collateral. Land is the most important asset in rural India, but its distribution is highly unequal, despite the huge body of land-reform legislation. This skewed the allocation of credit. Also, as mentioned above, it is not always easy to establish rights to a piece of land, which increases transaction costs for the lender.

Even those who do not own land often access it as tenants. Surely, their crops could have been considered collateral? But the nature of (well-intentioned) tenancy legislation got in the way. Most states in India had passed laws giving tenants protection against eviction and arbitrary rent increases, if they could demonstrate that they had occupied a piece of land for a certain length of time, sometimes just a few years. To prevent tenants from gaining protection, landlords often resorted to oral leases. Of course, such leases made it difficult for a tenant to prove his or her status and thereby obtain a loan against crops.[26]

The impact of bank expansion on rural poverty has been the subject of some controversy, because two careful pieces of statistical research have come to quite different conclusions. In general, it is difficult to isolate the benefit of major policy changes like the bank expansion, because they are usually only one piece of a broader package. Also, banks tend to locate in fast-growing areas, where they are more likely to be profitable. So it is difficult to establish causality: Is growth occurring because of the banks, or are banks popping up because of growth? In a seminal paper, Robin Burgess and Rohini Pande (2005) treated the change in trend created by the government's policy of greater expansion in unbanked areas as effectively random.[27] They found, using state-level data, that bank expansion had significantly reduced rural poverty and increased wages.

Anjini Kochar revisited this this issue using household-level data from Uttar Pradesh only.[28] Rather than rely on the broad policy discussed above, Kochar looked at the actual rules for implementation of the policy at the district level. The government had set up thresholds in terms of number of persons per bank. Districts that exceeded these thresholds would receive priority in branch expansion. Kochar exploited the discontinuity—areas just above the threshold would be favored over areas just below it—to isolate bank expansion that could be considered as good as random. She found that rural bank expansion had mainly benefited the better-off sections of rural society in Uttar Pradesh rather than the poor. Moreover, the "directed lending" to the poor had done little good. The difference in the findings of Burgess and Pande on the one hand, and Kochar on the other, remain to be clarified.

Recovery rates by banks were low, but how low depends on how we measure them. One standard approach has been to look at overdue loans in relation to "demand" (i.e., the fraction of currently due payments). By this measure, as table 4.6 shows, public sector finance, whether bank or cooperative, performed calamitously. A different approach, taken by the Agricultural Credit Review Committee (Reserve Bank of India 1990), often called the Khusro Committee, was to recognize that much of the money was eventually repaid, as shown in table 4.7. The committee assumed that 1 percent of all debts overdue less than three years would never be repaid, as would 15 percent of loans overdue between three and five years and 70 percent of those exceeding five years. Using this approach, the committee estimated that of the total loans outstanding, the percentage of bad debts was 4.3, 4.1, 8.1, and 3.3 percent for the commercial banks, the regional rural banks, short-term cooperative credit, and land-mortgage-backed long-term cooperative credit (provided by land development banks), respectively.

We might have expected that land development banks would have high repayment rates. To protect cooperatives from price fluctuations, the value of collateral

TABLE 4.6. Overdue loans of various credit institutions as a percentage of demand, 1975–1986

AGENCY	1975–1976	1980–1981	1985–1986
Commercial banks	48	47	43
Regional rural banks	NA	48	51
Short-term cooperative lending	34	43	41
Land mortgage-backed long-term cooperative lending	34	46	39

Source: Adapted from Reserve Bank of India (1990, 538).

TABLE 4.7. Breakdown of agricultural sector overdue loans, by loan age and institution, percent

AGE OF LOAN (YEARS OVERDUE)	COMMERCIAL BANK	REGIONAL RURAL BANK	SHORT-TERM COOPERATIVE LENDING	MORTGAGE-BACKED COOPERATIVE LENDING
Less than a year	11.5	13.1	16.7	16.2
1–4 years	57.9	65.7	50.4	33.9
4–6 years	15.5	15.5	20.8	32.8
More than 7 years	15.1	5.7	12.1	17.1
Total	100	100	100	100

Source: Adapted from Reserve Bank of India (1990, 596).

was much larger than the loan amount. However, recovery rates have been low, in part because it is difficult to foreclose. Landowners are members of rural communities and have been able to dissuade potential buyers from participating in auctions. The manipulation of land auctions is a phenomenon that goes back a long time in India and elsewhere.[29]

To what extent was bank credit also de facto insurance? The Khusro Committee pointed out that, for the first time, public sector banks were explicitly differentiating between "wilful defaulters" ("socially and politically important people") and "non-wilful defaulters" and treating them differently. When natural calamities occurred that reduced output in a specific region by 50 percent or more, defaulting borrowers were permitted to borrow afresh, despite not having repaid their old debts. Similar accommodation was provided to small and marginal farmers who were in default to a small extent. Policies to provide accommodation to borrowers who have faced natural calamities have been reiterated recently, and they reflect banks explicitly playing the credit-cum-insurance function mentioned earlier, when it comes to large observable aggregate shocks.[30]

A more controversial policy that has been repeatedly adopted is the unconditional debt waiver. In this case, the borrower does not repay, and the government compensates the bank. This may be the humane thing to do in the short run, when agriculture is in crisis in a region as a whole, and is a form of ex-post insurance. But the evidence suggests the waivers are not good policy, in part because they undermine the incentive to repay loans. The largest of these debt waivers occurred in 2008, targeting 60 million households and costing 1.7 percent of GDP. Gine and Kanz (2014) find no benefit for productivity, wages, and employment. They also find that beneficiaries of debt-relief were less likely to receive loans in the future.

In sum, the bank expansion likely alleviated poverty and provided some de facto insurance, but overall, its record was mixed. As the Indian economy became more market friendly after 1991, policies changed.

4. Liberalization and the Rise of Microfinance: 1991–2010

After 1991, the pace of rural bank expansion slowed down (see figure 4.2). Over the next decade, the share of rural credit provided by commercial and regional rural banks fell from 29 percent to 24.5 percent (see table 4.2). Policy has vacillated, with a renewed effort to double institutional lending between 2004 and 2006. Still, rural borrowers appear to have returned to moneylenders—33 percent of borrowing is from them as of 2013 (table 4.2). A new type of financial institution to help the poor has emerged: microfinance.

Microfinance in India began in the late 1980s with the self-help group (SHG), consisting of ten to fifteen women. The SHG is not-for-profit, often linked to a bank, and receives subsidies from the government. Membership is growing rapidly, from 9.23 million borrowers in 2003 to 57.85 million in 2013.[31] The SHGs are generally believed to have contributed to poverty reduction, and there is statistical support for this claim.[32] Several features seem to have contributed to their success. These include solidarity among group members, the combination of savings with credit, and the fact that the SHG also cooperated in other dimensions of economic life. However, SHGs are beginning to face problems of elite capture and increasing default, which, as we have seen, played such a big role in the cooperatives' story.[33]

Classical microfinance, with small groups and shared liability, along the lines of the famous Grameen Bank of Bangladesh, came to India somewhat later. But it is now growing rapidly, from 10 million clients in 2006–2007 to 27.5 million in 2012–2013. An important point is that Indian MFIs, unlike the Grameen Bank, are usually for profit. The for-profit MFI has been far more controversial than the SHG. Interest rates are often high. As noted, until recently the RBI permitted interest rates of up to 26 percent per year.[34] MFIs have also been criticized for using harsh methods in loan recovery.[35] Mihir Shah and coauthors write: "We suggest that while the Microfinance Institution (MFI) model is unsustainable and may actually end up worsening conditions for the poor, the Self-Help Group-Bank Linkage approach has the potential to make a decisive impact on security and empowerment of the most disadvantaged."[36] The best available statistical research shows very small benefits for the poor from MFI access.[37]

In 2010, the microfinance industry received a severe shock in Andhra Pradesh, the Indian state where it was most prominent. The crisis, as well as the regulatory response, is reminiscent of the Bombay Deccan story of the 1870s, with which I began this chapter. The Andhra MFIs had high rates of loan recovery, typical of MFIs in the subcontinent. And they were so profitable that they had attracted foreign capital. The number of lenders multiplied. Poor urban neighborhoods were being "carpet-bombed" with loans.[38] Borrowers were able to take out multiple loans, borrowing from one lender to repay another. A credit bubble emerged. The bubble burst when some lenders were accused of strong-arm tactics to recover loans, and borrowers allegedly committed suicide as a consequence. Local religious leaders began to advocate default, and borrowers complied in large numbers. The Andhra Pradesh government then intervened to regulate the MFIs.

The regulations were draconian. The Andhra Microfinance Bill's brief Statement of Objectives highlighted the need to prevent lenders from using "inhuman coercive measures." Coercion was defined broadly. For instance, it included "any act calculated to annoy or intimidate." The managers and employees of the MFI were liable for three years' imprisonment for any coercion. MFIs were forbidden from asking for collateral. The microfinance bill also contained the *damdupat* provision discussed earlier for DARA (1879): No borrower could be required to pay a total amount of interest that exceeded the principal. If he or she had already done that, the loan was extinguished, and the lender was required to repay the excess. Finally, "Fast Track Courts" would be set up to adjudicate disputes.

As repayment rates plummeted, the MFI industry in Andhra was severely affected. Worried that the baby was being thrown out with the bathwater, a large group of prominent economists felt compelled to write a newspaper article titled "Microcredit Is Not the Enemy."[39] "The new law," they pointed out, "clearly signals that borrowers need not repay their short-term loans." Eventually, the RBI stepped in, better regulation was passed, and the MFI industry is back on track, but MFIs remain controversial.[40]

I began this chapter by pointing out that the for-profit moneylender has historically been perceived as cruel in India. Public sector banks have been more humane but have needed subsidies and are subject to rent-seeking. We have now seen the same contrast emerge in microfinance, perhaps to a smaller extent—the for-profit MFI is perceived as exploitative, and the subsidized SHG is viewed more favorably. A highly respected commentator, formerly chief general manager of the National Bank for Agriculture and Rural Development, draws the obvious conclusion:

> The government seems to be making the playing field uneven by subsidizing the operations and cost of funds of one stream of microfinance,

that is, SHGs. With customers being common for MFIs and SHGs any reduction in cost of credit should be applied at the customer level and not to intermediary institution.[41]

The distinction between banks and MFIs is now beginning to blur. For instance, Bandhan, a major MFI operating in West Bengal, has now been given a license to open a private bank. Banks and MFIs are now competing for the same borrowers and are using similar methods for loan recovery. This convergence has probably contributed to the most visible symbol of agrarian distress in India over the past two decades: the high incidence of farmers' suicides. I conclude with a brief discussion of this issue.

Today, farmers' movements rage across the country. High input costs, low prices, and shocks to productivity have forced farmers into debt. Some have committed suicide, after being unable to repay. To whom are these farmers indebted? The National Crime Records Bureau reported, for the year 2015: "Among 3,097 suicides committed by farmers/cultivators due to 'Bankruptcy or Indebtedness,' 2,474 farmers/cultivators have taken loans from 'Financial Institutions like Bank/Registered Micro Financial Institutions' [80 percent] and 302 of them [10 percent] have taken loans from 'Money Lenders.'" The remainder had taken loans from both moneylenders and formal financial institutions.[42] Abhijit Sen, a former member of the Planning Commission, noted: "The latest data is interesting because all of us thought that moneylenders were the culprits of the piece. Even today, more than half the people take loans from moneylenders." How does he explain the low proportion of moneylender-borrowing-related suicides?

> The organised sector is less flexible because rules don't permit them flexibility. The microfinance sector is worse. They put pressure by telling others in self-help groups that their share would be cut if one person does not pay loans in time. This creates social pressure, as well. Many also send goons to the neighbourhood to scare borrowers.[43]

The cause-of-suicide figures needs to be taken with a large grain of salt, because the police, who record the information, have no particular expertise in this matter. The farmer's family may also be uneasy about blaming the moneylender, who might be in the village and whose help they might need again.[44] Still, these figures do shed doubt on a traditional narrative that identifies the moneylender as uniquely malevolent. The fundamental problem is that of low and variable incomes, in the face of which loan recovery by lenders who face bottom-line pressures, institutional or not, can be harsh. Humane lending can only be state-subsidized lending, which tolerates delayed repayment and sometimes default, with the attendant risks of rent-seeking. The rural credit sector has to tolerate one of these two evils. There is no case for singling out the private noninstitutional lender for especially punitive regulation.

There is surely a role for the legal system, which should not allow lenders to use fraudulent methods to induce borrowing or to apply coercion in loan recovery. It also needs to address cases like the one described by Meena Menon and Uzaramma in 2017, in which a lender was alleged to be charging more than 10 percent per month.[45] We can also hope that the Government of India's recently announced high-profile crop insurance scheme (Pradhan Mantri Fasal Bima Yojana) will defeat the conventional wisdom on the challenges of crop insurance and succeed. In this happy event, the level of default, and therefore controversy regarding methods for loan recovery, may die down, and India might get closer to, as Harold Mann put it, a "normal banking system."

My argument that, in relation to rural credit, the law is trying to do too much, is strengthened by a very recent Supreme Court judgment, whose implications have yet to play out. As we have seen, state governments have passed various pieces of legislation to provide ex-post debt relief to farmers who had borrowed from moneylenders. The farmer can be required to pay less than owed contractually, and the lender takes a "haircut." Also, under the Usurious Loans Act of 1918, a court could rule that the payment received by the lender would be less than the amount contractually owed, if the court thought this was excessive. However, the Banking Regulation Act of 1949 (Section 21A) protected banks from such legislation: "Notwithstanding anything contained in the Usurious Loans Act 1918, or any other law pertaining to indebtedness in any state, a transaction between a banking company and its debtor shall not be re-opened by any court on the ground that the rate of interest charged by the banking company in respect of such transaction is excessive." In *Jayant Kumar and Others versus Union of India and Others*, the Supreme Court ruled in February 2018 that section 21A would not apply to banks, so long as the debt relief legislation passed by the state specifically mentioned debt to banks. In other words, legislation that could reduce the amount courts would award a moneylender could now apply to a bank as well. It remains to be seen how this ruling affects banks' willingness to lend to rural borrowers.

Notes

This chapter is almost identical to chapter 3 of *Law and the Economy in a Young Democracy: India 1947 and Beyond* (jointly written with Tirthankar Roy) to be published by the University of Chicago Press in September 2021. I thank, but do not implicate, Jerry Caprio, Anjini Kochar, Benugopal Mukhopadhay, P. Sainath, and Aseem Shrivastava.

Epigraph: Harold Mann, review of "The General Report of the Committee of Direction: All India Rural Credit Survey," *Indian Economic Review* 3(4): 76–80.

1. A similar rule in Roman law was known as *Alterum Tantum*, or "Only Twice as Much."

2. See https://economictimes.indiatimes.com/opinion/interviews/for-profit-mfis-worse-than-money-lenders/articleshow/6973551.cms.

3. See https://economictimes.indiatimes.com/industry/banking/finance/microfinance-industry-is-out-of-an-unprecedent-crisis-thanks-to-regulations-diligent-borrowers/articleshow/51886097.cms. Also see Reserve Bank, https://www.rbi.org.in/scripts/BS_ViewMasCirculardetails.aspx?id=9827#II.

4. The parallel between the Deccan crisis of the late nineteenth century and the recent MFI crisis is described in more detail in Chaudhary and Swamy (2011).

5. For an analysis of the impact of DARA on borrowing, acreage, and investment, see Chaudhary and Swamy (2017).

6. The following extract is from a speech by R. Gandhi. See https://www.bis.org/review/r160217a.pdf.

7. See Quereishi (1947, 143).

8. Wadhwa (1989).

9. Reserve Bank of India (1954, 279).

10. Reserve Bank of India (1954, 279).

11. Thorner (1964, 83).

12. Bhende (1983).

13. Patil (2009, vii).

14. Srinivasan (2016, 84).

15. According to the Indian Constitution, the states have the right to regulate money-lenders. The acts passed included the Kerala Moneylenders Act of 1958, The Karnataka Moneylenders Act of 1961, and the Rajasthan Moneylenders Act of 1963. A full list is provided by the RBI in their 2007 publication, *Report of the Technical Group to Review Legislations in Money Lending*, p. 70. I have relied on this source for this paragraph.

16. Bombay (1954, 359).

17. See Government of Maharashtra (1960).

18. Vijay Kumar (1997) provides a useful overview.

19. The interest rate ceilings were put in place in 2004, http://sahakara.kar.gov.in/faqML&PB.html. In Andhra Pradesh, moneylenders can charge at most 2 percent more than do commercial banks: http://www.thehansindia.com/posts/index/Warangal-Tab/2017-08-22/Law-against-lenders-rarely-enforced/320732, accessed on March 24, 2018. A similar rule applies in Kerala: http://www.thehindu.com/news/national/kerala/provision-in-law-against-moneylenders-rarely-enforced/article6024791.ece.

20. See David Roodman, "Quick: What's the Grameen Bank's Interest Rate?" https://www.cgdev.org/blog/quick-whats-grameen-banks-interest-rate.

21. See http://www.thehansindia.com/posts/index/Warangal-Tab/2017-08-22/Law-against-lenders-rarely-enforced/320732.

22. See http://www.thehindu.com/news/national/kerala/provision-in-law-against-moneylenders-rarely-enforced/article6024791.ece.

23. Quereishi (1947).

24. See Bhende (1983) and Kochar (2011).

25. Cole (2009).

26. Under the Kisan (farmer) credit card scheme, tenants with oral leases can borrow against them. I have not been able to locate evidence on how often such loans actually happen.

27. The deviation from trend was the "instrumental variable" for the number of banks.

28. Kochar (2011).

29. I am grateful to Benugopal Mukhopadhyaya for this point. For the colonial period, see Roy and Swamy (2016, chapter 4).

30. The RBI issued a "Master Circular" collating existing rules in 2014.

31. Srinivasan (2016, 109).

32. Deininger and Liu (2008).

33. Srinivasan (2016, 110).

34. In 2014, the RBI altered the rules: The maximum rate charged would be the lower of the cost of funds plus a 10 percent margin or 2.75 times the base rate of commercial banks. See https://economictimes.indiatimes.com/news/economy/finance/rbi-removes-26-interest -rate-cap-on-mfi-loans/articleshow/30004542.cms.

35. See http://www.thehindu.com/news/national/karnataka/Women-allege-coercive -loan-recovery-by-microfinance-firms/article17000680.ece.

36. Shah et al. (2007, 2).

37. Banerjee et al. (2015) use a randomized controlled trial.

38. See Gokhale (2009).

39. Banerjee et al. (2010).

40. See https://economictimes.indiatimes.com/opinion/interviews/for-profit-mfis -worse-than-money-lenders/articleshow/6973551.cms.

41. Srinivasan (2016, 113).

42. See India, National Crime Records Bureau (2015, 267).

43. See http://indianexpress.com/article/india/farmer-suicides-due-to-debt-in-80-per -cent-cases-loans-taken-from-banks-not-moneylenders-4463986/.

44. I thank P. Sainath for this point.

45. See https://indiankanoon.org/doc/1879287/.

References

Banerjee, A., P. Bardhan, E. Duflo, E. Field, D. Karlan, A. Khwaja, D. Mookherjee, R. Pande, and R. Rajan. 2010. "Microcredit Is Not the Enemy." *Financial Times*, December 13.

Banerjee, A., E. Duflo, R. Glennerster, and C. Kinnon. 2015. "The Miracle of Micro-finance? Evidence from a Randomized Evaluation." *American Economic Journal, Applied Economics* 7(1): 22–53.

Bell, C. 1990. "Interactions between Institutional and Informal Credit Agencies in India." *World Bank Economic Review* 4(3): 297–327.

Bhende, P. J. 1983. "Credit Markets in the Semi-Arid Tropics of Rural South India." ICRI-SAT Economics Program Project Report 56, International Crop Research Institute for the Semi Arid Tropics, Hyderabad, India.

Bombay (India: State). 1954. *Gazetteer of Bombay State: Poona District*. Bombay: Government Central Press.

Burgess, Robin, and Rohini Pande. 2005. "Do Rural Banks Matter? Evidence from the Indian Social Banking Experiment." *American Economic Review* 95: 780–795.

Chaudhary, L., and A. Swamy. 2011. "Microfinance and Predatory Lending: The Same Old Story?" *Ideas for India*, http://www.ideasforindia.in/article.aspx?article=Microfinance -and-predatory-lending-The-same-old-story.

Chaudhary, L., and A. Swamy. 2017. "Protecting the Borrower: An Experiment in Colonial India." *Explorations in Economic History* 65: 36–54.

Cole, S. 2009. "Fixing Market Failures or Fixing Elections? Agricultural Credit in India." *American Economic Journal: Applied Economics* 1(1): 219–250.

Deininger, K., and Y. Liu. 2013 "Economic and Social Impacts of an Innovative Self-Help Group Model in India." *World Development* 43 (2013): 149–163.

Ghatak, S. 1976. *Rural Money Markets in India.* Delhi: Macmillan Company of India.

Gine, X., and M. Kanz. 2014. "The Economic Effects of a Borrower Bailout: Evidence from an Emerging Market." World Bank Policy Research Working Paper 7109, World Bank, Washington, DC.

Gokhale, K. 2009. "A Global Surge in Tiny Loans Spurs Credit Bubble in a Slum." *Wall Street Journal*, August 14. http://online.wsj.com/article/SB125012112518027581 .html.

Government of Maharashtra. 1960. *Maharashtra State Gazetteers: Kolhapur District.* Bombay: Directorate of Government Printing. https://gazetteers.maharashtra.gov .in/cultural.maharashtra.gov.in/english/gazetteer/KOLHAPUR/home.html.

Hoda, A., and P. Terway. 2015. "Credit Policy for Agriculture in India—An Evaluation." ICRIER Working Paper 302, Indian Council for Research on International Economic Relations, New Delhi.

India, National Crime Records Bureau. 2015. *Accidental Deaths and Suicides in India.* New Delhi: Ministry of Home Affairs.

Islam, M. M. 1995. "The Punjab Land Alienation Act and the Professional Moneylenders." *Modern Asian Studies* 29: 271–291.

Kochar, A. 2011. "The Distributive Consequences of Social Banking: A Microempirical Analysis of the Indian Experience." *Economic Development and Cultural Change* 59: 251–280.

Kumar, Vijay. 1997. "Hollowness of Debt Relief Laws." *Cochin University Law Review* (1997): 100–111.

Mann, H. 1957. "Review of the General Report of the Committee of Direction: All India Rural Credit Survey." *Indian Economic Review* 3(4): 76–80.

Patil, S. G. 2009. *Report of the High-Powered Committee on Cooperatives.* New Delhi: Ministry of Agriculture.

Pradhan, N. C. 2013. "Persistence of Informal Credit in Rural India: Evidence from All India Debt and Investment Survey and Beyond." RBI Working Paper Series, Reserve Bank of India, Mumbai.

Quereishi, Anwar Iqbal. 1947. *The Future of the Cooperative Movement in India.* Madras: Oxford University Press.

Reserve Bank of India. 1954. *All-India Rural Credit Survey: Report of the Committee of Direction: Vol. II: The General Report.* Bombay: Reserve Bank of India.

Reserve Bank of India. 1990. *A Review of the Agricultural Credit System in India.* Bombay: Reserve Bank of India.

Reserve Bank of India. 2007. *Report of the Technical Group to Review Legislations in Money Lending.* Mumbai: Reserve Bank of India.

Roy, T., and A. Swamy. 2016. *Law and Economy in Colonial India.* Chicago: University of Chicago Press.

Sarap, K. 1987. "Transactions in Rural Credit Markets in Western Orissa, India." *Journal of Peasant Studies* 15(1): 83–107.

Shah, M., Rangu Rao, and P. S. Vijay Shankar. 2007 "Rural Credit in 20th Century India: An Overview of History and Perspectives." *Economic and Political Weekly* 42: 1351–64.

Srinivasan, R. 2016. *State of Rural Finance in India: An Assessment.* New Delhi: Oxford University Press.

Thorner, D. 1964. *Agricultural Cooperatives in India: A Field Report.* New Delhi: Asia Publishing House.

Vaidyanathan, A. 2005. *Report of the Task Force on Revival of Rural Cooperative Credit Institutions.* New Delhi: Ministry of Finance.

Wadhwa, D. C. 1989. "Guaranteeing Title to Land: A Preliminary Study." *Economic and Political Weekly* 24(41): 2323–2334.

FORGOTTEN MARKETS
The Importance of Pawnshops

Marieke Bos, Susan Payne Carter,
and Paige Marta Skiba

As financial services and credit underwriting have become more automated and technologically advanced, one credit market has remained nearly unchanged for centuries: pawnbroking. The simple, nonrecourse loans that pawnshops offer are often the sole source of liquidity to smooth budget shortfalls for low-income households. A recent study estimated that 1.4 percent of US households have used pawnshops in the past year, with 4.3 percent of the unbanked population using them.[1] Despite the reliance on pawnshops by millions of households, economists and law and economics scholars have forgotten or all but ignored the most steady, unchanging source of credit. Here we present new, detailed data on the pawn industry and its customers, with the hopes of informing policymakers and social science researchers about the role pawnshops play in the financial lives of low-income households.

Pawn loans are small, collateralized loans. The pawnbroker makes a fixed short-term loan to a consumer who leaves collateral, most often jewelry or electronics, in the possession of the broker. Pawnbrokers typically offer a 50 percent loan-to-value ratio with a maturation term of three months. If the customer repays the principal amount plus interest and fees, the broker returns the collateral to the customer. In the United States, loans are small (most often less than $100) and come with interest rates ranging from 2 to 25 percent per month.[2] If the customer fails to repay the loan and interest by the maturation date, then, following a short grace period, the collateral becomes the property of the broker, and the customer's debt is extinguished. After this default occurs, the pawnbroker can then resell the item in their storefront.

Pawnshops have several unique features that have led to their continued popularity over centuries.[3] First, they occupy a unique position in that they are accessible to any consumer with collateral (and a valid government-issued ID). No credit check is conducted. This feature is not shared by other sources of credit, including perhaps the closest alternative, payday loans. Payday lenders who typically offer about $300 in cash, often at annualized interest rates of 400 percent, require a checking account statement, proof of employment, and in many cases a subprime credit check.[4]

The second unique feature is that the cost of default on a pawn loan is relatively low. Pawn credit is fully underwritten by the collateral that is handed to the broker at contract origination. Default is not reported to credit bureaus, nor will default affect one's ability to borrow subsequently on pawn credit. The consequences of default are limited to the loss of consumption (or sentimental) value of the collateral.[5] And although the average loan size is around $80, loans can be underwritten for collateral valued at as little as a few dollars. As long as the collateral is appraised accurately, this process eliminates any need on the part of the pawnbroking industry to evaluate its customers' credit risk or to use a credit bureau system that facilitates information sharing among banks. Together, these facts eliminate the risk that pawn-credit default will damage borrowers' mainstream creditworthiness and credit access. This fact is especially important, as credit scores are increasingly used to determine eligibility for employment (Bos et al. 2018a), rental apartments, phone plans, and insurance contracts. Pawn borrowers are less likely to become trapped in cycles of debt like that which has been reported in the payday lending industry.[6]

A final characteristic of pawn loans that makes them unique is that they are face-to-face transactions. Technology has changed nearly every type of credit to become more arm's-length and advanced. Sophisticated credit-scoring algorithms are used to determine someone's creditworthiness. With pawnshops, however, little has changed beyond the fact that the Internet has made it easier for pawnbrokers and customers to value collateral. Thus, going forward, the pawnshop market may serve as one of the only realms in which to study consumer and market behavior largely untouched and uninfluenced by technology.

Despite the many features that make pawnshops a popular resource for low-income households, the study of pawnshops is nearly nonexistent in the law and economics literature.[7] Lack of social science research on this topic stands in contrast to the exponential growth in understanding of the use and the consequences of regulation of other household financial products. For example, recent research includes numerous studies by economics scholars that help inform knowledge of a wide range of other financial products and services, including retirement instruments (e.g., Carroll et al. 2009), credit cards (e.g., Agarwal et al. 2015), mortgages (e.g., Padi 2018), student loans (Cox et al. 2018), and even alternative credit products (Bertrand and Morse 2011; Melzer 2011; Skiba and Tobacman 2019). Despite the importance of and recent interest in pawnshops (as evidenced by the success of reality TV shows like "Pawnstars"), research in this area is mostly absent from economic discourse. We hope to rectify the gap in understanding of the age-old practice of pawnbroking with new data that shed light on customer characteristics.

1. Data

This chapter utilizes large datasets of administrative records on the US and Swedish pawnbroking industries and their respective borrowers' social and financial backgrounds. The US data come from the administrative records of a large national payday lender operating in Florida and Texas that also offers pawnshop loans in many of its storefronts. We have observations from 1995 and 2004 on 9,124,865 and 398,722 pawn loan transactions from Texas and Florida, respectively.

The Swedish data consist of two samples from two data sources. The first sample consists of transactional pawn-credit data from the Swedish Pawnbroking Association, whose members cover 99 percent of the Swedish pawn-credit market—yielding 2.8 million pawn transactions involving 200,313 unique borrowers. These borrowers are matched with their complete credit bureau files from the leading mainstream credit bureau in Sweden (similar to Equifax or Transunion in the United States) in a bimonthly fashion from 2000 to 2005. The second sample functions as a comparison group and is a random sample of credit bureau files from the general Swedish population. The sample consists of 313,002 unique individuals for the period 2001 to 2005.

The Swedish data add a unique scope and depth of financial information not available in the US data. These two datasets make it possible to analyze detailed characteristics of pawnshop borrowers for the first time, offering an opportunity to begin to fill a long-standing lacuna in the literature on financial markets.

2. The Pawnbroking Industry in the United States and Sweden

The processes for taking out pawnshop loans in the United States and Sweden are very similar: individuals bring in items, called "pledges" that they would like to

TABLE 5.1. Industry characteristics

	UNITED STATES	SWEDEN
Ratio of pawnshop customers to adult population (%)	1.4	4.0
Interest rate ceiling?	In 42 states	None
Average monthly interest rate (%)	2–25	3–4
Average loan size (US dollars)	80	350
Most popular pledge	Jewelry	Gold/Jewelry
Average repayment rate (%)	80	90
Typical contract length (days)	120	90
Grace period (days)	30–90	60
Return excess proceeds	9 states	Always

Sources: Percent of Population: United States: 2017 Survey of the Unbanked. Loan Size, Most Popular Pledge, and Contract Length: Transactional Data from a US provider of financial services as described in section 1 (1995–2004). Swedish data: registered data from the Swedish Pawnbrokers Association described in section 1 (2001–2005).

pawn. The pawnbroker evaluates the item, gives a loan based on the value (often 50 percent of the resale value), and sets the interest and duration of the loan. Across both countries, jewelry is the most popular item pawned.

While the process for taking out a pawnshop loan, as well as the items used to pawn, are similar across the two countries, the pawnbroking industries in the United States and Sweden do differ in interest charged, average loan amount, and loan lengths. Tables 5.1–5.3 compare these characteristics across the two countries. In the United States, regulations capping average monthly interest rate vary widely: 2 percent per 30 days in some states, 25 percent per 30 days in other states, and no cap in others. In Sweden, where there is no cap on interest rates, competition has driven the interest rate down to a tight range of 3 to 4 percent.

Table 5.4 shows popular items pledged in Texas, Florida, and Sweden broken out by gender. Electronics and musical instruments are also popular, especially in the United States, and more so for men than for women.

The average loan value is much lower in the United States than in Sweden ($80 versus $350).[8] This difference may be driven by differences between the two countries, such as consumption of more expensive jewelry with which to pawn, or it may be a result of the lower interest charges.[9] Another difference between the two countries is that in Sweden, the initial contract is legally required to have a maximum maturity term of three months with an additional grace period of two months. In the United States, loans start at thirty days, and a borrower has to pay interest on the loan every month.

TABLE 5.2. Pawnshop borrower and general population demographics

	TEXAS		FLORIDA		SWEDEN	
AGE (YEARS)	PAWNSHOP BORROWERS	2000 CENSUS	PAWNSHOP BORROWERS	2000 CENSUS	PAWNSHOP BORROWERS	2000 CENSUS
18–24	9.05	14.69	18.75	10.79	7.9	9
25–34	29.1	21.13	33.74	16.86	18	17
35–44	33.17	22.2	30.32	20.15	25	18
45–54	20.35	17.45	12.82	16.78	22	17
55–64	6.45	10.68	3.34	12.64	16	16
65+	1.89	13.85	1.03	22.76	11	24
Total sample size N	416,628	14,965,061	8,992,145	12,336,038	1,336,408	313,002

	UNITED STATES		SWEDEN	
	PAWNSHOP BORROWERS	GENERAL POPULATION	PAWNSHOP BORROWERS	GENERAL POPULATION
Married	39	52	26	45
Divorced/Separated	20	13	27	11
Homeowner	45	70	8	43

Sources: US transaction data from a large pawnshop corporation and Swedish register data. Population data for Texas and Florida from the 2010 Census only includes the population older than 18 (the age when one is legally permitted to take out a pawnshop loan). The US statistics for marital status and homeownership are unweighted averages from the June 2011 Current Population Survey and include borrowers who had used a pawnshop in the past, not just to sell an item. All numbers are percentages in this table except for the total sample size *N*.

TABLE 5.3. Pawnshop borrower characteristics

	TEXAS	FLORIDA	SWEDEN
Average loan duration (days)	109	81.1	141
Average loan amount (US dollars)	$79.50	$75.80	$353.80
Average number of rollovers	3.6	2.7	1
Average loans per customer per year	3.5	7.7	4
Percentage who ever default	80	90	50
Percent who always default	33	17	14

Sources: US transaction data from a large pawnshop corporation and Swedish register data as described in section 1.

TABLE 5.4. Top pawnshop pledges for men and women

2000–2005			
MEN	%	WOMEN	%
UNITED STATES			
FLORIDA			
Jewelry	37	Jewelry	71
Electronics	29	Electronics	21
Tools	20	Tools	3
Sporting equipment	6	Sporting equipment	1.5
Guns	2	Household items	1
Musical instruments	3	Musical instruments	1
Household items	2	Cameras	1
Cameras	1	Guns	0.4
TEXAS			
Jewelry	33	Jewelry	61
Electronics	31	Electronics	28
Tools	22	Tools	4
Sporting equipment	4	Sporting equipment	1
Guns	3	Household items	2
Musical instruments	3	Musical instruments	1
Household items	3	Cameras	1
Cameras	1	Guns	1
SWEDEN			
Gold	62	Gold	85
Watches	12	Watches	4
Electronics	6	Silver	3
Musical instruments	6	Art	2
Cameras	4	Electronics	2
Miscellaneous	3	Cameras	1
Bonds	1	Musical instruments	1

Sources: United States, Transactional data; Sweden, Swedish Pawnbrokers Association as described in section 1.

3. Pawn Customers and Their Borrowing Behavior

Table 5.2 displays characteristics of individuals who take out loans and their borrowing behavior. The table shows that in both countries, the typical pawnshop borrower is most likely to be between the ages of 25 and 54 and is likely to be recently divorced or never married.

We measure mainstream creditworthiness by the pawn-credit borrowers' access to mortgages (proxied by home ownership), by income, and by credit scores. As noted above, creditworthiness in the mainstream credit market is independent of consumers' ability to borrow from a pawnshop. Access to pawn credit depends entirely on the resale value of the borrower's collateral.

The homeownership status of pawnshop borrowers is a good proxy for creditworthiness for several reasons. First, a consumer must have fairly good credit and a dependable income stream to obtain a mortgage. Second, homeownership represents an ongoing debt commitment that requires a fairly stable income stream to maintain, and the payment record is generally available to current credit grantors. Finally, homeownership represents an asset that can be used as collateral for a home equity loan. The bottom row of Table 5.2 shows statistics from the United States and Sweden on the homeownership status of pawnshop borrowers and of the general population. The homeownership rate in the pawnshop sample is much lower than that in the general population: 45 percent versus 70 percent for the United States and 8 percent versus 43 percent for Sweden. Similarly, Johnson and Johnson (1998) find a 26.4 percent homeownership rate for US pawnshop borrowers and a 65.4 percent rate in the United States generally. The difference between pawnshop borrowers and the general population may be influenced, in part, by the urban locations of pawnshops, where homeownership rates are likely lower in general, but also by the financial status of those who take out pawnshop loans. With respect to the US data, it is somewhat surprising that the homeownership rate among pawnshop borrowers is as high as it is. Further research into the use of pawnshop loans by homeowners would be fruitful.

Table 5.3 shows the borrowing behavior across the two countries. In our Florida and Texas samples, borrowers take out on average only $76 and $80, respectively. Meanwhile, the average amount in Sweden is just over $350 (in US dollars). US borrowers typically took out 3.5 to 8 loans per year, while borrowers in Sweden typically took out about 4 loans annually. Borrowers often returned to the lender to redeem their items: in Texas, only 33 percent of borrowers always defaulted; in Florida, 17 percent; and in Sweden, 14 percent. The National Pawnbroking Association similarly estimates that 80–90 percent of pawn loans are redeemed worldwide, implying a default rate of 10–20 percent.[10] Given that

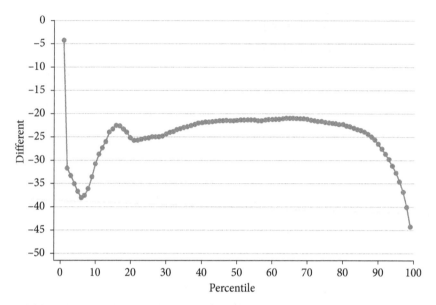

FIGURE 5.1.   Difference in total income over the income percentiles for the general Swedish population and pawnshop borrowers. Note: Difference=100% ×(income$_{\text{Pawnshop}}$ – income$_{\text{Swedish Population}}$) / income$_{\text{Swedish Population}}$.

defaulting on a pawnshop loan has no negative repercussions for a borrower's credit score, it is important to note that people are largely using pawnshops for short-term loans versus using pawnshops as a location to sell their items for cash.

We turn next to the Swedish data to examine income trends and mainstream credit scores of pawn-credit borrowers in Table 5.5. We believe that trends in the United States are likely to be similar. On average, pawnshop borrowers make only $13,500 per year, while our sample of the general population earns on average about $19,300 per year. Figure 5.1 documents the difference between the general population and the pawnshop borrowers in the Swedish sample by plotting the differences between these groups over the quintiles of the income distribution.[11] The figure reveals that the difference is always negative (pawnshop borrowers earn less than the general population, by 20 percent on average). As is to be expected, differences are larger at the top and bottom of the income distribution: The highest-income nonpawnshop borrowers have much higher credit scores than do the highest-income pawnshop borrowers, and the same holds true at the lower end of the income distribution.

Just as in the United States, Swedish credit scores measure default and delinquency risk. Unlike in the United States, however, Swedish scores range from 0 to 100, with lower scores representing a lower default risk. The cutoff point be-

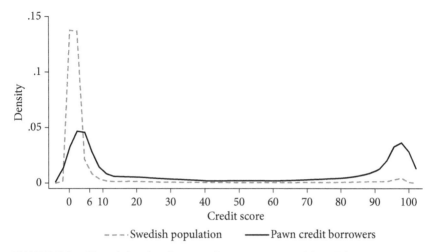

FIGURE 5.2.   Kernel density plots: credit scores, general Swedish population and pawnshop borrowers.

tween having a good versus bad credit score in Sweden lies between 6 and 10, where "good" implies a positive probability of obtaining mainstream credit. On average, pawnshop borrowers have higher (i.e., worse) credit scores. Figure 5.2 illustrates the different kernel density estimates of the mainstream credit scores for both the pawnshop sample and the general Swedish population. The density of the general population distribution lies almost completely on the "good" side of the cutoff range; in contrast, the density of the pawnshop borrowers falls about half on the good side and half on the bad side. These results confirm that pawnshop borrowers have a harder time accessing traditional forms of credit, leaving pawnshops in the role of lender of last resort.

4. Pawnshops and Other Types of Alternative Credit

Finally, we turn to a discussion of the importance of spillover effects between pawnshops and other types of credit. First, as noted above, one important benefit of pawnshops is their relatively small cost of default in comparison to other types of credit. Since they are collateralized loans, the costs of default are limited to surrendering the collateral. Default comes with no dunning calls, no reporting to credit bureaus, and no consequences on the ability to use pawnshop credit in the future. While the monetary or sentimental cost of losing one's collateral may in fact be large, the benefit of these costs being isolated from mainstream credit is potentially important. Bos et al. (2018a) document that pawn borrowers who default in the mainstream credit market are especially vulnerable to bearing the cost in both the credit market and the labor market as more and more actors check individuals' credit records.

Beyond the data we have shown here characterizing pawnshop borrowers, a couple of papers have examined the relationship between payday loans and pawnshop loans. Bos et al. (2018b) examine the use of pawnshop loans among consumers who also apply for payday loans. They find that being just below the subprime cutoff for receiving a payday loan increases pawnshop usage relative to those who do receive a loan. Carter (2015) also studies joint use of these products. She uses Current Population Survey data from the US Census Bureau to study the relationship between legal regulations on the frequency with which payday loan borrowers can roll over their loans and pawnshop- and payday-loan use. She finds some complementary use of payday loans and pawnshops given these regulations; however, the results depend on characteristics of the individual.

Beyond any interest in pawnbroking's effects on consumers per se, spillover effects exist across credit markets, a fact that policymakers should keep in mind as they contemplate regulation or restrictions on any subprime credit market.

In both the United States and Sweden, the pawnbroking industry has remained an important source of credit for centuries. The Great Recession coincided with an exponential growth spurt in pawnbroking in both countries, with annual growth rates of more than 20 percent starting in 2007 (see Figure 5.3). Surging gold prices likely supported this growth, as jewelry is a commonly used form of collateral for pawnshop loans.

Despite the rapid growth of the industry and the controversy surrounding other forms of alternative credit, such as payday loans, pawnshops have largely evaded regulatory scrutiny. Institutional features of the pawn market help borrowers, even those without a paycheck, avoid an extended debt cycle that can occur in payday lending. Defaulting on a pawnshop loan will not influence the individual's prime or subprime credit score. Campbell et al. (2011) suggest that one regulatory approach to dealing with high-interest credit products (such as payday loans) is to encourage alternatives. Pawnshop loans are likely one of those alternatives, and we stress the importance of better understanding the full picture of financial markets used by the millions of Americans operating outside the traditional banking system. Knowing who borrows and how is important for building a more complete understanding for the economics profession and public policy debates surrounding financial regulation.

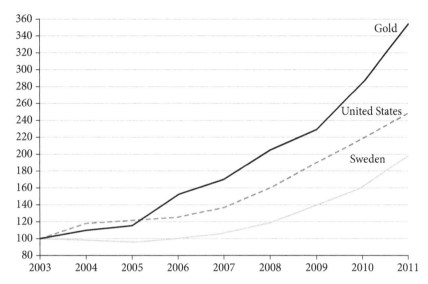

FIGURE 5.3.   Growth rate. Outstanding loan balance in the pawnbroking industry and the price of gold (deflated and indexed to 2003).

Notes: US data are from the financial statements of three publicly traded pawnshop companies, EZCash, Cash America, and First Cash, for the end-of-year pawn loans outstanding (on December 31) from 2003 to 2011.

TABLE 5.5.   Pawnshop borrower and general population credit and income characteristics, Sweden

	SWEDEN	
	PAWNSHOP BORROWERS	NON-PAWNSHOP POPULATION
Average Credit Score*	40.32	4.98
Average yearly income (Swedish krona)	90,100**	128,600***

Source: Swedish register data as described in section 1.
*Unlike FICO scores, credit scores in Sweden are default risks between 0–100, where low numbers reflect a low default risk.
**Approximately US$13,515.
***Approximately US$19,290.

Finally, the central question of interest to us as researchers, and one we are unable to fully address here, is the effect that pawnbroking has on consumer welfare. Are pawnshops good or bad for consumers? Despite the benefits laid out here relative to other sources of credit, pawnshops' seedy reputation seems indelible. It is difficult to judge pawnbroking's influence on consumer well-being, considering the small absolute amount of credit that is supplied through pawnshops; this amount is bound to be relatively modest compared to the credit supplied through regular banking channels. (Although the amount is small, pawn loans may in deed have a disproportionate effect on consumers' well-being due to pawn borrowers' largely low-income status.) We have shown that pawnshop borrowers have worse credit scores than the general population in Sweden and are less likely to be home-owners in the United States and Sweden. People who are excluded or have ex-hausted resources available from the credit supplied through the regular banking system have to rely on alternative financial services like those supplied by the pawnbroking industry. Thus, for those who are credit constrained, pawnshop bor-rowing may have a positive effect on welfare. Identifying the welfare consequences of pawnshops and other types of credit deemed "predatory" is an important task that we hope future work in law and economics will tackle. Our broader goal is to raise awareness of the importance of pawnshops and of the need for them to be considered more mainstream than "fringe."

Notes

1. Federal Deposit Insurance Corporation (2017).

2. For more detailed information on pawnshop regulation and usury laws, see Carter (2015).

3. The precise emergence of pawnbroking is unknown, but pawn loans are referenced in the Old Testament (Caskey 1994).

4. For more on the payday loan underwriting process, see Agarwal et al. (2009).

5. Carter and Skiba (2012) discuss the role of sentimentality and loss aversion in pawnshop repayment behavior.

6. The US Consumer Financial Protection Bureau reported in 2014 that four out of five payday loans were rolled over, meaning borrowers did not repay their debt in full on time. In rollover scenarios, payday borrowers can end up paying more in interest and fees than the original loan amount borrowed. See https://files.consumerfinance.gov/f/201403 _cfpb_report_payday-lending.pdf. Carter et al. (2020) also study payday loan rollovers.

7. Notable exceptions in the economics literature include Caskey (1991), Johnson and Johnson (1998), and Avery and Samolyk (2011).

8. These data come from our US and Swedish datasets described in section 1.

9. Caskey (1991) and Avery and Samolyk (2011) find that lower interest rates cause an increase in loan size to cover the high fixed costs of operating a pawnshop.

10. National Pawnbroking Association. 2017. "Pawnbroking around the World." https://www.nationalpawnbrokers.org/2017/pawnbroking-around-the-world/.

11. Difference $= 100\% \times ($income$_{Pawnshop} -$income$_{Swedish\ Population}) /$ income$_{Swedish\ Population}$.

References

Agarwal, Sumit, Paige Marta Skiba, and Jeremy Tobacman. 2009. "Payday Loans and Credit Cards: New Liquidity and Credit Scoring Puzzles." *American Economic Review Papers and Proceedings* 99(2): 412–417.

Agarwal, Sumit, Souphala Chomsisengphet, Neale Mahoney, and Johannes Stroebel. 2015. "Regulating Consumer Financial Products: Evidence from Credit Cards." *Quarterly Journal of Economics* 130(1): 111–164.

Avery, Robert, and Katherine Samolyk. 2011. "Payday Loans versus Pawn Shops: The Effects of Loan Fee Limits in Household Use." Working paper, September 2011. Available at SSRN: https://ssrn.com/abstract=2634584 or http://dx.doi.org/10.2139/ssrn.2634584.

Bertrand, Marianne, and Adair Morse. 2011. "Information Disclosure, Cognitive Biases, and Payday Borrowers." *Journal of Finance* 66(6): 1865–1893.

Bos, Marieke, Emily Breza, and Andres Liberman. 2018a. "The Labor Market Effects of Credit Market Information." *Review of Financial Studies* 31(6): 2005–2037.

Bos, Marieke, Susan Payne Carter, and Paige Marta Skiba. 2018b. "Balancing Act: New Evidence and a Discussion of the Theory on the Rationality and Behavioral Anomalies of Choice in Credit Markets." In Joshua C. Teitelbaum and Kathryn Zeiler (eds.), *Research Handbook in Behavioral Law and Economics*. Northhampton, NH: Edward Elgar Publishing.

Campbell, John Y., Howell E. Jackson, Brigitte C. Madrian, and Peter Tufano. 2011. "Consumer Financial Protection." *Journal of Economic Perspectives* 25(1): 91–114.

Carroll, G., J. J. Choi, D. Laibson, B. C. Madrian, and A. Metrick. 2009. "Optimal Defaults and Active Decisions: Theory and Evidence from 401(k) Saving." *Quarterly Journal of Economics* 124 (4):1639–1674.

Carter, Susan Payne. "Payday Loan and Pawnshop Usage: The Impact of Allowing Payday Loan Rollovers." 2015. *Journal of Consumer Affairs* 49: 436–456.

Carter, Susan Payne, and Paige Marta Skiba. 2012. "Pawnshops, Behavioral Economics and Self-Regulation." *Review of Banking & Financial Law* 32: 193.

Carter, Susan Payne, Kuan Liu, Paige Marta Skiba, and Justin Sydnor. 2020. "Time to Repay or Time to Delay? The Effect of Having More Time before a Payday Loan Is Due." Manuscript.

Caskey, John P. 1991. "Pawnbroking in America: The Economics of a Forgotten Credit Market." *Journal of Money, Credit and Banking* 23: 85–99.

Caskey, John P. 1994. *Fringe Banking: Check-Cashing Outlets, Pawnshops, and the Poor*. New York: Russell Sage Foundation.

Cox, James C., Daniel Kreisman, and Susan Dynarski. 2018. "Designed to Fail: Effects of the Default Option and Information Complexity on Student Loan Repayment." NBER Working Paper 25258, National Bureau of Economic Research, Cambridge, MA.

Federal Deposit Insurance Corporation. 2017. "2017 FDIC National Survey of Unbanked and Underbanked Households." Available at https://www.fdic.gov/householdsurvey/2017/2017report.pdf.

Johnson, Robert W., and Dixie P. Johnson. 1998. "Pawnbroking in the U.S.: A Profile of Customers." Washington, DC: Georgetown University School of Business, Credit Research Center.

Melzer, Brian. 2011. "The Real Costs of Credit Access: Evidence from the Payday Lending Market." *Quarterly Journal of Economics* 126(1): 517–555.

Padi, Manisha. 2018. "Consumer Protection Laws and the Mortgage Market: Evidence from Ohio." Working Paper.

Skiba, Paige Marta, and Jermey Tobacman. 2019. "Do Payday Loans Cause Bankruptcy?" *Journal of Law and Economics* 62(3): 485–519.

NEW TECHNOLOGY, INCREASING RETURNS, AND THE END OF THE ANTITRUST CENTURY

Kaushik Basu

With the latest technological revolution, it is becoming harder to apply some of our traditional laws and regulations pertaining to markets and trade. This is particularly true for antitrust law. With production chains that, thanks to digital linkages, span many countries and exhibit economies of scale never before seen, to apply antitrust laws mechanically could be the death knell for a nation's competitiveness and the manufacturing sector. But to refrain from using these laws with no complementary regulations put in its place is to leave consumers and workers vulnerable to exploitation.

This chapter is an attempt to spell out this dilemma clearly. To take stock of our current predicament, I go back to the original ideas of Augustin Cournot and Joseph Bertrand in the early and late eighteenth century, respectively, and to the antitrust revolution in the United States starting in the late nineteenth century. Over the past two or three years, I have commented on this problem in several places in a piecemeal manner. This chapter draws on these efforts[1] and discusses how to redo the theory in the light of these new technological developments. It also speculates about how we should respond in terms of regulation. The prescriptive part of the paper is indeed speculation, written while being fully aware that these are first thoughts and will have to be honed before they can be used by policymakers.

1. Technological Change and Regulatory Challenge

In large tracts of traditional economics, the "invisible hand" is treated as an ideological weapon. Adam Smith's discovery suggests that the order that we see in society does not necessarily imply the existence of a God or a ruler who orders our food to be delivered to our dining tables or clothes to be kept ready at stores for us to choose from. Instead, Smith's discovery that much of this can happen through the implicit workings of an invisible hand arising naturally from our urge to further our individual interests, gave rise to some of the finest research in general equilibrium analysis and economic theory. But it also provoked a large amount of overwhelmingly misleading debate on ideology. One group took Smith's theory to indicate that you can always leave decisions to the market, without the need for government intervention; and another group took that theory to be false, indicating that you always need state directive and regulation.

In reality, as modern economic theory has made amply clear, it all depends on the domain of the economy we are talking about. In some domains, it may be fine to leave it, largely, to individual motivations to maximize profit or utility. In others, you may need the law and regulation, in significant ways enforced by the agents of the state, to bring about order and optimality. Local food markets in villages clearly fall in the first category. The use of public goods and commons falls in the second category.

But what is rarely appreciated is that the same market that worked well once without the use of law's authority may cease to do so as a result of shifts in the underlying technology. Or, more generally, the kind of regulation that once worked may cease to do so as technology changes the strategic character of the game of life we are engaged in. In an ongoing research project of mine with Jorgen Weibull (Basu and Weibull 2020), we try to characterize the idea of slow drift, which, while expanding the production possibility frontier of humankind, nevertheless changes the strategic structure of interaction among human beings. As a result, if left to itself with no regulation, such an economy could collapse to a disastrous outcome that is referred to as the "dinosaur risk."

Human society has had to contend with many such turning points in the course of history. When 2.5 million years ago, our ancestors learned to make labor-saving tools, or when approximately 300,000 years ago, they learned to "domesticate" fire, these achievements marked dangerous turning points in our history (Harari 2011). At those times, there was no state or codified law, but there were norms and informal rules of behavior that had to change to convert these technological breakthroughs into advantages and higher standards of living. These changes could instead have become forces of destruction. The story was quite similar during the Industrial Revolution, from the roughly mid-eighteenth to the mid-nineteenth century. The arrival of new technology and machines to displace labor caused distress and turmoil. But as a result of new laws—such as Britain's various factory acts—to protect workers, and the novel idea of a sustained income tax in 1842, the Industrial Revolution became an asset that led to higher growth and ultimately higher living standards. It is also no coincidence that the period of the Industrial Revolution coincided with, arguably, the period of biggest breakthroughs in economics, from Adam Smith's *Wealth of Nations* in 1776, to the marginalist revolution led by Stanley Jevons (1871) and Leon Walras (1874) in the late nineteenth century.

It is arguable that we are at a similar juncture today, with new digital technology turning markets on their heads, causing the relative demand for labor to drop,[2] and prompting a political backlash and an increase in populism (Rodrik 2017). The mastering of long-distance sea travel in the late fifteenth century changed the landscape of the world economy and polity, bringing in new forms of trade and prosperity but also ushering in the age of colonialism. In the same way, today is a time of new opportunities and also new challenges. It is time to rethink the foundations of our discipline and also the modes and nature of market regulation. This chapter focuses on a segment of the regulatory challenge pertaining to antitrust laws and their implementation. It is, therefore, a small contribution to a large research agenda.

2. Antitrust Century

Even in the best of times, antitrust law was a controversial policy instrument for improving market efficiency and fairness. The pioneering work on this began in the United States, with the enactment of the Sherman Antitrust Act in 1890. The theory of oligopoly and monopoly, though they had been given mathematical structure several decades before that, starting with the seminal work by Cournot (1838), was still not a part of the regular discourse in economics. The antitrust law movement grew more out of political activism to protect the hapless consumer,[3] than from any formal theoretical understanding of markets. It was never very clear whether its primary motivation was to promote efficiency or fairness. It was recognized much later, at the time of enacting the Robinson-Patman Act in 1936, that the most exploitative monopoly (namely, one that perfectly price discriminates across consumers) may be as efficient as a perfectly competitive market (see Basu 1993).

To understand this, consider a standard demand curve as shown in Figure 6.1. Assume that the marginal cost of production is constant at k. Then, as is well known, the competitive equilibrium is at the point marked C. The amount pro-

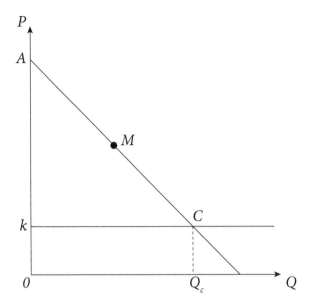

FIGURE 6.1. Standard demand curve.

duced will be Q_C, and the price charged will be the same and the marginal cost of production, k.

However, if the market was being provided for entirely by a standard monopolist, then the price would be higher, at p_M, and the quantity sold would be Q_M, as illustrated in Figure 6.1. Since the competitive equilibrium is efficient, standard monopoly, which supplies less than a competitive industry, clearly results in underproduction. It is in this sense that monopoly is known to be inefficient.

Now suppose that a certain market is served by one firm, the monopolist, and so the equilibrium is at the point marked M. There is inefficiency, as already seen. Interestingly, however, there are two ways to get to an efficient outcome. The first is to let many more firms enter the industry, as is typically attempted by antitrust laws and pro-competition laws. But what is not always appreciated is that there is another way to get to the efficient outcome—to enable or encourage the monopolist to become more exploitative, by discriminating across consumers perfectly. This in effect means that for each unit of the good sold, the monopolist extracts the highest price a consumer is willing to pay. In other words, the consumer's surplus is converted into the monopolist's profit. In such a case, the monopolist is able to collect the entire area beneath the demand curve as revenue. Such a monopolist will sell Q_C units and collect a total revenue equal to the area $OACQ_C$. Since the cost of producing this is $OkCQ_C$, the monopolist's profit is kAC, and the consumers earn zero surplus.

In brief, perfect competition (where consumers do well for themselves) or perfectly price-discriminating monopoly (where consumers are totally exploited) are both efficient outcomes. If our sole aim is efficiency, as is the case for many traditional economists, we should be indifferent to these two outcomes. Therein lies a big problem with conventional antitrust law as conceptualized by the "neoclassical" law and economics profession that emerged in the 1960s (see Basu 2018a for a discussion). Hence, if our main aim is to achieve efficiency, a monopolist should be nudged either to become competitive or more exploitative, using price discrimination to extract all consumer surplus from those buying the good or the service in question.

The morally unacceptable nature of this view becomes evident if one considers an extreme case, such as bonded labor or slavery. As a system of labor, slavery was in all likelihood "efficient." By pushing one group of people (namely, the slaves) to the wall, their owners were maximizing their own gains to the greatest extent possible. The result is Pareto optimal. It is not possible to make any person involved in this sinister system better off without making anyone else worse off.

Increasingly, economists who came to dominate the field of law and economics, certainly since the 1960s, emphasized that the main purpose of antitrust law was to promote efficiency, quite unmindful (or uncaring) of the fact that extreme exploitation can also promote efficiency. Fortunately, the economics profession seems to have now moved away from this Chicago School paradigm. I shall return to these two ways of getting to an efficient outcome in sections 4 and 5.

Turning to a different matter, it is interesting to note that our contemporary dilemma (namely, that the mechanical application of competition laws can do grave damage to industry) had been encountered earlier in a rather interesting way. This is captured by the fascinating history of the US Webb-Pomerene Act of 1918.

The years prior to and during World War I were a time of soul-searching and questioning about globalization, akin to what is happening now. There were dissenting voices during World War I expressing concern that the United States was unable to make enough profit out of foreign consumers, thanks to the restraining effect of these anti-monopoly laws, which were meant to protect all consumers. These were times of xenophobia, and some of the concerns aired stemmed from this. The Federal Trade Commission, which opened its doors in 1915, was entrusted with surveying the situation and coming up with policy recommendations. Its staff hit on a solution, one that was, effectively, an amendment to existing antitrust laws. The outcome was the Webb-Pomerene Act of 1918. In essence, this law allowed firms and corporations to collude and hike prices as long as they could show that the bulk of their goods was exported. In other words, the consumers they were exploiting were foreign consumers and not the domestic ones protected by the Sherman Act 1890 and Clayton Act 1914 (Diamond 1944).

We are at a similar juncture today, not because of foreign competition but because of the massively increasing returns to scale, made possible by the rise of new technologies. It is arguable that the steady and, in recent years, dramatic changes in technology, especially the rise of digital technology, is causing inequality to rise and the wages of workers to be depressed. If we do not want this trend to spin out of control, we need to rethink our regulatory structure and even the foundations of economics as deeply as we did during the Industrial Revolution.

In the sections that follow, I argue that the antitrust regime, which began in 1890, served reasonably well for a century. But if we persist with it now, it will become either irrelevant or an actual hindrance, thwarting the nation's manufacturing sector and markets and stalling development. It has been roughly a century of antitrust legislation, and now it is time to call it a day: the end of the antitrust century.

This immediately gives rise to questions about inequality and how its excesses can be curbed. As noted above, the original motivation behind the Sherman Act was to prevent arbitrary profiteering and to protect the small players and consumers in the market. If this law is now revoked because increasing returns to scale renders it irrelevant (or a hindrance), how do we ensure fairness and equity in the marketplace? For that, I believe, we need a different set of laws, those pertaining to direct action to promote greater equality and different kinds of profit sharing.

Before I go into these details, it is useful to articulate the problem with antitrust law in today's world.

3. Serrated Industries: A Description

While Adam Smith (2011 [1776]) and, later, Allyn Young (1928) were aware of the eventual arrival of increasing returns to scale and what this might do to markets, this was not a major concern until recent times. As a result of the relentless march of technology and the start and advance of digital connectivity, which allows us to ship fractions of a large project to distant lands, today we have economies of scale of a magnitude that was almost unimaginable even a few decades ago. Among the many implications of the digital economy is that search costs have gone down dramatically (e.g., see Goldfarb and Tucker 2017). You can be a producer in a small town in Vietnam and be known to those who need your product in Detroit.

This connectivity has one important consequence. In producing any slightly complicated goods for consumers—laptops, cars, toys, or music systems, for instance—it is now possible to consider components of the final product separately and have them produced in different places with relative advantages (and on a massive scale), so that each component is much cheaper than it would have been if everything was produced under one roof. I refer to this as a "vertically serrated industry" or simply a "serrated industry'" (Basu 2018b). This will be defined more formally in section 4.

Hence, the age we are entering is one in which there may still be thousands of firms involved in producing the same product, not because each of these firms produces the final good from start to finish (as in a traditional Cournot (1838) or Bertrand (1883) oligopoly or competitive model), but because each firm produces some tiny part of the final product. Take the example of the car industry. A standard oligopoly is one in which there are n producers of cars. A vertically serrated industry is one in which n firms may still be involved, but with one producing all the gears, one all the ignitions, one all the wheels, and so on. To make matters worse, these firms may be scattered around the world. One firm in one nation with cheap labor may be the master wheel maker, and another firm in another nation with sophisticated engineers may be the master gear manufacturer, with assembly taking place in yet another nation.

In the traditional oligopoly theory that comes down to us from Cournot's celebrated work of 1838, we know exactly how to characterize an equilibrium for an industry with n producers, for each n. If n is 1, we have a monopoly; if n is 2, it is a duopoly. As n increases and approaches infinity, we approach the competitive equilibrium, which we know from the First Fundamental Theorem of Welfare Economics, is Pareto efficient.

But how should one characterize an equilibrium in a serrated industry? The best way to do it is to first characterize a serrated industry formally. Once that is done, I propose to use the fundamental equilibrium idea that underlies both the contributions of Cournot and Bertrand, namely, that of a Nash equilibrium.

If this is done carefully, we get a surprising result. When $n = 1$, that is, there is only one firm producing cars (which means the full car is made by one firm), the outcome is, of course, the standard monopoly equilibrium. But when $n = 2$ in a serrated story, it is a very different situation from $n = 2$ in a standard oligopoly. In a standard oligopoly, this means a duopoly. In a serrated industry model, it means that one firm produces one part of the car (say, the front half) for all the cars being supplied, and another firm produces the other part (the rear half of the car) for all the cars. Assume that the assembly happens automatically and costlessly. In this case, the Nash equilibrium, far from moving from monopoly toward the competitive equilibrium, now moves in the opposite direction, with a smaller supply, resulting in a worse deal for consumers, with shrinking consumer surplus, and also exacerbating inefficiency. This scenario opens up an array of interesting questions and modeling options.

The next section illustrates these possibilities. Once this is done, we can see the problem of using conventional antitrust law to help consumers or to promote efficiency, which then leads to section 5, which speculates about the kind of law we will need in this new digital world.

4. Adapting Cournot: A Model of Serrated Industries

Consider a standard monopoly producing some goods, say, cars.[4] As we move toward competition, the number of firms producing cars increases. There is, however, another way in which we can have many firms involved. As discussed in section 3, we can have one firm producing wheels, another gears, another brakes, and so on. This is what I call a (vertically) serrated industry.

As technology advances and economies of scale increase, it is natural that we will move toward greater serration. Each of the, say n, components of the final product will be produced by one firm and components will be ever more finely defined.[5] Let the aggregate demand for cars be given by X, when the price of cars is P, and $A > 0$ and $B < 0$:

$$X = A - BP. \tag{1}$$

Suppose there are n firms producing n parts of the car. I make some strong symmetry assumptions purely for ease of analysis. Suppose firm j produces a certain component of the car at a cost of $c = c(n)$ for each unit of the component. Hence the cost of producing a car is $nc(n)$. It is assumed that fewer the tasks a firm does, the better it becomes at it. That is:

$$\text{If } m > n, \text{ then } nc(n) \geq mc(m). \tag{2}$$

Assume that firm i chooses a price p_i for its component. The competition, in other words, is over prices. Each firm tries to gouge out a bigger chunk of the total profit by pricing its component suitably. In a standard Cournot oligopoly, firms compete horizontally by taking shares of the product market. Here the competition is vertical; hence the term "vertically" serrated industry. The final price of a car will clearly be:

$$P = p_1 + p_2 + \ldots + p_n.$$

Hence, the profit function of firm i is given as follows, where π_i denotes profit earned by firm i:

$$\pi_i = [A - B(p_1 + p_2 + \ldots + p_n)](p_i - c).$$

A vertically serrated market is a game in which each firm chooses a price for its component. Maximizing profit gives us the following first-order condition for player i:

$$A - B(p_1 + p_2 + \ldots + p_n) - B(p_i - c) = 0. \tag{3}$$

We have n equations like (3). Given the symmetry of the model, it is obvious that when we solve all n equations, we will get

$$p_1 = p_2 = \ldots = p_n \equiv p^*.$$

Inserting these values in (3) and using P^* to denote the price of the final product $(P^* \equiv np^*)$, we get:

$$P^* = \frac{n(A + Bc)}{(n+1)B}. \tag{4}$$

It is easy to see that, if $n = 1$,

$$P^* = \frac{A}{2B} + \frac{c(1)}{2}. \tag{5}$$

Recall that $c(1)$ is the total cost of making a car. Note that (5) depicts the standard monopoly equilibrium. This is illustrated in Figure 6.2, in which the line shown as $\alpha\beta$ depicts the demand curve, $c(1)$ is the marginal cost of producing each car, and the equilibrium occurs at the point marked δ.

Starting from monopoly, if we move to a standard oligopoly and keep increasing the number of firms, in the limit, as is well known, the equilibrium goes to the point marked "competitive equilibrium." But in a serrated market, as n increases, P increases. The equilibrium moves toward the price equal to A/B. This is depicted by the point marked α in the figure. In essence, as vertical competition increases, the equilibrium moves away from the monopoly equilibrium in the opposite direction. In other words, consumer welfare decreases.

To see this formally, recall that c is a function of n. Hence, (4) can be written as:

$$P^* = \frac{nA}{(n+1)B} + \frac{c(n)n}{(n+1)}$$

From (2) we know that as $n \to \infty$, $P^* \to \frac{A}{B}$.

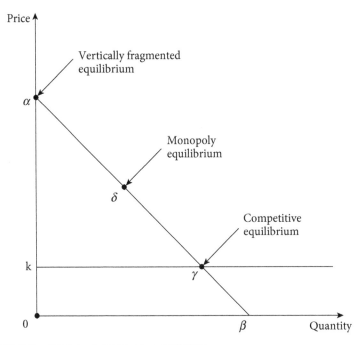

FIGURE 6.2.   Standard monopoly equilibrium.

Therein lies the problem for the consumer. With technological progress, the markets will tend to get even more exclusive, with prices rising and consumption falling. One reason this may not happen is that among the n producers, it is likely that not all will be playing the game as described above, choosing a price, and sitting back. Some will no doubt put on the mantle of a standard monopolist, who influences quantity along with the price.

If we assume, for instance, that the nth firm in the above industry is the retailer who assembles all the parts together and covers the last mile to the consumer, it is easy to show that the equilibrium will be at the standard monopoly equilibrium, that is, at δ, half-way between where the demand curve touches the vertical axis and the cost curve. For this to be formally modeled, we need to introduce the capacity for this n^{th} firm to use strategies that go beyond the pure choice of a price for each unit of its action.

Modern technology and the availability of consumer information also allows for discrimination of a kind that may not have been possible earlier. Sooner or later, some of the producers will learn the art of price discrimination. Once that happens, even as n keeps increasing, the number of cars produced will be the same as in the competitive equilibrium, but with one additional caveat—each consumer will be made to pay the highest price he or she is willing to pay. In other words (assuming, purely for reasons of analytical simplicity, that the income effect of the final product is zero), one or more of the producers will take the entire triangle below the demand curve and above the line k, as profit for themselves. The consumers will get to own many cars, but they would have paid up every penny they were willing to pay, with no consumer's surplus left over.

A formal proof of this is easy to give by assuming that the nth firm in the car industry, say, the final retailer, is able to price discriminate. Hence, while other firms choose their respective prices, firm n chooses a function $\phi(q)$, which says that this firm will charge a price of $\phi(q)$ for the act of retailing the qth car that it sells. In such a model, equilibrium occurs at the competitive equilibrium, marked γ in Figure 6.2, with the qth consumer being charged $p_1 + p_2 + \ldots + p_{n-1} + \phi(q)$. Hence, the entire consumer surplus is picked up by the retail firm. The nth firm will select:

$$\phi(q) = \frac{A}{B} - \frac{q}{B} - nc(n).$$

In brief, we have entered a world where small players—be they consumers or laborers—will either see a restriction of the market with prices rising or increasing price discrimination that extracts all their consumer surplus.

5. The Need for Regulatory Overhaul

The phenomenal success of the retailers in today's world may have something to do with the model described in section 4. Given the argument sketched above, it is not surprising that price discrimination is rampant in today's world. Of course, this has to be under camouflage, because most nations have anti-price-discrimination laws of some kind. In the United States, the Robinson-Patman Act of 1936 is supposed to deter price discrimination. But luckily for big corporations, this is one of the most poorly implemented laws, and for a good reason. A variety of ways can be used to price discriminate across consumers without admitting to doing so. We can use the traits of consumers and for each vector of traits, set a price. So, for example, all those who live on the upper west side of New York, live in a high-rise, and use a certain kind of computer to place an order will have to pay a certain price. And so on for other consumer groups. By this method, without having to name a consumer, you can price a commodity virtually for that consumer.

We can charge a rare air-traveler a much higher price per ticket and make it very cheap for those who fly a lot (which is called a frequent flyer program). We can vary the price of a taxi ride depending on what kind of phone you use to call the taxi. Prices can be made to vary depending on whether you are a good searcher or an impatient searcher. All these are common practices, where price discrimination is practiced under the guise of product differentiation.

In labor markets, something similar is happening: Salaries are varied by subtle means to extract much of the surplus that the laborer would have gotten by working. In areas where the poor live, wages are low. For many jobs, there is open wage-bargaining, which allows employers to tailor the wage they pay to different workers for the same job.

So with the march of technology and with greater vertical serration of the markets, we are moving towards an equilibrium where either prices are so high that most people are excluded from buying the product or they face a price discriminatory market, whereby their consumer surplus is taken out of their hands. They may buy a lot, and workers may work a lot, but the prices they pay for what they buy and the wages they receive for their work leave them with little surplus.

A part of the rise of inequality globally is caused by this mechanism. It is not a result of rising avarice or people getting meaner (though they may well be doing so) but the advance of technology changing the shape of market equilibria, as described in section 4. One sees in rich nations increasing evidence of bilateral bargaining, which allows sellers to charge different prices for different consumers. This happens nowadays in the United States whether one is buying a car, an airplane ticket, or even a medical service. The bazaar economy that one used to see in poor countries and village markets has at last arrived in rich nations.

The big policy challenge is: What should we do about this? Using the Sherman Act and forcing markets to be horizontally competitive (that is, competitive in the traditional way) is to forgo many of the benefits of technological advance, which have resulted in increasing returns to scale. If for each product, we insist that there must be thousands of producers, each supplying a small fraction of the demand, we would forgo all the benefits of modern technology and push society back to primitive times. Also, it is arguable that the Sherman Act does not apply in such situations, because this act is meant for artificially created monopolies and not natural monopolies that arise by the very nature of technology.

More specifically, a firm must control at least 70 percent of the market to be considered a monopoly; and to be considered guilty of monopolization, it must practice one or more "exclusionary practices." Whether something is a deliberate exclusionary practice is, of course, a questionable matter, and not surprisingly, the law has given rise to a lot of dispute (see Hovenkamp (1999) for a more detailed discussion). What I just showed, however, is that even if the law did apply to the kind of monopolies arising today, using it to create many competing firms would be undesirable. In brief, given the changing nature of modern industry, the Sherman Act and in fact all conventional antitrust laws have little role to play.

This leads me to the conclusion that some of the problems of large firms that Stiglitz (2017b) and many others have written about can no longer be solved by using our traditional antitrust laws. We have to look beyond these laws to novel interventions. The antitrust laws had a good century's run from 1890 but is turning out to be totally inadequate for today's world. The Robinson-Patman Act (1936), as already pointed out, can be destructive and cause output to decline in vertically serrated industries, which are becoming more and more common. It is time to draw the curtain on the whole gamut of antitrust and competition laws. This relates to the point broadly made in Basu and Weibull (2019), where we show with an illustratively constructed game how at times, the ground beneath our feet may shift slowly, which while expanding the production possibility frontier, also changes the strategic character of the game. It may thereby create a risk that unchanged behavior can cause a collapse. The slow shift may make us impervious to what is happening. But it is important for us to put our research hat on, understand the shift, and think outside the box, developing new regulations and new social conventions that may not have been needed before. (And in some cases, we may need to remove old laws and regulations.)

Note that in the face of the rise of digital technology, if we just watch it happen and leave all regulations unchanged, the global GDP will keep rising, but inequality will also rise in step, in fact sharply, with a few owners of firms cornering all the benefits and most of the population being impoverished. What we need is a different set of laws to counter this trend; we also need social conventions for different norms of behavior. My focus here is on the law.

If monopoly or oligopolies with few firms will be the market structure of the modern vertically serrated industries, how can we ensure an equitable income? A natural idea is that even if a few firms earn huge profits, there is no reason that only a few individuals should earn huge profits. To prevent this, we have to have laws that compel firms to diversify their shareholding. In short, the key is to ensure that the shares in each company are widely held. A monopoly of production must not mean a monopoly of income. Thus, the dismantling of antitrust laws, as suggested in this chapter, must be accompanied by new laws mandating a more radical dispersal of shareholding in each company. Not only will there no longer be a majority shareholder but shareholding in each company will be much more granular. How granular? How do we restrict the buying and selling of shares so that they do not end up with a few individuals holding a disproportionate amount of a firm or corporation? These are questions that need careful examination, and laws will have to be drafted with attention to details. The main point here is to note that once we have such a law, we will not have to worry about monopoly profits all flowing into a monopolist's hands. The profits will indeed accrue to one firm. But the firm being widely held, the profit will accrue to many individuals. The details of this mechanism will need a lot of thought to be effectively worked out. Every intervention has unexpected consequences, and it is important to try to think through these.[6]

One specific problem that can arise and deserves comment here is that a few individuals can hold few shares each in each firm, but they can do this for so many firms and corporations that they become disproportionately rich. With falling economywide wage shares and rising profits, this would result in very large profits accruing to a few individuals, even as we ensure that for each corporation shares are widely held. To correct this imbalance, we need a second intervention, this one at the level of the nation and not just the firm. The idea is to have some profit sharing at the national level. In brief, some fraction of profits in society should accrue to ordinary people, including workers (employed or unemployed).

The challenge is to create a blueprint for an equitable society that is viable. History is replete with systemic shifts that began with the right intentions but ended up with a few people capturing both political power and wealth. The clue is some form of profit sharing while respecting the laws of the market. We have to recognize that the market incentive and the profit motive are important drivers and must not be glossed over (or worse, centralized). What is needed is an intervention that respects this and still curtails inequality. So the suggestion is for a minimal profit-sharing within the nation, that is, to give all human beings a right to a certain fraction of the nation's profits. This idea has been around for a while, and variants can be found in the writings of Weitzman (1984), Steiner (1994), Hockett (2008), and recently, Matt Bruenig (2018) in a *New York Times* opinion piece. With the share of wages in society falling steadily, and the share of profits and rents rising in step with advancing technology and the creation of digital platforms for trade and exchange, some universal basic profit-sharing is critical.

Basically, what I am proposing is the twin dispersal idea: No firm must be disproportionately owned by one or a few individuals, and a fraction of the nation's shares should be widely dispersed. So as firms cut their demand for labor and profits rise, many individuals will share these higher profits, and furthermore, a part of these profit ends up with the workers, who own a share of the overall profits in the nation. And every time a worker is displaced by a robot, the workers' wages do not fully become the profit of the owner of the robot.

These are fledgling ideas that will have to be carefully worked out before they inform actual policy. It must be realized that human ingenuity is immense. For every law, there will be action to circumvent its intent. Good drafting of the law requires anticipating what these counteractions will be and creating mechanisms to minimize them; and all this will have to be done while making sure that market incentives do not get damaged.

To see some of the challenges that will no doubt have to be addressed, consider executive pay in companies. Once profits are dispersed widely by law and the CEO is unable to take a lion's share of it, a natural tendency will be to increase the salaries of the top echelons of a corporation, so that a part of the profit is indirectly siphoned off as salary. Further, what I have suggested are policies to allow industries to flourish and yet not have profits heaped on a few plates. But there is a global aspect to this problem that I do not address in this chapter.

All changes in regulation invariably provoke responses from individuals and corporations trying to navigate or even circumvent the new laws. I have argued (Basu 2018a) that this is bound to be an inexorable process, since human ingenuity is endless, with every new law provoking new and often unexpected strategies. The best we can do is to anticipate some of the reactions. In this case, some of the reactions are evident enough. As we try to set limits on inequality, there will be a tendency on the part of individuals to garner consumer's surplus, bypassing higher cash incomes. One way to do this is barter. If Picasso gives one of his paintings to Stravinsky and Stravinsky, in turn, composes a musical score especially for Picasso, both could be vastly better off. Indeed, even in current society, especially among the very poor and the very rich, there is much more barter or exchange of favors than most people (including trained economists) realize. I would expect this barter to increase with the new regulatory model suggested here.

Furthermore, groups will form to ensure that in their locality and for their collective interests, there are better public goods—more parks, cleaner air, better street lighting, and so on. This will enhance the group's well-being without showing up as enhancements to individual incomes.

Another issue is that of inter-country differences. Some profit-sharing and easing of antitrust laws within each nation can, as this chapter has suggested, curb some of the social ills that have brought us to our present predicament in each country. But inter-country inequality can increase, as some nations do better in solving their internal problems. This can cause migration and refugee flows, which can further fuel protectionism. In working out the details of the new regulatory framework, we will have to anticipate some of these problems and work them into the law. In particular, the problem of inter-country policy coordination and some minimal global rules of engagement are important matters that we cannot escape in today's globalizing world.[7]

This problem goes beyond the scope of the present chapter, not because it is not important but because I have no solutions to offer at this time. Clearly, it should figure prominently in our future research agenda.

Notes

This chapter benefited greatly from a presentation at the CRADLE conference held in New York on April 12 and 13, 2018. The comments and questions received at the conference helped me prepare this written version of the presentation. I express special thanks to Aviv Caspi, Kaniska Dam, Dominick Salvatore, and Haokun Sun for many valuable comments and suggestions.

1. In particular, I draw heavily on Basu (2018b).

2. See Autor et al. (1998), Karabarbounis and Neiman (2014), and Basu (2016).

3. There is a case for being similarly concerned about the hapless worker. While the exploitation of laborers has been a subject of long-standing interest to economists, it is heartening to see a recognition of this in the new legal literature in the context of antitrust law (see Naidu et al. 2018; Marinescu and Hovenkamp 2018). Sunstein (2018) refers to this as the "New Chicago School in town."

4. This section is drawn from Basu (2018b).

5. Models with similar results have been derived in the literature; see, for instance, Amir and Gama (2013). Such models are a part of the strategic complementarity literature in industrial organization theory: see Singh and Vives (1984) and Vives (1990). There is another direction in which markets are likely to move with technological change: toward greater entry deterrence (Dixit 1980), but I do not discuss that option here.

6. For an interesting critique of dispersed shareholding as strategy to counter the challenge of our new digital age, see Shroff (2018), who argues that the crux of the problem in India is the state-business nexus, which is becoming deeply embedded in India's polity.

7. For an engaging account of this challenge, see Stiglitz (2015; 2017a, chapter 4).

References

Amir, R., and A. Gama. 2013. "On Cournot's Theory of Oligopoly with Perfect Complements." Mimeo, University of Iowa.

Autor, D., L. Katz, and A. Krueger. 1998. "Computing Inequality: Have Computers Changed the Labor Market?" *Quarterly Journal of Economics* 113: 1169–1213.

Basu, K. 1993. *Lectures in Industrial Organization Theory*. Oxford: Basil Blackwell.

Basu, K. 2016. "Globalization of Labor Markets and the Growth Prospects of Nations." *Journal of Policy Modeling* 38(4): 656–669.

Basu, K. 2018a. *The Republic of Beliefs: A New Approach to Law and Economics*. Princeton, NJ: Princeton University Press.

Basu, K. 2018b. "The Rise of Trump and an Agenda for Regulatory Reform." *Journal of Policy Modeling* 40(4): 546–558.

Basu, K., and J. Weibull. 2020. "The Dinosaur Game: A Fable of Civilization Collapse." Work-in-progress, New York and Stockholm.

Bertrand. 1883. "Researcher de la Theorie Mathematique sur la Richesse." *Journal des Savants* 48: 499–508.

Bruenig, M. 2018. "The Massive US Inequality Problem." *New York Times*, December 6, p. 14.

Cournot, A. 1838. *Researches sur les Principles Mathematiques de la Theorie des Richesses*. Paris: M. Riviere & Co.

Diamond, S. 1944. "The Webb-Pomerene Act and Export Trade Associations." *Columbia Law Review* 44(6): 805–836.

Dixit, A. 1980. "The Role of Investment in Entry Deterrence." *Economic Journal* 90: 95–106.

Goldfarb, A., and C. Tucker. 2017. "Digital Economics." NBER Working Paper 23684, National Bureau of Economic Research, Cambridge, MA.

Harari, Y. N. 2011. *Sapiens: A Brief History of Humankind*. London: Penguin.

Hockett, R. 2008. "Toward a Global Shareholder Society." *Journal of International Law* 30(1): 101–187.

Hovenkamp, H. 1999. *Federal Antitrust Policy: The Law of Competition and Its Practice*. St. Paul, MN: West Group.

Jevons, W. S. 1871. *The Theory of Political Economy*. London: Macmillan & Co.

Karabarbounis, L., and B. Neiman. 2014. "The Global Decline of the Labor Share." *Quarterly Journal of Economics* 129(1): 61–103.

Marinescu, I., and I. Hovenkamp. 2018. "Anticompetitive Mergers in Labor Markets." Mimeo, University of Pennsylvania.

Naidu, S., E. Posner, and E. G. Weyl. 2018. "Antitrust Remedies for Labor Market Power." *Harvard Law Review*, forthcoming.

Rodrik, D. 2017. "Populism and the Economics of Globalization." NBER Working Paper 23559, National Bureau of Economic Research, Cambridge, MA.

Shroff, J. 2018. "Can Laws Mandating Dispersed Shareholding Counter Entrenched Inequality in India?" University of Oxford, Faculty of Law, https://www.law.ox.ac.uk /business-law-blog/blog/2018/05/can-laws-mandating-dispersed-shareholding -counter-entrenched.

Singh, N., and X. Vives. 1984. "Price and Quantity Competition in a Differentiated Duopoly." *Rand Journal of Economics* 15(4): 546–554.

Smith, A. 2011 [1776]. *The Wealth of Nations*, A. S. Skinner (ed.). Cambridge, England.

Steiner, H. 1994. *An Essay on Rights*. Oxford: Blackwell.

Stiglitz, J. 2015. *The Great Divide: Unequal Societies and We can Do about Them*. New York: Penguin.

Stiglitz, J. 2017a. *Globalization and Its Discontents Revisited: Anti-Globalization in the Era of Trump*. New York: W. W. Norton & Company.

Stiglitz, J. 2017b. "America Has a Monopoly Problem—and It's Huge." *The Nation*, October 23.

Sunstein, C. 2018. "A New View of Antitrust Law That Favors Workers," https://www.law .uchicago.edu/news/cass-sunstein-eric-posners-new-view-antitrust-law.

Vives, X. 1990. "Nash Equilibrium with Strategic Complementarities." *Journal of Mathematical Economics* 19: 305–321.

Walras, L. 1874. *Elements d'economie Politique Pure, ou Theorie de la richesse sociale*.

Weitzman, M. L. 1984. *The Share Economy: Conquering Stagflation*. Cambridge, MA: Harvard University Press.

Young, A. A. 1928. "Increasing Returns and Economic Progress." *Economic Journal* 38(152): 527–542.

LAW AND INTERNATIONAL
MONETARY POLICY REGIMES

Yair Listokin

In this chapter, I explain why asking more of law can expand the choice set available to international economic policymakers. Specifically, law, in the form of currency unions, capital controls, or even price controls, provides a macroeconomic adjustment mechanism otherwise unavailable to countries seeking to reap the benefits of trade by synchronizing their currency with a trading partner.

The "impossible trinity" of international macroeconomics is usually considered to offer governments a stark choice. They can either promote trade through shared or fixed currencies or they can promote macroeconomic stability by retaining control over monetary policy, but not both.

To retain some control over monetary policy while retaining fixed exchange rates, countries can enact capital controls—the third prong of the impossible trinity. With capital controls, jurisdictions pass laws to impede the movement of capital across borders, going so far as to deny the enforcement of an otherwise valid contract when enforcement would enable a violation of another country's capital control regime. Capital controls complicate law. From a traditional microeconomic perspective, such controls are strongly disfavored as inefficient restrictions on trade. But capital controls allow jurisdictions to access the trade-promoting benefits of fixed exchange rates as well as the credibility enhancement associated with pegging an unreliable currency to one with a sturdier international reputation—without relinquishing control over monetary policy. Using capital controls to enable stable exchange rates and monetary flexibility is a perfect example of the possibilities opened by law and macroeconomics—by asking more of law, regimes with capital controls, such as the Bretton Woods regime of 1944–1971, enable better macroeconomic outcomes.

The usual discussion of the impossible trinity also elides the distinction between currency pegs and currency unions. Currency pegs are relatively reversible. A country with a peg can alter the level of the peg or go off the peg entirely simply by changing a law. By adjusting a peg, a country regains some control over monetary policy. The enhanced reversibility of a currency peg reduces the hands-tying value of a fixed exchange rate, which may mitigate some of the credibility benefits associated with an exchange rate pegged to currencies with strong international reputations.

Currency unions, by contrast, are extremely difficult to reverse without incurring significant economic and constitutional dislocation. A currency union is therefore highly credible, but at the cost of a loss of macroeconomic flexibility. In most currency unions, both capital controls and devaluations are impossible. Monetary policy is set for the union as a whole, rather than being tailored to individual jurisdictions. In these instances, policymakers in jurisdictions suffering from extreme macroeconomic dislocation should consider even more radical legal policies, such as wage and price controls. The costs of price controls are high; they impose extreme microeconomic harms on the economy. But when macroeconomic factors, rather than supply-side constraints, hold back the economy, even wage and price controls may be efficient.

Consider Greece. I argue that, in the course of a disastrous recession ongoing since 2010, Greece should have imposed a uniform mandatory deflation of all prices and domestic debt contracts.[1] Conventional international macroeconomics suggests that the first best remedy for Greece's ills would have been to devalue its currency. Doing so would have made Greek labor more internationally competitive by making Greek goods and services cheaper relative to the costs of similar products produced in nearby countries. As a member of the Eurozone, however, Greece was unable to devalue its currency; nor was Greece able to restrict capital flows, so instead, Greek wages and other prices needed to fall in absolute terms. As Milton Friedman predicted, this internal price adjustment imposes much higher macroeconomic costs in terms of unemployment and lost output than would a currency devaluation. Compared with Greece's never-ending recession, I argue that Greece should have designed a legal package of price controls and other legal measures to mimic a currency devaluation.

In short, law offers a mostly unexplored tool of international macroeconomic policy. Using law to "tie hands" may enable a country to expand its set of macroeconomic policy options and better coordinate its policy with those of other countries. Creative use of law, in the form of capital controls and even price controls, can enable easier macroeconomic adjustment than more traditional channels can, though at the cost of significant microeconomic dislocation. Lawyers, as well as macroeconomists, deserve an important role in the making of international macroeconomic policy, as they enjoyed during the Bretton Woods era.

1. Monetary Policy Institutions and International Macroeconomics

1.1. Law, Institutions, and International Macroeconomic Policy

Many countries limit their macroeconomic policy options by fixing exchange rates with other jurisdictions.[2] For example, a currency peg with an important trading partner mitigates exchange-rate risk that hinders trade between the two countries. At present, currency pegs are used by Saudi Arabia and (to a lesser extent) China. Both countries peg their currencies to the U.S. dollar, an important trading partner. Similarly, many countries on the periphery of Europe, such as Bulgaria and Morocco, peg their currencies to the euro. During the Bretton Woods era (1944–1971), most of the developed world enjoyed the trade-promoting benefits of fixed exchange rates.

In addition to promoting trade, currency pegs can enhance macroeconomic credibility. By pegging their currencies to the euro, Bulgaria and Morocco reset expectations of monetary growth to rates similar to those of the euro, rather than to previous domestic expectations. Currency unions go even further than currency pegs in removing exchange-rate risks from trading relationships and reducing transaction costs associated with trade (such as the costs of exchanging currencies). Shared currencies also provide a powerful symbol of economic and political integration. If these benefits are large enough, then jurisdictions may choose to share a currency, at the cost of losing the ability to tailor monetary policy to conditions in the jurisdiction. Anticipating these trade-enhancing benefits, the members of the Eurozone relinquished control over monetary policy in order to join the euro. Likewise, US states belong to a currency union (the dollar)[3] that eliminates exchange-rate risks and costs from interstate trade at the price of each state's inability to use monetary policy to respond to macro conditions.

While each jurisdiction in a currency union (e.g., countries in the Eurozone and the states in the United States) loses the ability to use monetary policy to address macroeconomic fluctuations, monetary policy in a currency union reflects economic conditions in the union as a whole. If the Eurozone as a whole, or the US economy as a whole, suffers from inadequate aggregate demand, then the European Central Bank (ECB) or the Fed expands the money supply to lower interest rates and stimulate aggregate demand. Because the central bank pursues monetary stabilization for the currency union as a whole, jurisdictions in a currency union don't forgo monetary policy completely. Instead, they each lose the ability to tailor monetary conditions to macroeconomic conditions in their jurisdiction. If macro conditions in a jurisdiction differ from conditions in the union as a whole, then the jurisdiction cannot rely on monetary policy to bring the economy back into balance.

Currency pegs and currency unions amplify the international spillovers of monetary policy. If, for example, US interest rates move lower in response to recession in the United States, then monetary conditions in all countries with exchange rates fixed relative to the US dollar must also lower interest rates to maintain the currency peg and keep capital flows in balance. To coordinate these spillovers, fixed rate international macroeconomic regimes need strong institutions, such as the International Monetary Fund (IMF) under the Bretton Woods System (see below).

CURRENCY PEGS VERSUS CURRENCY UNIONS

To this point, the discussion has treated two different institutional arrangements—currency pegs and membership in a currency union—as identical. But they are not the same, even if they are often conflated in discussions of international macroeconomics. Currency pegs are relatively reversible—a jurisdiction with a peg can simply change the peg or allow its currency to float. As a result, a jurisdiction in a currency peg can regain control over monetary policy relatively easily if the need for monetary policy stabilization proves to be greater than expected. Moreover, countries with a currency peg may retain some control over monetary policy and enjoy the benefits of fixed exchange rates by imposing capital controls (see below). Currency unions, by contrast, are much harder to reverse. To reverse its membership in a currency union, a jurisdiction has to demonetize its economy of the old currency and introduce a new one. Such systematic disruption to the money supply is almost certain to cause a profound recession.[4]

The relative irreversibility of currency unions versus currency pegs offers advantages as well as disadvantages to jurisdictions. If a jurisdiction was formerly viewed as inflation prone, then its entry into a relatively irreversible currency union reduces inflation expectations by more than would the adoption of a currency peg, which is easier to reverse. In addition, the trade facilitated by a currency peg should fall short of the trade facilitated by a currency union. With the peg, there remains some risk of the peg getting altered or removed. Finally, if the purpose of a currency union is to indicate deeper political integration between two jurisdictions, then irreversibility is a virtue.

In short, a currency peg offers a more modest combination of benefits and costs than a currency union. If the cost-benefit analysis associated with a fixed exchange-rate regime proves to be unrealistically optimistic in encouraging adoption, then a currency peg is much easier to reverse than a currency union. Absent economic catastrophe, jurisdictions considering currency unions should first enter into pegged exchange-rate relationships for several full turns of the business cycle. If the currency peg has been successful, only then should jurisdictions enter into a currency union.

Both currency pegs and currency unions, however, generally entail a significant loss of monetary policy autonomy for a jurisdiction. Given the inevitability of shocks to aggregate demand, these jurisdictions need alternative tools for mitigating macroeconomic harms.

THE IMPOSSIBLE TRINITY OF INTERNATIONAL MACROECONOMICS

As noted above, the "impossible trinity" of international macroeconomics requires a trade-off between the trade-promoting benefits of fixed exchange rates, the investment-promoting benefits of free capital flows, and the macroeconomic stability benefits of control over the money supply.[5] The impossible trinity demonstrates that it is impossible for a country to simultaneously have all of (a.) fixed exchange rates (with correspondingly low trading costs), (b.) control over monetary policy (interest rates), and (c.) free capital flows. Wedded to the notion of free capital flows, many jurisdictions therefore allow their currencies to float rather than lose the ability to use monetary policy to facilitate macroeconomic adjustments. This decision impedes trade flows by introducing exchange-rate risks and expenses.

1.2. Capital Controls

In his book, *The Globalization Paradox*, Dani Rodrik argues against a binary choice between forgoing monetary policy and impeding trade with floating exchange-rate regimes. Instead, Rodrik argues for capital controls, the often overlooked third prong of the impossible trinity. With capital controls, jurisdictions get the benefits of monetary policy and the benefits of stable exchange rates. Jurisdictions lose the benefits of free international flows of capital, but Rodrik asserts that these benefits are smaller and more uncertain than commonly perceived.

Law and macroeconomics assume a much more important role in a fixed exchange rate/ capital control regime than they do when currencies float or jurisdictions have a shared currency. Capital controls are legal instruments, imposed by the government. The capital controls of the Bretton Woods regime pervaded law. IMF Article VIII.2(b), for example, obliged member nations to make foreign exchange dealings that violated one country's capital controls "unenforceable" in another member country. According to the IMF legal department, this meant that "the courts in members' territories must not lend their assistance to implement the obligations of such contracts" that violated another member's capital controls.[6] The necessity of capital controls to the international macroeconomic system superseded the ordinary enforcement of contracts—one of the most fundamental commitments of most legal systems. Bretton Woods thus entailed an important change in law to facilitate macroeconomic ends.

Many economists assume that capital controls are doomed to failure, because they are subject to "evasion and circumvention."[7] This assumption entails economists spurning a policy option because of legal, rather than economic, reasons.

The economist's critique of capital controls also proves too much; every law is subject to evasion and circumvention. Indeed, it is only with elaborate legal regimes that governments retain control over monetary and fiscal policy.

Monetary policy depends on government control over currency and the payments system. This control can be evaded. When people counterfeit currency, they undermine the government's control over the currency. To protect confidence in the payments system more generally, governments offer a diverse array of subsidies and regulations. Deposit insurance, for example, enables the government to retain more effective control over monetary policy but also gives financial institutions many opportunities to exploit government guarantees for private gain. Instead of giving up on monetary policy because of incentives to evade and circumvent, governments impose anticounterfeiting laws, capital requirements, and a wide array of other complicated regimes.

Fiscal policy similarly depends on the government's ability to raise funds and spend them effectively. Taxes are evaded, and government spending is subject to all kinds of abuse, but we don't abolish taxes or spending, even though the incentives for individuals to evade taxes or fleece the government seem overwhelming. Instead, governments criminalize evasion and circumventions. The regimes introduced to mitigate evasion can be intrusive and clumsy. In recent years, for example, the United States adopted an intrusive reporting regime, known as the Foreign Account Tax Compliance Act (FATCA) for foreign financial institutions holding offshore accounts of US taxpayers.[8] The regime was so costly for the foreign financial institutions that some simply terminated the accounts of US taxpayers.[9] But the United States chose to enforce the costly regime in order to reduce opportunities for tax evasion and circumvention.

Like paying taxes or using government-provided fiat-money, capital controls can be enabled by a government regime that reduces incentives for evasion or circumvention. It may be true that capital controls are easier to evade, more costly to enforce, or provide less benefit than the regimes that protect monetary and fiscal policy. But legal experts, and not just economists, need to help make this determination. Unfortunately, legal experts usually don't take part in this discussion, because they don't know the macroeconomic stakes well enough to balance the costs of enforcing capital controls against the benefits.

1.3. Capital Controls in Currency Unions

Most countries that combine capital controls with fixed exchange rates (such as China) peg their currencies to a reference currency. Jurisdictions in a currency union, by contrast, seldom restrict capital flows in the currency union. Capital controls limit economic integration between jurisdictions, whereas currency unions reflect a strong desire for both economic and political integration.

But jurisdictions in a currency union (and the central banks that run monetary policy in those unions) should consider capital controls in some circumstances. In particular, capital controls may be desirable if a jurisdiction's economy is out of tune with the rest of the currency union's economy.

Consider Greece. The term "Great Recession" fails to convey Greece's struggles from 2009 to the present. Unemployment there peaked at a remarkable 29 percent in 2013 and remained well above 20 percent into 2018. Seven years into the Great Recession, Greek output was 26 percent smaller in real terms than at its pre-recession height. By comparison, US output during the Great Depression bottomed out at 25 percent below its peak. Seven years after the onset of the Great Depression, real output in the United States had fully recovered. Greek social indicators, such as plummeting birthrates and a sharp increase in the incidence of depression and suicide, testify to the human cost of Greece's economic tragedy.

One reason for this horrific performance was Greece's inability to use many of the most effective macroeconomic stimulus tools. Expansionary fiscal policy was precluded by Greece's parlous state of public finance. Expansionary monetary policy was limited by Greece's membership in the Eurozone. The ECB, which sets monetary policy for the Eurozone, implemented policies for the zone as a whole. As a result, the ECB's policies aimed to stimulate much less than they would have done had monetary policy been targeted at Greece exclusively. The ECB kept its benchmark policy interest rate, known as the refinancing rate, (slightly) above 0 percent through 2014, a period during which the Greek depression was at its worst. The inadequate policy response to Greece's macroeconomic crisis meant that Greece's misery was deeper and longer than it might have been.

Greece could have regained control over monetary policy by exiting the Eurozone. "Grexit," however, was viewed as an anathema to Greek leaders, the leaders of other important European countries, and the leaders of the EU's institutions.

Rather than leaving the Eurozone, Greece and the ECB might have considered imposing temporary capital controls on the movement of capital between Greece and other EU nations. Capital controls would have loosened the macroeconomic policy straightjacket that hinders the response to the Greek economic catastrophe. With capital controls, the ECB could have set a lower short-term interest rate in Greece than in other EU countries, providing desperately needed stimulus to the Greek economy without unduly stimulating the rest of the Eurozone.

Why didn't the EU and Greece consider establishing capital controls? One critical factor was law. Free movement of capital represents one of the four "fundamental" freedoms articulated in the EU's governing Treaty of Lisbon. Articles 63–66 of the Treaty ban capital controls between member countries. Even Article 66, which permits the establishment of capital controls in "exceptional circumstances," applies only to "third countries." Thus, Greece was prohibited by treaty from imposing capital controls on capital movements within the EU, precluding this "solution" to Greece's macroeconomic policy problem. Yet again, we see the deep connection between law and the making of international macroeconomic policy.

2. Using Wage and Price Controls to Address Extreme Macroeconomic Imbalances in the Face of Fixed Currency Regimes: The Case of Greece

Greece's depression was so bad that even more extreme legal interventions, such as wage and price controls, should have been considered.

Wage and price controls have a justifiably poor reputation as instruments of macroeconomic policy. When the United States instituted such controls under the Emergency Stabilization Act in the early 1970s, for example, microeconomic imbalances abounded, while inflation continued to increase.[10]

But even wage and price controls are worth considering if the macroeconomic alternatives are sufficiently dire. Under the right conditions (which will be rare), price controls offer a powerful tool for overcoming price rigidities that keep output below potential in depressed economies. If even the most unlikely tools of law and macroeconomics (such as price controls) occasionally have their uses, then we should never dismiss law and macroeconomic interventions absolutely. Instead, we need to compare legal solutions to macroeconomic problems with fiscal and monetary alternatives.

Many economists blame Greece's astronomic unemployment rates on prevailing wages. Greeks who do work are paid too much in relation to overall labor productivity, and those who don't work demand too much to get back into the labor market. Since Milton Friedman's seminal analysis of this issue, the conventional macroeconomic prescription for a country in Greece's position has been currency devaluation, which would be accomplished by expansionary monetary policy.[11] By devaluing its currency, Greece would, in a single stroke, make its labor and capital more competitive, enabling it to increase exports and mitigate the depression.

However, as a member of the Eurozone, Greece does not control its own currency. It cannot unilaterally loosen monetary policy, even by imposing capital controls. Instead of devaluing its currency, Greece was forced to "internally devalue" by allowing wages and other prices to decline. A market-led process of wage declines, however, moves fitfully and painfully, leading to further reduction in output. Because the market system cannot coordinate rapid wage and price adjustments, inefficiencies, such as sky-high unemployment, also follow. As Friedman explained, "Wage rates tend to be among the less flexible prices. In consequence, . . . a policy of permitting . . . [wages] to decline is likely to produce unemployment rather than, or in addition to, wage decreases."[12]

Greeks have borne witness to the accuracy of Friedman's prediction. Instead of lowering wages, many Greek employers chose to keep nominal wages fixed and instead cut employment. Prices and wages have since decreased, but the process has been agonizingly slow and economically painful.

Even with currency devaluation off the table, Greece need not have left macroeconomic management to market forces: There are other ways of combating the notorious downward inflexibility of wages. Law—in particular, price controls— offers an alternative, an instrument for lowering real wages and prices rapidly and in a more coordinated fashion than isolated market actors can achieve. If Greece passed a law requiring all nominal wages, prices, and domestic debts to be briefly reduced by a significant amount—say, 10 percent for three months—then real wages and prices would have adjusted as quickly as if Greece had devalued its currency. At a stroke, a regime of price controls would have made Greek labor and production more competitive relative to the other Eurozone countries.[13]

As one might expect, there are trade-offs. Any deflation—whether through currency devaluation or legally imposed deflation—can put the financial system at risk. Greek banks' domestic assets would lose value, but foreign liabilities wouldn't, taxing the banks' solvency. A financial meltdown would, of course, exacerbate the depression. In addition, Greek products include inputs from outside the country. The cost of these inputs would not change, even as the domestic revenues of those firms would lose value. Either Greek businesses would have to bear this painful shock—which might cause many to collapse—or be able to adjust their individual price deflation to reflect the foreign component of their inputs, which would make legally imposed deflation very complex. More broadly, devaluation squeezes the profits of importers who charge consumers in domestic currency but pay their suppliers in foreign currency. Finally, there is no simple way to determine what debt is domestic, and therefore subject to devaluation, and what is foreign. Thus, lawyers would have to draw fine lines between which accounts are subject to devaluation and which are not.

Other risks are unique to legally imposed deflation. While importers in a country that has devalued can simply raise their prices, price controls would restrict the ability of Greek importers to adjust. Preventing a vicious squeeze on Greek importers therefore requires a somewhat more flexible program of mandated deflation (with price decreases differing for imports versus domestically produced goods), which greatly increases complexity. Most importantly, price controls, however short lived, deprive a market economy of its primary coordinating mechanism—price.

But desperate times call for desperate measures. Greece is suffering an unprecedented economic cataclysm, with both supply-side (uncompetitive labor costs) and demand-side (aggregate demand short of supply capacity) dimensions. European monetary policy is now stuck at the zero lower bound, limiting monetary stimulus. Greek monetary stimulus options would anyway be limited to stimulus appropriate to the Eurozone as a whole because of Greece's membership within it and the illegality of capital controls between Greece and the rest of the EU. Greek fiscal policy also has no scope for stimulus, as national debt levels are astoundingly high. And in spite of the horrendous costs, neither Greece nor the "troika" of the IMF, ECB, and European Commission are willing to accept a Greek exit from the Eurozone, which would enable direct devaluation. (Like a legally imposed domestic deflation, "Grexit" would also require difficult determinations of what assets would remain denominated in euros versus drachmas).

Legally mandated deflation doesn't have to be perfect. It just has to be better than internal devaluation, which has been incredibly costly. Mandated deflation would use law to coordinate a rapid change in prices, potentially facilitating less painful adjustment to the problem of wages disproportionate to productivity. And unlike the Nixon-era price controls in the United States, which targeted inflationary symptoms rather than demand causes, mandated deflation in Greece would directly address one of the central problems of Greek macroeconomic underperformance: the downward rigidity of prices. As a result, mandated deflation is more likely to be effective over the long run than are price controls that attempt to tame inflation.

Amid the worst economic crisis in modern history, a short period of legally mandated deflation probably is worth the accompanying risks, although these risks also can be mitigated to an extent. Cooperation between the troika and the

Greek government would help, particularly in reducing the threat of a financial crisis. The troika's expertise would be essential in crafting partial solutions to the problems of deflating Greek assets without unduly affecting assets held in other Eurozone countries. In addition, the ECB must offer a strong backstop to Greek financial institutions as they cope with the one-time harm of a sudden devaluation of their assets relative to their liabilities. Finally, Greece and the troika would need to develop solutions for the inevitable tensions that arise between mandated deflation and the EU's comprehensive system of rules and regulations.

Wage and price controls demonstrate the power and the peril of law and macroeconomics. By intervening in the price system, law can respond directly to the most pressing macroeconomic problems. At its best, law can coordinate macroeconomic rebalancing when other tools for such coordination, such as monetary or exchange-rate policy, prove wanting. But given the major downsides of wage and price controls, they should be used only when the macroeconomic policy toolkit is almost bare, as in Greece today.

Notes

1. For related suggestions, see Emmanuel Farhi, Gita Gopinath, and Oleg Itskhoki (2014), "Fiscal Devaluations," *Review of Economic Studies* 81(2): 725–760.

2. The theory of optimal currency areas examines the trade-offs between larger and smaller currency unions. See R. A. Mundell (1961), "A Theory of Optimum Currency Areas," *American Economic Review* 51(4): 657–665.

3. During the "free banking" era in the United Srares (1837–1864), states, not the federal government or a national bank, regulated the issue of currency.

4. Even if the quantity of money stays constant, the uncertainty is almost certain to cause a pronounced decrease in the velocity of money. (Velocity measures how frequently a given unit of currency changes hands.) With constant quantity of money and a decrease in velocity, the quantity "theory" of money, $MV = PY$, requires either deflation of a decrease in output.

5. For a lucid explanation of the impossible trinity, see Paul Krugman (1999), "O Canada—A Neglected Nation Gets Its Nobel," *Slate* (October), available at http://www.slate.com/articles/business/the_dismal_science/1999/10/o_canada.html.

6. See https://www.imf.org/external/pubs/ft/wp/2016/wp1625.pdf.

7. See https://www.imf.org/external/pubs/ft/wp/2016/wp1625.pdf.

8. See "FATCA" at https://www.irs.gov/businesses/corporations/foreign-account-tax-compliance-act-fatca.

9. See https://www.theguardian.com/money/2014/sep/24/americans-chased-by-irs-give-up-citizenship-after-being-forced-out-of-bank-accounts.

10. For a review and critique from the General Counsel of the agency established to oversee wage and price controls, see https://nixonswageandpricefreeze.files.wordpress.com/2011/07/forty-years-after-the-freeze.pdf.

11. See Milton Friedman (1950), "The Case for Flexible Exchange Rates," in *Essays in Positive Economics*, 157–203. Chicago: University of Chicago Press.

12. Friedman, "The Case for Flexible Exchange Rates," 165.

13. See Tyler Cowen (2010), "Are Wage and Price Controls a Solution for Greece?" *Marginal Revolution*, February 19, at https://marginalrevolution.com/marginalrevolution/2010/02/is-this-a-solution-for-greece.html. Farhi et al. show that a combination of an increase in import taxes and an increase in export subsidies can also replicate a currency devaluation. See Farhi et al., "Fiscal Devaluations." Note, however, that EU single market rules would prevent Greece from pursuing this policy with respect to its EU counterparts.

8

WHY ECONOMICS IS A MORAL SCIENCE

Lifting the Veil of Ignorance in the Right Direction

Gaël Giraud

Economics is essentially a moral science. That is to say, it employs introspection and judgement of value.

—Lord Keynes, writing to Sir Roy Harrod, July 4, 1938

In Atkinson (2009, 792), the late British economist acknowledged that "not only is welfare economics a legitimate exercise, but it is an exercise to which economists should devote more time and attention. Economics *is* a moral science. Welfare economics should be a central part of the discipline. But it is not. While welfare economics was a subject of importance half a century ago, today it has largely disappeared from the mainstream. . . . Yet economists go on making welfare judgments." Economics, however, deals (or, at least, should deal) with ascertainable facts, while ethics focuses on valuations and obligations.

This dichotomy between values and facts—which, regarding social sciences, goes back at least to Max Weber (1988)—raises a specific challenge for decision theory. Decision theory and game theory, indeed, claim to deal with behavioral patterns free of judgments and have permeated the body of normative theories of justice, rather than been inspired by the latter. Rawls (1971) and Harsanyi (1953, 1955, 1975), for instance,[1] have constructed theories of social justice based on the "rational" choices that representatives would make for society in what Rawls names the "original position," behind a veil of ignorance that prevents people from knowing their own future social positions.

In this chapter, I suggest that attitudes toward risk can actually be deduced from some broader ethical options. Rawls (1971) views preferences in the original position as being of a different nature from "ordinary" preferences for consumption, for risk, or for the distribution of social goods to others. He specifies that the parties in the original position are concerned only with citizens' share of primary social goods, which include basic rights as well as economic and social advantages. Rawls also argues that the representatives in the original position would adopt the maximin rule as their principle for evaluating the choices before them (i.e., making the choice that produces the highest payoff for the least-advantaged position). One interpretation of this classical viewpoint consists of understanding the agnosticism of representatives behind the veil as the hallmark of, and the guarantee for, ethical choices, while the rationality of their decision itself would be entirely based on some positive behavioral theory. The Maximin criterion then appears as only one possible option among many others, characterized by some extreme risk aversion.

If Rawls and Harsanyi come to quite different conclusions about the form ethical preferences should take behind the veil of ignorance—respectively, the Maximin and the utilitarian criteria—this is mainly due to their different views on the attitude of people toward uncertainty or risk behind the veil of ignorance. Nevertheless, both scholars agree to view the original position as a thought experiment in which ethical preferences should conform anyway to some rationality requirements analogous to the ones used by people when making decisions *in front of the veil* (i.e., in full knowledge of their social positions).

It is therefore only natural to inquire whether some of these requirements are not common to both the hypothetical discussion taking place behind the veil of ignorance and the daily decisions presumably made in front of it. Kariv and Zame (2008) have indeed introduced a framework encompassing both risk, and social and ethical preferences, where they show that, under some assumptions, ethical preferences in the original position are entirely determined by risk and social preferences (i.e., by preferences that are not hypothetical at all). Moreover, according to revealed preference theory, risk preferences should be deducible from observational facts and experiments keeping at bay any moral consideration. To carry the Rawlsian metaphor further, according to these authors, preferences behind the veil of ignorance can be deduced from preferences in front of the veil. Because these authors view risk and social preferences as being essentially arbitrary, they conclude that "there is no conceptual reason to expect that moral preferences should be consistent with any particular notion of rationality—or theory of justice." Thus, at variance with both Rawls and Harsanyi, they reach a conclusion rather similar to that of Hayek (1976), according to whom social justice is a "mirage." Their argumentation, though, is quite different from the one put forward by the Austrian thinker: In the same way, they argue, that in a liberal polity one should not discuss the tastes of consumers and investors (*de coloribus et gustibus non disputandum est*), one should also refrain from discussing the ethical principles underlying, say, the writing of the law, the basic distribution of goods, and so forth. For such principles are all but arbitrary.

This chapter challenges this viewpoint by reexamining the framework introduced by Kariv and Zame (2008) and later developed by Zame et al. (2019). I consider the situation of a representative who can face three types of decision problem: (1) Behind the veil of ignorance, her preferences will be called "ethical";[2] (2) in a risky individual decision problem (in front of the veil), her preferences will be termed "risk preferences"; (3) finally, in a social choice problem (still in front of the veil, where the Representative is assumed to know her position), her preferences will be "social." I then ask whether it is possible to deduce attitudes toward risk from ethical preferences. Starting with the same setting as the authors just mentioned, but adopting different assumptions (which encompass a broader spectrum of classical preferences than do the assumptions needed by these authors for their argument to go through), I provide an extremely simple proof of exactly the opposite result: Under fairly weak assumptions, risk and social preferences can be uniquely deduced from ethical ones. Thus, I agree with Kariv and Zame (2008) that there is a linkage between preferences behind and in front of the veil of ignorance. But, according to the viewpoint defended here, the implication goes in the reverse direction: Decision theory toward risk does not boil down to a descriptive theory (how people actually behave de facto) but embodies normative views (how people ought to choose). Risk and social preferences belong to prescriptive theories.

This theoretical finding complements the laboratory experiment run by Hörisch (2007) to implement and test the Rawlsian original position. Her experimental design allows for a separation of the effects of risk and social preferences behind the veil of ignorance. Though only a minority acts according to maximin preferences, subjects prefer more equal distributions behind than in front of the veil of ignorance. Men prefer more equal allocations mostly for insurance purposes, women also due to social preferences for equality. These results contrast the utilitarian's claim that behind the veil of ignorance, maximin preferences necessarily imply infinite risk aversion. Indeed, the results are compatible with any degree of risk aversion as long as social preferences for equality are sufficiently strong. This suggests that ethical preferences behind the veil cannot be deduced from attitudes toward risk in front of the veil.

Needless to say, the consequences of such a statement can hardly be overestimated regarding, say, climate change (see, e.g., Llavador et al. 2010). Depending on the level of risk aversion and time impatience, it is well known that one can reach completely different conclusions as to whether and at what pace a strong mitigation policy should be put into practice. The punchline of this chapter is that these postures toward risk and time themselves depend on ethical options that are questionable and should become part of the public debate.

Section 1 introduces my framework. Section 2 proves that, under weak restrictions, attitudes toward risk and social choice problems can be deduced from ethical options. Finally section 3 discusses further Kariv and Zame (2008) and provides two counterexamples. The first one illustrates an instance where risk preferences can be deduced from ethical preferences, but the converse is not true. The second example provides a situation where neither of the two implications hold: In this case, the veil of ignorance simply cannot be lifted.

1. Choice Environments

Following Kariv and Zame (2008), society consists of $n \geq 1$ citizens, of whom there is no loss of generality in assuming that the Representative is citizen 1. Three environments are considered. In the first, termed the "ethical choice environment," the objects of choice are allocations of prospects for all members of the society, including the Representative, but in a setting in which the Representative does not know her position in the society, nor the positions of others. In the second environment, called the "social choice environment," the objects of choice are (deterministic) allocations of prospects for all members of society, including the Representative. By contrast with the ethical one, in this second environment, the Representative knows her social position before making a decision. In the third, which is termed the "risk environment," objects of choice are random individual prospects for the Representative. As for prospects, they may designate a huge variety of items: quantity of basic goods, utility levels, income, poverty indices, and so forth.[3]

Choice spaces are formalized as follows:

- The choice space $\mathcal{R}$ in the individual risk environment consists of all lotteries, that is, collections

$$(p_h; x_h)_{h=1,\dots,k} \tag{1}$$

  where $(p_h)_h$ is a probability vector,[4] and each $x_h \in \mathbb{R}$ is a prospect, where a prospect can designate a large variety of items: utility level, income, wealth, poverty index, relational capability index (Lhuillier et al. 2017), and so forth. The lottery (1) yields the Representative prospect x_h with probability p_h.
- The choice space $\mathcal{S}$ in the social choice environment consists of all allocations of prospects $x^j = (x_i^j)_i \in \mathbb{R}^n$ for society.

Let $N = \{1, \dots, n\}$, and S_N be the group of permutations $\sigma: N \to N$. Given some vector $x \in \mathbb{R}^n$ and some permutation $\sigma \in S_N$, the composition σx is again an allocation $\mathbb{R}^n$ assigning prospect $x_{\sigma(i)}$ to citizen i.

- The choice space ε in the ethical choice environment consists of all lotteries $(p_\sigma ; \sigma x)_{\sigma \in S_N}$,
  where (p_σ) is a probability distribution on the finite set S_N, and $x \in \mathbb{R}^n$.
  This lottery yields individual i prospect $x_{\sigma(i)}$ with probability p_σ.

In the risk environment, the Representative is simply a decision maker who is to choose a random prospect for herself. In the social choice environment, the Representative is to choose a deterministic prospect for every individual in the society. In the ethical choice environment, she is to choose a deterministic distribution of prospects across society but with the random assignment of individuals to places in society. When probabilities $p_\sigma = 1/n!$ are identical, this ethical choice environment coincides with Harsanyi's (1953, 1955) formalization of ethical decisions.[5]

In the ethical choice, social choice, and risk environments, the Representative's preference relations are written $\succeq_e$, $\succeq_s$, and $\succeq_r$, respectively. To be able to shift from one environment to the other, we need to consider a global environment encompassing ε, $\mathcal{S}$, and $\mathcal{R}$. Let us therefore denote by $\mathcal{L}$ the space of lotteries over allocations:

$$(p_j; x^j)_j, \tag{2}$$

where each $x^j \in \mathbb{R}^n$ is an allocation. In particular, the lottery given by (2) yields x_i^j to the Representative with probability p_j.

Obviously, $\mathcal{S} \subset \varepsilon \subset \mathcal{L}$. As in Kariv and Zame (2008) and Zame et al. (2019), let us suppose that there is an injection $\iota \colon \mathcal{R} \to \mathcal{L}$ and some preference relationship $\succeq$ on $\mathcal{L}$, which allow us to view every individual lottery $(p_h; x_h)_h \in \mathcal{R}$ as the truncation of some lottery of allocations $(p, (x^j)_j)$ in $\mathcal{L}$ and verify:

$$\iota[(p_h; x_h)_h] \succeq \iota[(q_h; y_h)_h] \Rightarrow (p_h; x_h)_h \succeq_r (q_h; y_h)_h.$$

For instance, one could think of a "selfishness" property analogous to the one introduced by Kariv and Zame (2008):

B1 Selfishness. $(p, (x^j)_j) \sim (p, (x_1^j, 0, \ldots, 0)_j)$ for every $(p, (x^j)_j) \in \mathcal{L}$.

Selfishness identifies $\mathcal{R}$ with the subset of $\mathcal{L}$ consisting of lotteries that yield all individuals other than the Representative the 0 prospect with probability 1. However, any other injection from $\mathcal{R}$ into $\mathcal{L}$ would work for our purpose, so that no "selfishness" property (whose ethical content is arguably questionable) is necessary here. All that is needed is a way to "deduce" attitude toward risk from some preferences over $\mathcal{L}$.[6]

2. Deducing Risk Attitude from Ethics

In what follows, let us make the following rather innocuous restrictions about preferences.[7] The first ones concern global preferences $\succeq$ on $\mathcal{L}$. Since they are standard, we gather them into a single assumption, **A0:**[8]

A0. (i) Transitivity. The relation $\succeq$ on $\mathcal{L}$ is transitive.

(i) Reduction of compound lotteries. Any compound lottery in L is indif-fferent to a simple lottery, their probabilities being computed according to the ordinary calculus. In particular, if each $L_h = (p_h^i; x_h^i)_i$, is a lottery for $h = 1, \ldots, k$, then there is no loss of generality in assuming that they all involve the same finite set $(x^j)_j$ of allocations, and moreover

$$(q_h; L_h)_h \sim (\tilde{p}_j; x^j)_j,$$

with $\tilde{p}_j := \sum_h q_h p_h^i$.

(ii) Continuity. Given any collection of allocations $(x^1, \ldots, x^k) \in \mathcal{S}^k$, ordered so that $x^i \succeq_s x^{i+1}$ for every $1 \leq i \leq k-1$, then every x^i is indifferent in $\mathcal{L}$ to some lottery involving only x^1 and x^k, that is, there exists a probability $p_i \in [0,1]$ such that

$$x^i \sim ((p_i, 0, \ldots, 0, 1-p_i); (x^1, \ldots, x^k)) := X^i. \tag{3}$$

(iii) Substitutability. In any lottery $(p_k; x^k)_k$ in $\mathcal{L}$ and for every i, X^i (as defined by (3)) can substitute for x^i, that is:

$$((p_1, \ldots, p_k); (x^1, \ldots, x^i, \ldots, x^k)) \sim ((p_1, \ldots, p_k); (x^1, \ldots, X^i, \ldots, x^k)).$$

(iv) Weak independence. For every probability $(p_j)_j$ and arrays of allocations $(x^j)_j$ and $(y^j)_j$, one has:

$$x^j \succeq_s y^j \; \forall j \;\Rightarrow (p_j; (x^j)_j) \succeq (p_j; (y_j)_j).$$

A0 (v) is a weakening of the familiar independence axiom, and does not im-ply expected utility (even combined with the rest of assumption A0).

The next assumption concerns only ethical preferences. For every pair $x, y \in \mathcal{E}$, denote by $U_e(x, y)$ its upper contour set in ε defined by:

$$U_e(x, y) := \{(z, \sigma) \in \mathcal{S} \times \mathcal{S}_N \mid z \succeq_s x \text{ and } \sigma z \succeq_s y\},$$

while its lower contour set is defined similarly by

$$L_e(x, y) := \{(z, \sigma) \in \mathcal{S} \times \mathcal{S}_N \mid z \preceq_s x \text{ and } \sigma z \preceq_s y\}.$$

A1. Weak convertibility. Social preferences, $\succeq_S$, are complete and transitive. Moreover, for every $x, y \in S$, there exist (z^+, σ^+) and $(z^-, \sigma^-) \in U_e(x, y)$ and $L_e(x, y)$ respectively, such that

$$z^+ \preceq_s z \text{ and } \sigma^+ z^+ \preceq_s \sigma' z, \text{ for every } (z, \sigma') \in U_e(x, y),$$

and

$$z^- \succeq_s z \text{ and } \sigma^- z^- \succeq_s \sigma' z, \text{ for every } (z, \sigma') \in L_e(x, y).$$

A1 says, first, that to any pair (x, y) of allocations in S an auxiliary pair of allocations, $(z^+, \sigma^+ z^+)$, can be associated that are related to each other by a permutation, σ^+, and constitute, so to say, a "minimum" of the upper contour set of (x, y). Second, **A1** says that to every such pair in S, another auxiliary pair of allocations in ε can also be associated, but they constitute a "maximum" of $L_e(x, y)$.

Remark. This assumption on ethical preferences is satisfied both by Rawls's Maximin criterion:[9]

$$(p_\sigma, \sigma x)_\sigma \succeq_e (q_\sigma, \sigma y)_\sigma \Leftrightarrow \min_j x_j \geq \min_j y_j, \tag{4}$$

as well as by the utilitarian criterion:

$$(p_\sigma, \sigma x)_\sigma \succeq_e (q_\sigma, \sigma y)_\sigma \Leftrightarrow \sum_j \lambda_j \mathbb{E}^p(x_j) \geq \sum_j \lambda_j \mathbb{E}^q(y_j) \text{ for some } \lambda_j \geq 0 \text{ all } j, \tag{5}$$

where $\mathbb{E}^p(\cdot)$ designates the expectation operator with respect to probability p. Indeed, with regard to the Maximin criterion, suppose without loss of generaliy that $x \succeq_s y$, take

$$z^+ := (\min_j x_j, \ldots, \min_j x_j), \, z^- := (\min_j y_j, \ldots, \min_j y_j),$$

and any permutations, $\sigma^+, \sigma^- \in S_N$. Concerning the utilitarian case, whenever $u(p, x) := \sum_j \lambda_j \mathbb{E}^p(x_j) = u(q, y) := \sum_j \lambda_j \mathbb{E}^q(y_j)$, it suffices to take the Dirac masses $z_j^+ = z_j^- := u(p, x)$ for every j and the trivial permutations $\sigma^+ \equiv \sigma^- \equiv \mathrm{Id}_N$. Suppose, next, that $u(x) > u(y)$. For every $\sigma \in S_N$, the subset

$$K(x, y, \sigma) := \{z \in \mathbb{R}^n \,|\, (z, \sigma) \in U_e(x, y), u(z) \geq u(x) \text{ and } u(\sigma z) \leq u(x)\}$$

is compact. It therefore admits at least one point in $\mathbb{R}^n$ which minimizes $u(\cdot)$ over $K(x, y, \sigma)$. Since S_N is finite, it suffices to take for (z^+, σ^+) a minimum over these minima for $\sigma \in S_N$. The maximum z^- can be constructed in an analogous way.

For lack of a better term, let us call "reasonable" any risk preference, $\succeq_r$, that can be viewed, thanks to ι, as the restriction of global preferences $\succeq$ fulfilling **A0**. The main result of this chapter is now straightforward.

Theorem.—For all ethical preferences $\succeq_e$ and for social preferences satisfying **A1**, there is a unique global preference relation $\succeq$ on $\mathcal{L}$ verifying **A0** and such that its restriction to ε coincides with $\succeq_e$. Hence, social preferences verifying **A1** and reasonable risk preferences are both uniquely determined by ethical preferences.

Proof. Since $\mathcal{S} \subset \varepsilon$, social preferences can be deduced from ethical ones.[10] What we have to prove is that global preferences over $\mathcal{L}$ can be deduced in a unique way from ethical preferences $\succeq_e$ (although, obviously, $\mathcal{L}$ is not a subset of ε). Given assumption **A0** (i)–(iv) on global preferences $\succeq$, they verify the following property:[11] For any lottery $(p_j; x^j)_{j=1,\ldots,k} \in \mathcal{L}$, it is possible to find a lottery involving only x_1 and x_k, and to which it is indifferent. That is, there exists $p \in [0,1]$ such that

$$(p_j; x^j)_j \sim ((p, 1-p); (x^1, x^k)).$$

Therefore, for our purposes, it suffices to prove that the restriction of global preferences $\succeq$ on simple lotteries of the form $(p, (1-p); (x, y))$ can be deduced in a unique way from $\succeq_e$. Given ethical preferences $\succeq_e$, and courtesy of Assumption **A1**, let us therefore define global preferences by:

$$((p, 1-p); (x_a, y_a)) \succeq ((q, 1-q); (x_b, y_b))$$
$$\Leftrightarrow ((p, 1-p); (z_a^+, \sigma_a^+ z_a^+)) \succeq_e ((q, 1-q); (z_b^+, \sigma_b^+ z_b^+)),$$

Clearly, global preferences defined this way will coincide with ethical preferences when restricted to ε, hence with social preferences when restricted to $\mathcal{S}$. However, since by construction, global preferences satisfy the weak independence property **A0**(v) together with (i)–(iv), they are uniquely defined. Therefore, their restriction to $\mathcal{R}$ thanks to ι yields a unique preference relation, $\succeq_r$, in the risk environment.

Following Harsanyi, one could argue that the risk preferences induced by (4) in the $\mathcal{R}$ setting are hardly realistic. On the contrary, both theoretical investigations (see, e.g., Artzner et al. 1999) and empirical practices of stress tests in the financial industry suggest that behaviors at least close to the ones dictated by the Maximin criterion are not relegated to exotic matters, even in the highly specific set-up of individual risk. On the social choice side, such an egalitarian criterion has been advocated in various ways, among which by Fleurbaey and Maniquet (2006) in a purely ordinal setting. As regards the utilitarian criterion, in terms of individual risk, it corresponds to the requirement of risk neutrality, which is widely used for pricing and hedging financial derivatives. In the field of social choice, it has received a purely ordinal axiomatic foundation by Mertens and Dhillon (1999). There has been considerable controversy over "utilitarian ethics" in the way it is defended by Harsanyi, as in the debate between Sen (1976, 1977, 1986) and Harsanyi (1975, 1977). It suffices here to state that it is perfectly consistent to deduce attitudes toward risk and social choice from an ethical conversation.

Finally, Nussbaum (2006, 17) criticizes the social contract theorists, and Rawls among them, inasmuch as they see the society as a contract for mutual advantage between human beings who are free, equal, and independent. This perspective does not take into account people who suffer from impairments and disabilities. One could add: Nor does it acknowledge the possibility that some parties may represent natural ecosystems to which new rights have been entrusted (Giraud 2020). Even though I agree with Nussbaum's criticism and with the ecological concern for the rights of nonhuman natural ecosystems, these issues are not addressed in this chapter: The parties that are behind the veil of ignorance are assumed not to possess such serious physical or mental impairments that would prevent them from exhibiting "preferences" fulfilling axioms **A0** and **A1**. The prospect of welcoming nonhumans behind the veil of ignorance opens a new question that goes far beyond this chapter: Can one conceive of a theory of justice based on weaker rationality requirements than **A0** and **A1**?

3. Further Discussion

Our framework $(\mathcal{E}, S, R)$ being identical to that introduced by Kariv and Zame (2008), let us recall the restrictions on social preferences introduced by these authors. In addition to being complete, transitive, reflexive, and continuous (in the sense of **A0** (iii)), they need to verify:

B2 The worst outcome: $x \succeq_s (0, \ldots, 0)$ for every $x \in S$,
and

B3 Self-regarding: For each $x \in S$, there exists $t \in \mathbb{R}_+$ such that $(t, 0, \ldots, 0)$ $\succeq_s x$.

Clearly, "selfishness" (**B1**) is a strengthening of "self-regarding" (**B3**). The result proved in Kariv and Zame (2008) that is of interest to us is the following:

Proposition (Kariv and Zame 2008):

1) For all risk preferences and social preferences that satisfy **B2** and **B3**, there is a unique preference relation $\succeq$ on $\mathcal{L}$ verifying **A3** and such that

its restriction to $\mathcal{S}$ (resp. $\mathcal{R}$) coincides with $\succeq_s$ (resp. $\succeq_r$). Hence, if $\succeq$ verifies weak independence, then ethical preferences $\succeq_e$ are determined by risk, $\succeq_r$ and social preferences $\succeq_s$.

2) If social preferences are selfish (i.e., satisfy **B1**), then for all lotteries $(p; (x^j)_j)$, $(q; (y^j)_j)$ in $\mathcal{L}$, one has:

$$(p; (x^j)_j) \succeq (q; (y^j)_j)$$

$$\Leftrightarrow ((p_j)_j; ((x_1^j, 0, \ldots, 0))_j) \succeq_r ((q_j)_j; ((y_1^j, 0, \ldots, 0))_j).$$

The second part of the proposition says that, if the Representative is perfectly selfish (in the sense of **B1**) in the social choice environment, then preferences in the risk environment coincide with ethical ones. Given the widespread use of expected utility as a formalization of attitude toward risk, this seems to promote a definition of ethical preferences as being given by the expected utility of random allocations in $\mathcal{E}$—which is just Harsanyi's understanding of "ethical utilitarianism." Notice, however, that the abovementioned proposition is hardly compatible with a genuinely utilitarian definition of social choice preferences, because the utilitarian criterion (5) satisfies the self-regarding **B3** requirement but does not verify selfishness **B1** unless the weights, λ_i, attributed to citizens verify $\lambda_1 > 0$ and $\lambda_i = 0$ for every $i \neq 1$. In the latter case, utilitarianism simply reduces to dictatorship. However, the Maximin criterion (4) fails to fulfil **B1** and **B2**.

I conclude this chapter with two examples.

Example 1.[12] Take $N = 2$, and adopt the injection ι provided by **B1**. Let g: $\mathbb{R} \to \mathbb{R}$ be any continuous, strictly increasing function with the property that $g(t) = t$ for $t \leq 0$. Define the global utility function $W_g \colon \mathcal{L} \to \mathcal{R}$ by:

$$W_g((p_1, p_2); ((x_1, y_1), (x_2, y_2))) := p_1 g(-e^{x_1} + y_1) + p_2 g(y_2),$$

for any simple lottery in $\mathcal{L}$ involving the two allocations (x_1, y_1) and (x_2, y_2). (By the same argument as in the proof of our Theorem, it suffices to consider such simple lotteries.) The restriction of W_g on $\mathcal{R}$ does not depend on g, since $g(t) = t$ for $t \leq 0$, and $y_1 = y_2 = 0$ on $\mathcal{R}$. The social preferences induced by W_g on $\mathcal{S}$ do not depend on g because g is strictly increasing. However, the ethical preferences induced by W_g on $\mathcal{E}$ do depend on g: The weight given to inequality between citizens depends on g. Hence, ethical preferences cannot be deduced from risk and social choice preferences, so that the Proposition above fails. This is due to the failure of **B3**: Preferences induced by W_g on S are not self-regarding. By contrast, an easy manipulation shows that W_g fulfils **A1** (while **A0** is obvious): Whatever (x_1, y_1) and (x_2, y_2), it is always possible to find $(x, y) \in \mathbb{R}^2$ such that

$$\begin{cases} -e^x + y = -e^{x_1} + y_1 \\ x = -e^{x_2} + y_2 \end{cases}$$

and to take $z^+ = z^- = (x_1, y_1)$ while $\sigma^+ z^+ = \sigma^- z^- = (x_2, y_2)$.

Thus, from ethical preferences of the form

$$W_e ((p_1, p_2); ((x, y), (y, x)) := p_{1g}(e^x + y) + p_{2g}(e^y + x),$$

it is possible to reconstruct global preferences, W_g, from which both social choice and risk preferences are deduced.

Example 2. Suppose, as in Kariv and Zame (2008), that $\mathcal{R}$ can be restricted to nonnegative prizes, that is, $\mathcal{R} = \{(p_h; x_h)_h \mid x_h \geq 0 \ \forall h\}$. Again, take $N = 2$. Let $f: \mathbb{R} \to \mathbb{R}$ be continuous and strictly increasing, with the property that $f(t) = t$ when $t \geq 0$. Define the global utility function $U_{f,\lambda}: \mathcal{L} \to \mathbb{R}$ as follows. For every lottery $L = ((p_1, p_2); ((x_1, y_1), (x_2, y_2)))$,

$$U_{f,\lambda} (L) := p_1 f(x_1 - y_1) + p_2 \lambda f \left(\min_{i=1,2} |x_i - y_i| - \min_{i=1,2} |x_i - y_i| \right),$$

for a given parameter $\lambda \in (0, 1)$. The risk preferences induced by $U_{f,\lambda}$ on $\mathcal{R}$ do not depend on f (as $f(t) = t$ for $t \geq 0$), nor do social choice preferences (because $f(0) = 0$, so that, for every allocation (x_1, y_1), $U_{f,\lambda}(x_1, y_1) = f(x_1, y_1)$, and f is strictly increasing). However, the ethical preferences induced by $U_{f,\lambda}$ on $\mathcal{E}$ do depend on f, again because the weight given to inequality depends on f. Thus, once again, the Proposition above fails, so that ethical preferences cannot be deduced from risk and social choice preferences. This time, it is **B2** that is violated: There is no worst outcome. At variance with Example 1, however, $U_{f,\lambda}$ does not verify our convertibility assumption **A1** either, so that our Theorem fails as well.

Indeed, for every allocation, $z = (x, y)$, $U_{f,\lambda}((p, 1-p); (z, \sigma z)) = pf(x - y)$, whatever the probability $p \in (0,1]$. Hence, ethical preferences do not depend on λ, while global preferences do. And since risk preferences depend on λ as well, they cannot be deduced from ethical ones either.

Notes

Centre d'Economie de la Sorbonne, University Paris-1 Panthéon-Sorbonne, gael.giraud@univ-paris1.fr. Support from the Energy and Prosperity Chair is gratefully acknowledged.
    1. Another example is Binmore (1994, 1998).
    2. Following Ricœur's (1992, 170) classical distinction between *ethics* as the aim of an accomplished life in a teleological perspective, and *morality* as the set of norms related to a deontological point of view, I prefer here the term "ethical" to "moral."

3. Notice that I nowhere require preferences to be increasing with respect to prospects.

4. That is, $p_h \geq 0$, for each h, and $\sum^{P}_h p_h = 1$.

5. We could enlarge the ethical choice environment to include lotteries with random assignment without changing the analysis.

6. Zame et al. (2019) perform this deduction by considering an abstract (finite) set Ω of social states, a subset $P \subset \Omega$ of which have consequences only for the Representative.

7. Notice that we do not require global preferences to be complete or reflexive.

8. Remember the definition of compound lotteries: Suppose that $L_1, \ldots, L_k$ are k lotteries, and $(p_h)_{h=1,\ldots,k}$ is a probability distribution. Then $(p_h; L_h)_h$ denotes a compound lottery in the following sense: One and only one lottery will be the prize, and the probability that it will be L_h is p_h.

9. A stronger requirement would require, e.g., that (z^+, σ^+) and (z^-, σ^-) coincide with some (z, σ) such that $z \sim x$ and $\sigma z \sim y$. This property, however, would not be fulfilled by the Maximin criterion. Weak convertibility is also implied by (but does not imply) the Selfishness property quoted above.

10. So that the restriction A1 on social preferences actually can be viewed as a constraint put on ethical preferences.

11. See Luce and Raiffa (1957, 28).

12. This is a variant of Example 2 in Kariv and Zame (2008).

References

Artzner, P., F. Delbaen, J.-M. Eber, and D. Heath. 1999. "Coherent Measures of Risk." *Mathematical Finance* 9(3): 203–228.

Atkinson, A. B. 2009. "Economics as a Moral Science." *Economica* 76: 791–804.

Binmore, K. 1994. *Game Theory and the Social Contract*. Vol. 1, *Playing Fair*. Cambridge, MA: MIT Press.

Binmore, K. 1998. *Game Theory and the Social Contract*. Vol. 2, *Just Playing*. Cambridge, MA: MIT Press.

Fleurbaey, M., and F. Maniquet. 2008. "Fair Social Orderings." *Economic Theory* 34: 25–45.

Giraud, G. 2021. *Composer un Monde en commun: théologie politique de l'Anthropocène*. Paris: Seuil, forthcoming.

Harsanyi, J. 1953. "Cardinal Utility in Welfare Economics and in the Theory of Risk-Taking." *Journal of Political Economy* 61: 434–435.

Harsanyi, J. 1955. "Cardinal Welfare, Individualistic Ethics, and Interpersonal Comparisons of Utility." *Journal of Political Economy* 63: 309–321.

Harsanyi, J. 1975. "Can the Maximin Principle Serve as a Basis for Morality? A Critique of John Rawls' Theory." *American Political Science Review* 69: 594–606.

Harsanyi, J. 1977. "Nonlinear Social Welfare Function: A Rejoinder to Professor Sen." In R. Butts and J. Hintikka (eds.), *Foundational Problems in the Special Sciences*. Boston: D. Reidel Publishing Company, 293–296.

Hayek, F. 1976. *Law, Legislation, and Liberty*. Vol. 2, *The Mirage of Social Justice*. Chicago: University of Chicago Press.

Hörisch, H. 2007. "Is the Veil of Ignorance only a Concept about Risk? An Experiment." Discussion paper, University of Munich.

Kariv, S., and W. Zame. 2008. "Piercing the Veil of Ignorance." Working paper 2009-06, University of California, Berkeley.

Lhuillier, H., G. Giraud, and C. Renouard. 2017. "Crisis and Relief in the Niger Delta (2012–2013). Assessment of the Impact of a Flood on Relational Capabilities." *Oxford Development Studies* 46(1): 113–131.

Llavador, H., J. Roemer, and J. Silvestre. 2010. "Intergenerational Justice When Future Worlds Are Uncertain." *Journal of Mathematical Economics* 46: 728–761.

Luce, R.D. and Raiffa, H. 1957. *Games and Decisions*. New York, Wiley.

Mertens, J.-F., and A. Dhillon. 1999. "Relative Utilitarianism." *Econometrica* 3: 471–498.

Nussbaum, M. 2006. *Frontiers of Justice*. Cambridge, MA: Harvard University Press.

Rawls, J. 1971. *A Theory of Justice*. Cambridge, MA: Harvard University Press.

Ricœur, P. 1992. *Oneself as One Another*. K. Blamey (trans.). Chicago: University of Chicago Press.

Sen, A. K. 1976. "Welfare Inequalities and Rawlsian Axiomatics." *Theory and Decision* 7: 243–262.

Sen, A. K. 1977. "Non-linear Social Welfare Functions: A Reply to Professor Harsanyi." In R. Butts and J. Hintikka (eds), *Foundational Problems in Special Sciences*. Boston: D. Reidel Publishing Company, 297–302.

Sen, A. K. 1986. "Social Choice Theory." In *The Handbook of Mathematical Economics*, vol. 3, K. Arrow and M. Intrilligator (eds). North-Holland, Elsevier, 1073–1181.

Weber, M. 1988. "Die Objektivität' sozialwissenschaftlicher und sozialpolitischer Erkenntnis." In Johannes Winckelmann (ed.), *Gesammelte Aufsätze zur Wissenschaftslehre*. Tübingen: J.C.B. Mohr.

Zame, W. R., B. Tungodden, E. Ø. Sørensen, S. Kariv, and A. W. Cappelen. 2019. "Linking Social and Personal Preferences: Theory and Experiment." mimeo.

EXCHANGE CONFIGURATIONS AND THE LEGAL FRAMEWORK

Peter A. Cornelisse and Erik Thorbecke

Exchange is a fundamental part of economic behavior. And yet, remarkably little attention has been given in the economics literature to analyses of processes of exchange. Only in the past few decades have two strands of the literature (game theory and transaction cost theory) contributed significantly to a better understanding of these processes. Game theory has helped clarify the effects of information asymmetries and differences in bargaining power among actors in various forms of exchange. Transaction cost theory explains why economic actors bring transactions under different "governance structures," such as markets, firms, and families.

In this chapter, we propose a new paradigm, the exchange configuration approach, which allows a detailed analysis of various forms of exchange in different settings and at different levels of aggregation or disaggregation in developing and developed countries alike. This approach aims to identify the very building blocks of transactions and to explain how transactions obtain their form and content. In doing so, we frequently draw on our recent book, *Exchange and Development* (Cornelisse and Thorbecke 2010), and an abbreviated version of it (Thorbecke and Cornelisse 2014).

It should be emphasized that one of these building blocks and key determinants affecting the form and content of transactions is the prevailing legal framework, which can vary enormously across different settings. In section 1, we discuss some alternative approaches to the exchange process. Next, we present in section 2 our exchange configuration approach before focusing more specifically on the relation between market failures and the legal framework in section 3. The chapter concludes by giving an example of an exchange configuration and the multiple types of transactions and legal contracts that might ensue.

1. Alternative Approaches to the Exchange Process

In spite of the centrality of exchange to the operation and performance of any given economy, it is not easy to find a conceptual framework in which to study exchange that reflects and explains the enormous diversity of transactions that take place in the real world. Exchange that takes place in formal markets is best studied in the economics literature, yet even such a basic concept as "market" lacks a widely accepted definition.[1] Moreover, insufficient attention is generally paid to transactions that take place outside of formal markets. In developing countries, in particular, many forms of nonmarket exchange relations are both socially and economically important.

Different approaches to modeling the exchange process are available in the literature, some more general and some more specifically directed to modeling developing countries. Neoclassical models of markets predominate. The assumptions in these models regarding exchange are familiar: Property rights are fully determined, all actors are perfectly informed, and their capacity to process this information is unlimited. Therefore, transaction costs are excluded in neoclassical models. By assumption, only production costs are covered. In reality, transaction costs represent the aggregation of a number of costs that are generally not included in the concept of production costs, such as information costs, negotiation costs, monitoring costs, coordination costs, and enforcement costs. These costs—many of which are directly or indirectly related to the prevailing legal framework—are significant, and they have a strong impact on economic behavior.

The main contribution of the New Institutional Economics (NIE) has been to incorporate transaction costs as a major determinant of the exchange process. NIE explicitly recognizes the fact that information is imperfect and that economic actors are "intendedly rational, but only limitedly so" (Simon 1957, xxiv). So transaction costs cannot be avoided. North (1987) argues that the addition of transaction cost analysis to the standard economic approach makes it a useful tool for analyzing the whole range of allocation systems in history (Eggertson 1991). Polanyi's various "transaction modes"—administered trade, reciprocal obligatory gift giving between kin and friends, and householding, for instance—are not purely social and psychological institutions, according to North. Polanyi's transaction modes are in fact alternatives to price-making markets and are used instead of markets to allocate resources, because they economize on costs—particularly transaction costs—in the particular environments where they are found.

But it is mostly Williamson, who, in a series of publications, developed a coherent theory of Transaction Cost Economics. He identified three characteristics of transactions, each having a specific impact on transaction costs, which determine the preferred transactional mode (the so-called governance structure, such as markets, families, and firms). These characteristics are uncertainty, asset specificity, and frequency. He also introduced the concept of opportunistic behavior (i.e., self-interest seeking with guile), which seriously enhances uncertainty. Such behavior follows logically when it is recognized that economic actors are imperfectly informed and can, therefore, be deceived. Economic actors thus have strong incentives to select for their intended transactions the particular transactional mode that helps reduce their transaction costs (Williamson 1975, 1985, 1996, 2000).

2. The Exchange Configuration Approach

Transaction Cost Economics can account for the existence of broad categories of forms of exchange, but it does not explain the immense variety of forms and content of economic transactions within these categories. Hence it is desirable and necessary to develop a more general framework in which one can organize, analyze, and evaluate the myriad existing exchange settings but which still remains manageable. Such a general framework would not only have analytical merit; it could also contribute to improved policymaking. By laying bare the foundations of transactions, it would allow a more precise identification of characteristics that cause desirable and undesirable results.

The approach presented here traces exchange relations back to their building blocks—that is, to the specific combination of characteristics that jointly shape the form and content of a given exchange.[2] We call these building blocks *elements of exchange*. These are:

1. the *item* exchanged;
2. the *actors* engaged in decisions related to the item being exchanged; and
3. the *environment*—physical, social, technological, legal,[3] and so forth—in which the actors operate.

We postulate that the characteristics of these elements, in different combinations, shape distinct types of exchange relations and help explain their content and operation. We term each particular combination of elements together with the formation process of the exchange considered an *exchange configuration* (see figure 9.1).

Each of the three elements of an exchange configuration must be further broken down into an array of *characteristics*. The *item* at the heart of a transaction can be a product (e.g., a consumer good, an intermediate input, and a capital good, a service, a residential or nonresidential building, a financial asset, land, or foreign exchange). Differences in the nature of these items strongly influence the corresponding transactions.[4] It can easily be seen, for example, why a transaction involving an ocean liner differs from one where a bottle of beer changes hands. The power of discrimination of the item traded is also illustrated by the fact that markets are generally distinguished and named according to the items traded within these markets.

Attributes of *actors* consist of their preferences and objectives and other characteristics, on one hand, and the instruments available to them in pursuing their objectives, on the other. Such instruments include income, wealth, skills, education, social position, and information. There are many groups of actors. Producers, consumers, traders, and investors are examples of market actors; a branch manager of a vertically integrated firm and members of a farm household, operating within a firm and a family, respectively, are examples of nonmarket actors.

The *environment* is the third element of an exchange configuration. Characteristics of the environment impose various kinds of constraints on actors' decisions and their choice of transactions. For example, property rights, laws, and regulations have direct and indirect influences on actions culminating in transactions—as discussed in section 3. Other examples are behavioral and cultural codes inspired by the norms and values generally accepted in a given society; restrictions relating to the physical environment, encompassing among others, location, soil, and climate characteristics as well as the underlying infrastructure. These characteristics determine the type of goods that can be produced (e.g., what crops are suited for production in a given agro-ecological setting), transported, and marketed. Further, the overall level of economic development of a region or country acts as a constraint on purchasing power and on the volume exchanged, which in turn, affect the degree of specialization that a market can support. Finally, the available technological shelf acts as a bound on the feasible range of market decisions. Thus, as defined here, the environment includes political and legal, cultural, physical-geographical, technological, and organizational dimensions, as well as the underlying socioeconomic structure.

Having come to this point in the presentation of our analytical framework, we have to confront and address a potential problem. The problem relates to the total number of characteristics of the three exchange elements that might conceivably be relevant as building blocks for all transactions one can imagine. A complete list of these characteristics must be almost endless. So the question is: Can the concept of exchange configurations be of any use, if it is based on myriads of potentially relevant data and variables? The answer, fortunately, is relatively simple. For it appears that in any analysis of specific transactions (individual or aggregated, and whatever the type), only a few elements from the universe of potential features dominate the formation process and have discriminative power (in the sense that they are highly intercorrelated with other features). It also appears that these relevant and discriminating features suggest themselves fairly easily when considering the transaction being studied.

Experience shows that, for each transaction or group of transactions, a reasonably small number of properties (a dozen, at most) can effectively describe the key features of the item traded, the participating actors, and the environment in which the transaction takes place. Or, turning the argument around, a given subset of properties of elements can be used to explain the form and content of an exchange that embody the terms of exchange, the actual transfer of the item traded, and payment or settlement according to the agreed terms. The argument applies to market as well as nonmarket transactions in developing and developed countries alike.

Figure 9.1 shows graphically and in general terms the logic underlying the exchange configuration concept.[5] The relevant characteristics of the three exchange elements that have been identified for the transaction(s) under consideration appear at the bottom of the figure (a few of which are represented as dots in the ovals). In the formation process from a specific combination of characteristics to the resulting transaction(s), the actors play a crucial role as they activate the transaction(s). In other words, actors, as one of the elements of exchange, differ fundamentally from the item exchanged and the transactional environment, the other two elements. Actors consider, create, decide, and execute. They use their knowledge and experience of other transactions, take account of the prevailing properties of exchange elements, consider the terms of a possible transaction, and adjust them when possible in negotiations with their counterparts. Only when they make a positive decision does the transaction become a fact; and it is left to the actors to execute the agreed-on transaction. Note that it is the actors who convert the exchange elements into transactions.

An entire constellation—composed of a combination of the characteristics of elements, the shaping of ensuing transactions, and the resulting set of homogeneous transactions—is what we call here an *exchange configuration*. Exchange configurations can be thought of as channels through which specific transactions are effectuated. Given the constraints they face and their own attributes, the properties of the item transacted, and their environment, actors will choose to operate in (or will invent or initiate) the configuration and corresponding transaction that minimizes the sum of production and (perceived) transaction costs.

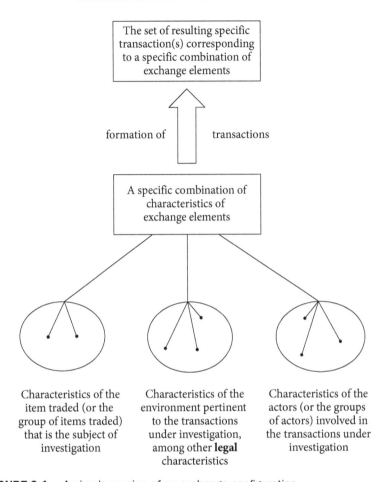

FIGURE 9.1.   A simple version of an exchange configuration.

Source: Cornelisse and Thorbecke (2010, 27).

3. The Use of Legal Measures to Address Market Failures

The fundamental importance of the legal framework on the ultimate form and nature of the transactions generated in a given exchange configuration should be obvious to any researcher. Students of comparative law know very well that different legal systems can yield very different transactional outcomes. In turn, the noncompliance with, or the absence of, a legal system is more than likely to lead to a failed state. In what follows, we give a few examples of how the state can intervene through legal means to influence and, ultimately, shape transactions with the objective of addressing market failures.

Market transactions are a particular and, in many respects, refined type of economic exchange. Elsewhere we have defined these transactions as bargaining transactions with full quid pro quo occurring frequently with a spillover of information.[6] Such an exchange can come about only after a long period of disciplining to promote trust and cooperation and to reduce uncertainty. In other words, it is inconceivable that market transactions can evolve and flourish without a set of legal arrangements relating to property rights and commercial law and without an authority to devise such arrangements and enforce compliance. The importance of these basic conditions can hardly be overestimated in a world where nearly all economies are guided by the market principle.

But there is more action on the interface connecting economic exchange with legal systems and state intervention. The reason is that markets often fail even under the best of conditions, and that they do so in different ways. Public sector intervention[7] is often needed to improve market performance and even to replace markets altogether, a subject that is less well known than the one mentioned above. In this section, we discuss briefly some major forms of market failure, and the (sometimes even imperative) policies that they have generated. It will appear, not surprisingly, that all market failures can be traced back to specific aspects of the three exchange elements discussed in section 2.

3.1. Public Goods

Public goods are characterized by two properties that separate them from other goods. One property is called nonrivalry. It applies when consumption by one user does not impede consumption of the same good by other users. This is an uncommon phenomenon, as consumers of most products are one another's rivals for that product: the ice cream I eat cannot also be consumed by somebody else (or perhaps only by my little daughter). But consider a street light. Its light helps me find my way as well as all other passers-by. The other property is nonexcludability, which refers to the fact that the provider of a good cannot exclude consumers from using that good. This property is also an unusual one, as most products are typically excludable: If I do not pay for my ice cream, the vendor will not sell it to me. The provider of a city street, in contrast, cannot stop all users of the street to demand due payment.

As pure public goods are both nonexcludable and nonrival, markets cannot (will not) provide them efficiently. Nonexcludability implies that suppliers cannot collect revenues to compensate for the costs incurred, so market actors opt out. In the case of nonrivalry, the marginal costs of using the good are zero, as the use by any additional consumer involves no extra costs. So any positive price that is charged is arbitrary and does not reflect the marginal costs, an inefficient outcome.

There are only few pure public goods, but their provision is very costly. One example is a national defense system. It is clearly nonrival, as it covers an entire nation, and the protection it provides to one citizen does not diminish the protection for others. It is also nonexcludable, as it is practically impossible to limit protection to those willing to pay for it. Other examples are roads and bridges and infrastructures protecting against flooding. Note further that pure public goods come in one size only. Individual preferences cannot be taken into account, and hence, dissatisfaction among users is inherent.

It follows from this discussion that public goods belong to the realm of the public sector, which must not only decide how much of them is provided but which must also finance the costs of investment and maintenance. Different levels of government occupy themselves with these tasks, depending on the reach, or geographical span, of the public goods concerned. For example, local governments will take care of public gardens, while the larger parks are, generally speaking, the responsibility of provincial governments. Because public goods are meant to serve the general public, it is only natural that they are financed by taxes. So public goods are directly connected to the vast range of rules that regulate the collection of general taxes. But other complex types of policies are also involved, such as expropriation procedures for infrastructure projects overriding private property rights. Further, because of the vast sums involved and the ever-present danger of corruption, public tenders need to comply with intricate and elaborate procedures that are meant to discriminate objectively among potential suppliers.

3.2. External Benefits and Costs

In some cases, the private production or consumption by one actor or group of actors has a positive or negative impact on the well-being of other actors. For example, inoculation against a specific disease protects not only the recipient but also other people, including those who cannot be inoculated because of an intolerance. This is a case of an external benefit or positive externality. The costs of the inoculation do not take account of this beneficial effect and are therefore higher than they should be. It may be a reason for a government to subsidize the inoculation or even to make it compulsory if the subsidy is not sufficiently effective. External costs or negative externalities are the counterpart of external benefits. In terms of the number and monetary impact of governmental countermeasures, they are much more spectacular. The most familiar example relates to the air, water, and soil pollution resulting from production of a variety of products with harmful health effects for the neighboring population and for the vitality of the environment in general. Governments may decide to tax such production activities and thus to internalize the external costs. Alternatively, considering that lives are at stake, such damaging activities may be prohibited entirely.

3.3. Uneven Market Power

Markets tend to fail when they are dominated by one or only a few actors on the supply or demand side, as in monopolies and monopsonies. The benefits from transactions in such markets are likely to be distributed very unevenly, such that there may even be outright exploitation. Furthermore, dominating-actor groups have little incentive to improve their own performance; on the contrary, their natural objective is to maintain the status quo. Governments have an array of measures at their disposal to combat uneven market power and promote competition, of which we mention only a few, such as laws against cartels and collusion, and measures to strengthen the position of the weaker actor groups or to prohibit intended mergers.

3.4. Income Redistribution

The income distribution generated by markets that are left unconstrained may be considered undesirable and at the limit, even unacceptable for a variety of reasons, among which moral judgments figure prominently. Governments may address this problem in different ways at three different levels: the primary, secondary, and tertiary level of personal income distribution. The primary level is concerned with the personal distribution of income obtained from production activities, such as wages, profits, and interest payments. This distribution tends to be typically very skewed, but it can be made less uneven, for example, by introducing minimum wage levels. The remaining unevenness can be reduced further through progressive income taxes and social security benefits. The resulting distribution is called the "secondary income distribution." In many countries, still further redistribution is achieved by means of income-dependent subsidies on consumption of certain products. Examples of such products are education, housing, and health care. The accumulated effect is reflected in the tertiary level of income distribution. The size and complexity of the administrative burden entailed by all these measures taken together are particularly impressive.

3.5. Goods and "Bads"

There are markets that function well in the limited technical sense but that still invite state intervention, because they deal with undesirable goods (sometimes called "bads"). In the estimation of society as a whole, consumers, if left to themselves own, tend to use much more of these bads than they should. Governments have a wide array of measures at their disposal to discourage consumption, ranging from relatively mild information programs (for example, about health hazards), excise taxes (as on tobacco and alcoholic drinks) to outright prohibition. Violation of the prohibition measures is a continuous threat, so government involvement does not stop here. It must be added that there also exist goods that are considered to be undervalued by individual consumers, so that their use deserves to be promoted. Government measures applied here are the inverse of those mentioned above. Examples in this case are subsidies on opera performances and museums and the obligatory use of safety belts and crash helmets. We see the public sector operating here in a paternalistic role.

A special case illustrating the powerful effect that culture in general and religion in particular can have on the social desirability of a product (and thereby on economic exchange) derives from the prohibition of interest on credit in Islamic countries. Especially since the 1970s, alternative financial instruments have been developed that are consistent with the principles of Islamic law. In practice, however, market actors prefer to remain as close as possible to traditional financial forms.

3.6. Second-Order Market Failure

Different countries respond in different ways to the challenges that market failures present. These variations may be the result of differences in judgment regarding the seriousness of the situation or regarding the most effective measures that need to be taken, or the range of measures available. So over the course of time, a complex mosaic of national policies combating market failures has come into existence. Ironically, all these policies give rise to a new type of market failure—which can be called a second-order market failure—as they cause serious impediments to international trade by requiring actors in international transactions to adapt to different transactional moulds. National governments realize that it is in their common interest to mitigate the effect of this second-order inefficiency and to negotiate with other nations so as to reduce the disparity among transactional moulds. The World Trade Organization provides a framework for such international agreements based mainly on the principles of nondiscrimination and reciprocity. The rules established through this mechanism have achieved, among other things, a reduction of barriers to trade resulting from national technical and safety standards. Member countries of the European Union even go several steps further by accepting more stringent measures that are decided on by majority vote.

3.7. Dynamics of the Relations between Law and Market Exchange

In the above discussion, we have argued as if rules, regulations, and laws precede market transactions, such that the latter have to adjust to existing legal moulds. In reality, the situation is somewhat different. For example, actors might create new transactions that are designed to circumvent existing rules while remaining within the law. This is an attractive course of action if these rules are found to be oppressive in one way or another. Alternatively, entirely new products might be developed for which there does not yet exist pertinent legislation, a situation that occurred with the introduction of internet services. Over the course of time, these new types of market transactions (new form or new content) may appear to have undesirable outcomes. This may then be the start of the long process of devising and applying new rules to correct the failure. In this case, regulation follows after exchange innovations.

Any exchange transaction is based on an agreement among participants. This agreement is embodied in the implicit (verbal) or explicit contract entered into by the parties involved. The exchange configuration for the use of an automobile provides a good illustration of the large number of different transactions and underlying contracts that may ensue, depending on the different characteristics of the actors (users and providers of this service), the characteristics of the item (the exact nature of the service to be provided), and the environment (in particular, the prevailing legal framework). Let's review briefly some of the options, resulting transactions, and contracts available to potential users of the service of a car

In the setting of an advanced country, such as the United States, the simplest transaction could be purchasing the car outright from a dealer or private party, entering into a sales contract, and receiving the title. A second option could be a lease agreement with a car manufacturer (or its dealer) over a given extended period with or without the option to purchase the car at the end of the lease period. A third option, if the potential user only required the car for a short period, would be to rent a car from a rental company such as Hertz or Avis. A fourth option, if the user only needed a one-time ride to a nearby destination, would be to call a cab or an Uber driver. There are still other alternatives available, such as "ride sharing" and car pools.

The point is that the selected transaction depends on the characteristics of the *actors* (particularly the tastes, needs, and wealth of the potential users), the characteristics of the *item* (such as cost, length of time service is needed, and accessibility), and the characteristics of the *environment* (especially the legal environment). The actors will select that transaction that minimizes transaction costs. The contract or legal instrument covering a given selected transaction can be argued to *embody* (reflect and capture) all the specific characteristics of our three elements of exchange. This is why we believe that the exchange configuration approach should be of operational usefulness to researchers focusing on the interface between law and economics.

Notes

1. One can find literally dozens of definitions of "market" in the literature emphasizing different characteristics and thereby illustrating the lack of common ground.

2. For details, see Cornelisse and Thorbecke (2010).

3. In section 3, we explore more specifically the link between the legal environment (legal characteristics) and market transactions.

4. In fact, a more detailed disaggregated distinction is often necessary. For example, agricultural commodities differ in so many respects (e.g., degree of perishability, their uses, their seasonal production pattern) from, say, industrial products that the exchanges involving these product (sub)groups will be influenced by different sets of product or factor characteristics.

5. In Thorbecke and Cornelisse (2014), we present two almost polar examples of very different configurations—one in the setting of a village economy (a "friends and family" credit exchange configuration) and one in the setting of the global economy (a financial exchange configuration mimicking the 2007 financial crisis)—following the schema shown in figure 9.1.

6. For a full discussion of this subject, see Cornelisse and Thorbecke (2010, 59 and subsection 3.2.3).

7. The public sector is defined here as consisting of national, state/provincial, and local governments.

References

Cornelisse, P. A., and E. Thorbecke. 2010. *Exchange and Development*. Cheltenham, UK: Edward Elgar.

Eggertson, T. 1991. *Economic Behavior and Institutions*. Cambridge: Cambridge University Press.

North, D. C. 1990. *Institutions, Institutional Change and Economics*. Cambridge: Cambridge University Press.

Simon, H. A. 1957. *Models of Man*. New York: John Wiley & Sons.

Thorbecke, E., and P. A. Cornelisse. 2014. "Exchange and Development." *Revue d'Économie du Développement* 22: 5–24.

Williamson, O. E. 1975. *Markets and Hierarchies: Analysis and Antitrust Implications.* New York: Free Press.

Williamson, O. E. 1985. *The Economic Institutions of Capitalism.* New York: Free Press.

Williamson, O. E. 1996. *The Mechanisms of Governance.* New York: Oxford University Press.

Williamson, O. E. 2000. "The New Institutional Economics: Taking Stock and Looking Ahead." *Journal of Economic Literature* 38: 595–613.

REIMAGINING GOVERNANCE THROUGH THE ROLE OF LAW

A Perspective from the *World Development Report 2017*

Luis F. López-Calva and Kimberly B. Bolch

The chapters in this volume cover a fascinating range of topics—from the need to reimagine antitrust laws in the face of changing technology to the historical importance of social connections for doing business in China. Each chapter prompts us to think more critically about the fundamental links between law, economics, and development. In this commentary, we view the ideas presented in these chapters through the lens of the "functionalist" approach to law developed in the *World Development Report 2017 on Governance and the Law* (World Bank 2017; referred to as WDR 2017 in this chapter)—and encourage the reader to think more precisely about commonly invoked (but rarely defined) concepts, such as "law," "governance," and "elites."

A Functionalist Approach to Law

What do we mean by "law"? Throughout the chapters in this book, the term is somewhat broadly applied to mean state-enacted rules. It is important, however, to recognize that not all rules are created equal. Following a simple classification structure proposed by Acuña and Tomassi (1999), we can think about rules as belonging to three different levels. Low-level rules refer to specific policies (such as the antitrust legislation discussed in chapter 6), mid-level rules refer to organizational structures (such as membership in the European Union, as discussed in chapter 7) and high-level rules refer to "rules about making rules" (such as election processes, as discussed in chapter 1). Fundamentally, all three types of these rules are the result of agreements among actors. We can think of the bargaining process through which actors—state and non-state actors—design and implement these rules as "governance."

Typical debates on governance center on the notion of the rule of law. While an unequivocally admirable objective, the "rule of law" is not necessarily the best analytical category for understanding the links between law and development—as it represents an ideal state rather than a process. The rule of law implies that rules are applied impersonally and that the rulers are also subject to the rules. As such, it is a norm in itself, an agreement among actors, an outcome. Thinking about the "role of law," however, helps us to trace the various pathways through which rules can potentially influence economic, social, and political outcomes. As argued in the WDR 2017, we can think about three primary—though not unique—roles that law plays in promoting development: ordering power, ordering behavior, and ordering contestation.

One role that law plays is *ordering power*—by conferring and limiting the power given to different state actors. In this volume, chapter 1 by Monga reflects on this role of law—and the consequences when it is ineffectual. In his discussion on the global disillusionment taking place within many "democratic" countries around the world, Monga draws attention to the failure of law in many of societies to hold politicians accountable when they act beyond their legally granted powers. This scenario is encapsulated in his opening description of "Terror Tuesday" in the White House—during which the US president makes executive decisions regarding the targeted killings of suspected terrorists around the world.

Another role that law plays is *ordering behavior*—by establishing a common set of economic and social rules to coordinate the action of individuals and organizations. Chapter 2 by Hoff and Walsh specifically zooms in on this role of law. In the authors' exposition of what they refer to as "the schematizing function of law" (the way law constructs or deconstructs our cultural categories), they explore how law serves as a focal point for coordinating behavior. One key result of this, they argue, is the potential to reduce harmful social biases. They show, for example, how laws reserving political leadership positions for women in villages in India helped to collectively shift discriminatory gender norms against women serving in such positions.

Law also plays a role in *ordering contestation*—by serving as a peaceful tool to challenge undesirable rules or to adapt rules to changing circumstances. Chapter 4 by Swamy engages with this role of law at various points. In his analysis of the changing history of rural credit markets in India, he describes the extensive legal tug of war over the rural credit markets. In one example that he details about the pursuit of greater autonomy of credit cooperatives from the state, after the failure of petitioners to achieve a favorable verdict by the Supreme Court, they go so far as to enact a constitutional amendment. This use of law to contest institutional practices stands in stark contrast to the historical episode Swamy describes at the beginning of the chapter—in which Deccan peasants "rioted" and attacked moneylenders in their frustration with the status quo.

Strengthening the different roles that law plays is essential to helping societies move toward a stronger rule of law. While an extensive literature exists that explores transitions to democracy, we know much less about how transitions to the rule of law take place (Fukuyama 2010; Mungiu-Pippidi 2017). Moreover, understanding this transition may be more universally meaningful for societies. As Monga argues, in today's world, the term "democracy" is hardly robust to the myriad ways in which democracy actually functions around the world. Rather than focusing on organizational "forms," such as democracies or autocracies— we should take a more functionalist approach to law. We should focus on how specific laws—in their different roles—reinforce or undermine the key governance functions that allow individuals to sustain agreements (commitment function), voluntarily abide by the rules (cooperation function), and react to other people's expected actions in a socially constructive manner (coordination function).

Law in a Changing World

A key contribution of this volume is how it grapples with law and economics in the context of a rapidly changing world characterized by massive technological advancements and increasing globalization. Without careful attention to how these new forces are changing the nature and sustainability of agreements among actors, societies may miss out on taking full advantage of the different roles of law in promoting development. It is quite possible that the "best solution" in the past may no longer be a good solution for the future—and may even be a detrimental solution.

In particular, chapter 6 by Basu and chapter 1 by Monga critically engage with the need to revisit our laws in this new context, asking if and how different laws need to be adapted for the future. As Basu reflects on how digital technology has reshaped firms' production into vertically serrated markets, he questions how well antitrust policies are aging. He argues that the consequences of applying historical antitrust laws in today's market may lead to an equilibrium in which price discrimination excludes most potential buyers while taking the full consumer surplus of those who do buy—with consequences for rising inequality. Thus he argues for the need to replace old antitrust laws with a "twin dispersal" approach, in which firm ownership is dispersed more broadly among individuals and firm profits are dispersed more broadly among individuals in the nation.

Monga (chapter 1) explores these changing dynamics in his reflection on the longevity of constitutions. Drawing attention to what he refers to as an "intrinsic contradiction of democracies," he asks why people should be bound by historical political rules designed for a different era—often an era in which many groups were explicitly excluded from the process that made those rules. While constitutions with long lifespans can be critical for promoting credible commitment and coordination within societies, if they do not support a stable and fair bargain, their unquestioned persistence may lead to conflict. Monga raises the question of the relevance of "giving the right to vote to dead people," but here we argue that in today's world, we need to think a step further. As we face increasing long-term cooperative challenges, such as climate change, not only do we need to think about the undue weight we are giving to voices from the past in our policy arenas today; we also need to consider the lack of voice of future generations who will be affected by contemporary political decisions. The recent wave of youth protests against the lack of action on climate change reflects these rising frustrations with a political process that fails to take into account the interests of all groups.

In Greta Thunberg's 2018 speech to world leaders at the 24th Conference of the Parties to the United Nations Framework Convention on Climate Change (COP24) in Katowice, Poland, the fifteen-year old climate change activist spoke to these concerns: "In the year 2078, I will celebrate my 75th birthday. If I have children maybe they will spend that day with me. Maybe they will ask me about you. Maybe they will ask why you didn't do anything while there still was time to act. You say you love your children above all else, and yet you are stealing their future in front of their very eyes."[1]

The Danish physicist Niels Bohr is quoted to have remarked that "it is very hard to predict, especially the future."[2] Yet, how laws adapt to our constantly changing world is at the heart of imagining what our future looks like. While research in this area may necessarily be somewhat speculative, it is a critical area that we need to seek to understand in greater depth. Discussions about changing technology tend to focus on "the future of work," but we also want to argue that we need to give equal attention to technology's potential impacts on the "future of governance."

In our world today, there are at least three essential confusions that technology has created in our political process: people take access to information as equivalent to knowledge, people take popularity as equivalent to legitimacy, and people take digital identity as equivalent to political voice. As technology lowers the cost of access to information, public debates are increasingly based on unfiltered information. As information is increasingly not appraised for its depth of "truth," institutional legitimacy is vulnerable to being weakened by popularity based on reductionist approaches to identity. As technology makes it easier for people to participate in social networks, public deliberation is increasingly limited to online spaces, while meaningful political engagement—including even voter turnout in electoral democracies—weakens. That favors the rise of clientelistic movements against the strengthening of programmatic party structures. These trends pose serious questions for the future of governance.

However, technology also presents incredible opportunities for the future of governance. It carries with it the potential to broadly restructure power relations and empower citizens—for example, through its role in promoting transparency, enabling collective action, and spreading norms and ideas across borders. While we cannot know what the future holds, we need to critically understand the challenges and opportunities presented by technology for the ways in which it alters how people interact to reshape mindsets, and to reach and sustain agreements— what we call governance.

Changing Law to Reshape the World

In every context, when existing rules are no longer effective in pursuing social objectives, it is time for change. While many scholars emphasize narratives of institutional persistence, our institutions are changing all the time. Such changes, however, often take place in incremental ways at the margins of formal law. Rather than the "big" changes that we sometimes see at "critical junctures" following rare episodes of shocks, this type of "small" change happens as the agreements among actors must adapt to frequently changing circumstances—such as changes in actors' preferences and beliefs or in their incentives.

Chapter 2 by Hoff and Walsh describes the iterative process of how laws can change actors' beliefs and preferences (by changing our cultural categories), which can in turn lead to new laws, which again change beliefs and preferences. This can be a virtuous circle (in which biases are reduced) or a vicious one (in which biases are reinforced). However, as Hoff and Walsh note—some norms can be quite "sticky." In the case of public leadership in Indian villages, changes in discriminatory norms against women did not begin to take place until after seven years of exposure to women leaders. The inelasticity of these types of social norms can make certain changes a very long-term process. This challenge is also reflected in Long's discussion in chapter 3 about anticorruption efforts in China. As she argues, "the long tradition of reliance on personal relationships dies hard in a traditional society, adding more challenge to the task of corruption fighting."

Where newly introduced laws are in conflict with existing norms, formal or informal, changing the rules on paper may be insufficient to promote the desired outcomes. In some cases, they may even lead to worse outcomes. For example, as

Hoff and Walsh note in chapter 2, while political reservations for women in Indian villages helped change the culture in terms of reduction in gender discrimination, political reservations for Scheduled Castes actually ended up leading to greater harassment of Scheduled Caste students in schools.

Adding to the pertinence of the chapters in this book, Basu's text (chapter 6) makes a central contribution in the context of thinking about how change happens, namely, its nod to game theory. Through the careful acknowledgment of the strategic interaction and responses of individuals and corporations, Basu concedes that change is rarely easy or straightforward—for every action, there is a reaction. Indeed, the process of changing laws and reaching new agreements among actors (what the WDR 2017 refers to as "the rules game") is a dynamic and iterative process. It is also a process informed by the subsequent impact of the rules on social and economic outcomes for the actors (what the WDR 2017 refers to as "the outcome game"). Together, these two games form an infinite loop. If power is too tightly concentrated in the hands of the few, this neverending loop can potentially undermine democracy by institutionalizing inequality.

The discussion of inequality implicitly encompasses the role of certain elites. "Elites" is another term that is widely invoked but rarely defined. While the term "elite" tends to have a negative connotation, it is in fact a neutral descriptor of relative power. In a way, everyone has some degree of "elite-ness" depending on how much we can influence decisions in certain realms. If we define elites as those who can directly influence decisions in the policy arena, then the definition is one based on an objective indicator. The rest of us, the citizens, can only influence decisions indirectly, for example, through our vote, through social organization, through political organization, or through public deliberation. Although change can be driven from the "top-down" (elite-led) or from the "bottom-up" (citizen-led)—it always results from a bargaining process that involves elite actors behaving in their own interests. Indeed, as Francis Fukuyama (among others) has argued—no peaceful social change has been brought about by citizens alone. In that sense, peaceful change tends to emerge from coalitions between citizens and change-friendly elites.

All the chapters in this volume emphasize important aspects of law for development and discuss potential ways in which it can or should be changed—ranging from greater regulation to greater deregulation. Few of them, however, pay sufficient attention to how the existing power relations in society could support the necessary coalitions for key actors to promote the desired changes. Who will lead these changes? What is the nature of the elite bargains in a given society?

It is generally more common to think in abstract terms about the rules required to solve economic or social problems, than to think seriously about how power asymmetries manifest themselves in the political arena and how these reforms may either be infeasible or vulnerable to capture. As Basu cautions in chapter 6, "the challenge is to create a blueprint for an equitable society that is viable. History is replete with systemic shifts that began with the right intentions but ended up with a few people capturing both political power and wealth." In the language of the WDR 2017, we need to think about reforms that create a "virtuous circle"—in which the "rules game" and the "outcome game" reinforce each other in promoting a more equitable, prosperous, and peaceful society. The chapters in this book contain eloquent examples of how to think seriously, and realistically, about these reforms.

Notes

1. From speech transcript "Ms. Greta Thunberg - High-level Segment Statement COP 24." United Nations Framework Convention on Climate Change. December 21, 2018. https://unfccc.int/documents/187780.

2. While the origin of this saying is contested, the remark is attributed to Bohr in several texts, including Stanislaw M. Ulam's 1976 book *Adventures of a Mathematician.*

References

Acuña, C., and M. Tommasi. 1999. "Some Reflections on the Institutional Reforms Required for Latin America." In *Institutional Reforms, Growth and Human Development in Latin America.* Conference Volume. New Haven, CT: Yale Center for International and Area Studies.

Fukuyama, F. 2010. "Democracy's Past and Future: Transitions to the Rule of Law." *Journal of Democracy* 21(1): 33–44.

Mungiu-Pippidi, A. 2017. *Transitions to Good Governance: Creating Virtuous Circles of Anti-corruption.* Cheltenham, UK: Edward Elgar Publishing.

World Bank. 2017. *World Development Report 2017 on Governance and the Law.* Washington, DC: World Bank.

BEYOND LAW AND ECONOMICS

Legitimate Distribution without Legislation?

Nicole Hassoun

Traditionally, scholars of law and economics apply the principles of economics to analyze legal problems (or consider how legal principles can guide market development). Some of this analysis has gone beyond positive modeling and prediction to the normative task of recommending policy based on the relevant analysis. In chapter 7 of this volume, for instance, Yair Listokin argues that central banks should consider using capital and/or price controls to achieve policy objectives. Kaushik Basu suggests requiring that firms share profits with everyone in the nation when anti-trust legislation is neither effective nor efficient at protecting consumers against monopoly power (Basu 2019).[1] The current chapter suggests that we might best advance the new field of law and economics by applying philosophical, as well as legal and economic, analysis to possible policy proposals derived from economic models in evaluating and advancing them. It illustrates this idea by considering when technocrats may legitimately implement policy proposals along the lines suggested here. In doing so, it aims to advance the field primarily by raising some new concerns and considering how to address them.

When a central bank raises interest rates, trade ministers decide to put countries on intellectual property watch lists, or a specialist at the Global Fund decides how to calculate the lives saved with its interventions, their decisions can greatly affect the allocation of resources within, and between, societies. The Global Fund's calculations, for instance, go into its aid allocation formula. So, with one swipe of his or her pen, the specialist charged with doing the calculations drastically affects the lives of millions. When a central bank raises interest rates or a trade minister lists a country on its intellectual property watch list, millions of people may benefit, while millions may also suffer.

When is it legitimate for technocrats to make such decisions? That is, when is this exercise of political power morally permissible? What follows considers this question.

First, a few words about *legitimacy*, who qualifies as a *technocrat*, and what constitutes a *decision with significant allocative consequences*. Let us say an entity is *legitimate* only if "it is morally justified in wielding political power" (Buchanan 2002, 689). In this sense, legitimacy is normative as opposed to descriptive and moral as opposed to legal. Moreover, if decisions are legitimate, those subject to them may have to abide by them, but in what follows, I will not assume that legitimacy generates an obligation to abide by the decisions.[2] I use the term *technocrat* broadly to include executives, policymakers, and others who make allocative decisions but are neither democratically elected nor directly appointed by elected officials.[3] Most technocrats, as I use the term, have some relevant skill that may help them make good decisions, but this need not be the case. Similarly, they need not have expertise in science or industry. I will suppose that a decision that affects the distribution of resources necessary for many people to live well will qualify as a *decision with significant allocative consequences*. Such "technocratic" decisions can include changing tax laws, increasing international aid, raising tariffs, and so forth. These decisions' consequences can be more or less significant, depending, for example, on the number of lives they affect.

There are many classical philosophical theories about what makes governments legitimate, and some of the principles they offer clearly apply to technocratic decisions. Some believe, for instance, that a decision is legitimate when those subject to it cannot do better than to abide by the decision (Raz 1986). According to these theories, whenever decisions are essential for people to reap large benefits from coordinating our actions, people should follow them regardless of their origin. It matters that someone decides whether we should all drive on the left- or right-hand side of the road, and once someone decides, we all have good reason to abide by the decision, but it does not matter who decides (Simmons 1976; Locke 1980; Kant 1999; Rawls 2007; Hassoun, 2008; Peter 2013).

It is less clear that other classical philosophical theories have any bearing on what individual technocrats can legitimately do. On some theories, the process that generates the decision is essential to its legitimacy (Benhabib 1994; Buchanan 2002; Estlund 2008; Peter 2008). For instance, some endorse theories on which only democratic processes legitimate the rules—that is, the rules are only legitimate when they are the rules of the majority (Rousseau 1974 [1712–1778], I:6 sec. 3.3; Christiano 1996; Valentini 2012). It is not obvious that these theories tell us what individual technocrats can legitimately do (unless we assume democratic theories proscribe all nondemocratic allocative decisions).

Perhaps many classical accounts of legitimacy do not tell us when technocratic decisions are legitimate because, traditionally, philosophers have supposed that laws specify all significant allocative decisions in democratic societies. Government officials may run on platforms focused on changing tax rates or welfare spending. When they are able to pass legislation that affects these changes, their actions have at least faced legitimacy. That is, they may be illegitimate, but the burden of proof falls on those who would argue that the action violates important substantive or procedural constraints on democratic decision making (Estlund 2008; Peter 2013).

Today, however, many decisions affect the allocation of resources outside of legislation (and technocratic decisions may have much more drastic effects on allocation than many legislative decisions that focus expressly on resource allocation). As Allen Buchanan puts it, "a technocratic elite, lacking in democratic accountability . . . is playing an increasingly powerful role in a system of regional and global governance," and I believe the same is true within countries (Buchanan 2003, 289). In many countries technocrats regulate health and safety, the quality of goods and services, the terms of trade, social discrimination, and more. Moreover, technocrats often make decisions implicitly, if not expressly, aiming to affect the distribution of resources.

More recently, however, philosophers have started to consider legitimacy beyond governments, and these debates also bear on the legitimacy of technocratic decisions. For instance, consider debates about the legitimacy of nongovernmental organizations (international institutions, aid groups, and corporations) that influence the distribution of resources in or between societies. There are ways in which some of these organizations' decisions are determined by governments. Many international institutions' decisions and funding streams, for instance, depend directly on government support. So, some maintain that it suffices if states consent to the general structure of international rules these organizations promulgate (Beitz 1998; Rawls 1999; Cavallero 2003). But some argue that corporations, nonprofit groups, and even international organizations' officials cannot make legitimate decisions about allocation, because they are not appropriately democratic (Benhabib 1994; Held 1995; Buchanan 2002; Caney 2006; Valentini 2012, 2014; Hassoun 2018). Others point to the consequences of the decisions in trying to determine whether they are legitimate or hold that the decision makers must only appropriately represent their constituents' interests (Held 1995; Stilz 2009). Yet others insist that the organizations' officials must make decisions through appropriate procedures and respect basic rights (Cohen and Sabel 2005; Buchanan and Keohane 2006; Abizadeh 2008; Valentini 2012).

It seems hard to deny that some technocratic decisions are legitimate. Likely, this seems plausible because the decisions are so widespread that denying their legitimacy may amount to, unintuitively, denying most governments' legitimacy. But there are also plausible theoretic reasons to endorse this conclusion. Likely, the legitimacy of the decision will vary, depending on the nature of the decision itself. Plausibly, it matters how significant the decision is and what other options are available. At least in the absence of fully just institutions, there may be some room for technocrats to make decisions that can improve allocation significantly (Buchanan 2003; Caney 2006; Dietsch 2017). Even if a given decision has some negative consequences, the alternative may be so bad that it is legitimate (Adler 2005). Imagine, for instance, that reducing interest rates is essential for a country to avoid a recession. If doing so is legal, does not have unintended bad effects, and there are no better options, then the central bank might be justified in reducing the rate.[4]

Technocrats may have more license to make decisions when there are just institutions in place to compensate for any unjust consequences. Some observers endorse the institutionalist thesis, which holds that individuals subject to just institutions should be free to make decisions within the confines of whatever laws they face (Waldron 1987; Murphy 1998). The idea is that society should divide moral labor so that background institutions provide rules within which individuals may generally pursue their interests (Rawls 1971; Nagel 1991, ch. 6, 9; Murphy 1998). For "people lead freer and better lives . . . if they can devote most of their concerns to their own affairs" (Murphy 1998, 258). Perhaps we can extend the idea so that technocrats should be free even to make significant allocative decisions, as long as laws can compensate for any unjustified consequences of their actions (Edmundson 1998; Greene 2016). Imagine, for instance, that a trade policy makes it more difficult for many poor farmers in Scotland to export wool. The Scottish government might compensate these people by taxing wool imports and redistributing the gains to exporters (if that is what justice requires).[5]

Still, many observers worry that technocracy (the proliferation of technocratic decisions) is incompatible with democratic values, public participation, representative governance, flexibility in the face of crises, or responsiveness to subjects' values. Others worry that technocracy cannot register discontent appropriately, restricts debate to those well versed in technical language, only represents the interests or values of the elite, and so forth (Tucker 2018, 219).

I might propose a minimal (necessary) condition for legitimate technocratic decisions with significant allocative consequences: Those affected by the decision should have a say in the process by which it is made, so that the allocation is appropriately responsive to their interests, at least when aspects of the decision exceed the decision maker's expertise.[6] It is plausible that these decisions will be better and fairer than those that do not take into account the affected people's interests.[7] Moreover, this principle might elicit an "overlapping consensus" amongst those with very different philosophical views on legitimacy (Christiano 1996).[8] After all, most stronger principles either strengthen requirements on the outcome of the decision (perhaps only correct decisions are appropriately responsive to interests) or on the process by which the decision is made (perhaps everyone should have an equal say in the process of making the decision). A notable exception is the account of legitimacy with which we started, where a decision is legitimate whenever those subject to it cannot do better but to abide by the decision (Raz 1986). Even those who accept this account can get on board, however, if we weaken the principle so that it just requires consultation and responsiveness to interests whenever that helps technocrats make better decisions.

Many questions remain: Do the legitimacy of technocrats' decisions hang on whether elected representatives can make these decisions? Can a central bank change interest rates on its own if it cannot get government approval to do so on time to avoid a recession, for instance? Can technocrats ever make legitimate decisions that go against democratically endorsed laws (Beitz 1979; Hassoun 2018)? Can a central bank ever legitimately change interest rates to prevent a recession if doing so is illegal, for example? Does it matter if the express purpose of policies is distributive or whether people understand the distributive consequences of their policy choices (Blake 2001)? Should technocracy constitute a separate sphere from politics (that is, be free, and perhaps insulated, from direct political control)?[9] How much (if any) discretion should technocrats have when their decisions do not contravene the law?[10] Even if, in principle, some technocrats can make legitimate significant allocation decisions outside (if not against) the law, does it matter *who* in these organizations is making the decision?[11] Does it matter if these decisions are made by executives, policymakers, scientists, or philosophers?[12]

It is impossible to address these questions further here. Considering them is, however, extremely important in our time, when technocratic decisions affect the fates of millions and their allocative consequences may be much more significant than those expressly determined by law. More generally, applying philosophical, as well as legal and economic, analysis to possible policy proposals may be essential for evaluating and advancing them.

Notes

1. In other work, Kaushik Basu also suggests redistributing firms' profits to those who are discriminated against in markets perhaps instead of enforcing laws against discrimination, although this might be affected in many ways (Basu 2018). Although both outcomes might be affected by a change in law, he might be amenable to market-based mechanisms for achieving them that are implemented by technocrats.

2. Let me further explain the kind of legitimacy at issue. I am asking: When is it *morally permissible* for technocrats to make decisions with significant allocative consequences? The answer to this question may have some bearing on when people should abide by the decisions, but I am not asking: When do most people think it is morally permissible for technocrats to make decisions with significant allocative consequences and when do they think they should abide by such decisions? (Weber 1964; Dworkin 1986; Raz 1986; Rawls 1993; Wellman 1996; Blake 2001; Buchanan 2002; Ripstein 2004; Hassoun 2008). Nor am I asking: When are these decisions legal? (Although it may turn out that it is morally permissible for technocrats to make decisions with significant allocative consequences whenever they are legal.)

3. Perhaps a better word would be "functionary" or "administrator," as even unelected members of the judiciary or military may qualify under this definition. But each term has its drawbacks, so I will continue to use the term "technocrat" in what follows. A related question is: When (if ever) are administrative agencies' decisions legitimate when they are not determined by elected representatives?

4. In evaluating decisions, it may also be helpful to distinguish between decisions that are unconstrained and those that are constrained by law, guidelines, and principles. It may also matter whether the decision is executive, legislative, or judicial, and the degree to which it is subject to elected representatives' control.

5. This is so even though laws are often imperfect, and institutions are rarely fully just—fair taxation etc. may rarely compensate for the allocative consequences of technocratic decisions (Buchanan and Keohane 2006; Dietsch 2017).

6. Note that this requirement is more stringent than requiring that the decision provide gains over those normally available via direct control by elected representatives—who may not be able to implement or maintain their decisions over time, given the changing tides and demands of politics. It also requires that the decisions appropriately respond to the affected party's interests and not just that they are accountable to those who are capable of judging the decisions (Wallach 2016).

7. Here one might appeal to arguments that democratic theorists use to establish democracy's instrumental value—for example, grounded on the Condorcet Jury Theorem. For discussion, see Christiano (1996).

8. My argument here is not that (normative) legitimacy requires an overlapping consensus among those with different perspectives on legitimacy (never mind politics more broadly). Where those perspectives are mistaken, it is not clear that they always merit consideration. Still, the principle may secure wide support. For a different perspective, see Tucker (2018), which also nicely considers how technocrats in independent agencies can threaten democratic decisions in practice. I agree, however, that the condition for legitimacy I propose is not sufficient for full legitimacy. Moreover, it is essential to consider institutional stability and implementation when setting out an account of legitimacy. See also Ackerman (2000).

9. Woodrow Wilson (1887) argued for this conclusion in his classic "Study of Administration."

10. Must they adhere to something like constitutional principles and support the rule of law, separation of powers, and so forth (DeMuth 2016; Tucker 2018)?

11. Alternately, it may matter which organizations are at issue—both their records as well as their mandates (contra Tucker 2018, 213).

12. It is also important to consider how decisions should be made (e.g., by committees or individuals with staggered terms) and what protections the groups and individuals making technocratic decisions have in doing so—budgetary control, job security, and so forth (Strauss 1984; Tucker 2018).

References

Abizadeh, Arash. 2008. "Democratic Theory and Border Coercion: No Right to Unilaterally Control Your Own Borders." *Political Theory* 36(1): 37–65.

Ackerman, Bruce. 2000. "The New Separation of Powers." *Harvard Law Review* 113(3): 633–729.

Adler, Matthew D. 2005. "Justification, Legitimacy, and Administrative Governance." *Issues in Legal Scholarship*. Available at: https://scholarship.law.duke.edu/faculty_scholarship /2588.

Basu, Kaushik. 2018. *Republic of Beliefs*. Princeton, NJ: Princeton University Press.

Basu, Kaushik. 2019. "Antitrust Law in the Age of New Technology: Is It Time to Call It a Day?" Available at https://www.iza.org/publications/pp/146/new-technology-and -increasing-returns-the-end-of-the-antitrust-century.

Beitz, Charles. 1979. *Political Theory and International Relations*. Princeton, NJ: Princeton University Press.

Beitz, Charles. 1998. "International Relations, Philosophy of," in Edward Craig (ed.), *Routledge Encyclopedia of Philosophy*. London: Routledge.

Benhabib, Seyla. 1994. "Deliberative Rationality and Models of Democratic Legitimacy." *Constellations* 1(1): 25–53.

Blake, Michael. 2001. "Distributive Justice, State Coercion, and Autonomy." *Philosophy and Public Affairs* 30(3): 257–296.

Buchanan, Allen. 2002. "Political Legitimacy and Democracy." *Ethics* 112(4): 689–719.

Buchanan, Allen. 2003. *Justice, Legitimacy and Self-Determination*. Oxford: Oxford University Press.

Buchanan, Allen, and Robert O. Keohane. 2006. "The Legitimacy of Global Governance Institutions." *Ethics and International Affairs* 20(4): 405–437.

Caney, Simon. 2006. "Cosmopolitan Justice and Institutional Design: An Egalitarian Liberal Conception of Global Governance." *Social Theory and Practice* 32(4): 725–756.

Cavallero, Eric. 2003. "Popular Sovereignty and the Law of Peoples." *Legal Theory* 9(3): 181–200.

Christiano, Thomas. 1996. *The Rule of the Many: Fundamental Issues in Democratic Theory*. New York: Westview Press.

Cohen, James, and Charles Sabel. 2005. "Global Democracy?" *New York University Journal of International Law and Politics* 37(4): 763–797.

DeMuth, Christopher. 2016. "Can the Administrative State Be Tamed?" *Journal of Legal Analysis* 8(1): 121–190.

Dietsch, Peter. 2017. "Normative Dimensions of Central Banking: How the Guardians of Financial Markets Affect Justice." In Lisa Herzog (ed.), *Just Financial Markets? Finance in a Just Society*. Oxford: Oxford University Press, ch. 10.

Dworkin, Ronald, 1986. *Law's Empire*. Cambridge, MA: Harvard University Press.

Edmundson, William A., 1998. *Three Anarchical Fallacies*. Cambridge: Cambridge University Press.

Estlund, David, 2008. *Democratic Authority*. Princeton, NJ: Princeton University Press.

Greene, Amanda. 2016. "Consent and Political Legitimacy." In David Sobel, Peter Vallentyne, and Steven Wall (eds.), *Oxford Studies in Political Philosophy*. Oxford: Oxford University Press, 71–97.

Hassoun, Nicole. 2008. "World Poverty and Individual Freedom." *American Philosophical Quarterly* 45 (2): 191–198.

Hassoun, Nicole. 2018. "The Evolution of Wealth; Democracy or Revolution?" In Jack Knight and Melissa Schwartzberg (ed.), *Wealth: NOMOS LVIII*. Oxford University

Press Scholarship Online. Available at: https://www.universitypressscholarship
.com/view/10.18574/nyu/9781479827008.001.0001/upso-9781479827008.

Held, David. 1995. *Democracy and the Global Order*. Palo Alto, CA: Stanford University Press.

Kant, Immanuel. 1999. *Practical Philosophy*. In Mary J. Gregor (ed.), *Cambridge Edition of the Works of Immanuel Kant in Translation*. Cambridge: Cambridge University Press.

Locke, John. 1980 [1690]. *Second Treatise on Civil Government*, C. B. MacPherson (ed.). Indianapolis: Hackett, 1990.

Murphy, Liam. 1998. "Institutions and the Demands of Justice." *Philosophy & Public Affairs* 27(4): 251–291.

Nagel, Thomas. 1991. *Equality and Partiality*. New York: Oxford University Press.

Peter, Fabienne. 2008. *Democratic Legitimacy*. New York: Routledge.

Peter, Fabienne. 2013. "The Procedural Epistemic Value of Deliberation." *Synthese* 190(7): 1253–1266.

Rawls, John. 1971. *A Theory of Justice*. Cambridge, MA: Harvard University Press

Rawls, John. 1993. *Political Liberalism*. New York: Columbia University Press.

Rawls, John. 1999. *The Law of Peoples*. Cambridge, MA: Harvard University Press.

Rawls, John. 2007. *Lectures on the History of Political Philosophy*. Cambridge, MA: Harvard University Press.

Raz, Joseph. 1986. *The Morality of Freedom*. Oxford: Oxford University Press.

Ripstein, Arthur. 2004. "Authority and Coercion." *Philosophy and Public Affairs* 32(1): 2–35.

Rousseau, Jean-Jacques. 1974 [1712–1778]. *The Essential Rousseau: The Social Contract, Discourse on the Origin of Inequality, Discourse on the Arts and Sciences, The Creed of a Savoyard Priest*. New York: New American Library.

Simmons, A. John. 1976. "Tacit Consent and Political Obligation." *Philosophy and Public Affairs* 5(3): 274–291.

Stilz, Anna. 2009. *Liberal Loyalty: Freedom, Obligation, and the State*. Princeton, NJ: Princeton University Press.

Strauss, Peter L. 1984. "The Place of Agencies in Government: Separation of Powers and the Fourth Branch." *Columbia Law Review* 84(3): 573–669.

Tucker, Paul. 2018. *Unelected Power: The Quest for Legitimacy in Central Banking and the Regulatory State*. Princeton, NJ: Princeton University Press.

Valentini, Laura. 2012. "Assessing the Global Order: Justice, Legitimacy, or Political Justice?" *Critical Review of International Social and Political Philosophy* 15(5): 593–612.

Valentini, Laura. 2014. "No Global Demos, No Global Democracy? A Systematization and Critique." *Perspectives on Politics* 12(4): 789–807.

Waldron, Jeremy. 1987. "Theoretical Foundations of Liberalism." *Philosophical Quarterly* 37(147): 127–150.

Wallach, Philip A. 2016. "The Administrative State's Legitimacy Crisis." Center for Effective Public Management, Brookings Institution, Washington, DC. Available at: https://www.brookings.edu/wp-content/uploads/2016/07/Administrative-state-legitimacy-crisis_FINAL.pdf.

Weber, Max. 1964. *The Theory of Social and Economic Organization*, Talcott Parsons (ed.). New York: Free Press.

Wellman, Christopher. 1996. "Liberalism, Samaritanism, and Political Legitimacy." *Philosophy and Public Affairs* 25(3): 211–237

Wilson, Woodrow. 1887. "The Study of Administration." *Political Science Quarterly* 2(2): 197–222

Kaushik Basu is Carl Marks Professor of International Studies at Cornell University and is currently president of the International Economic Association. He was formerly chief economist at the World Bank. His most recent book is *The Republic of Beliefs: A New Approach to Law and Economics* (Princeton University Press, 2018).

Kimberly B. Bolch is a doctoral candidate in International Development at the University of Oxford and a consultant for the United Nations Development Programme. Previously, she worked with the World Bank Group as a core team member of the *World Development Report 2017* on governance and the law and as a junior professional associate in the Poverty and Equity Global Practice. Her primary research interests focus on the political economy of poverty, inequality, and social policy. Her current research explores processes of inclusive state-building, with an emphasis on the role of conditional cash transfer programs in Latin America.

Marieke Bos is an economist and deputy director at the Swedish House of Finance at the Stockholm School of Economics. She also holds a visiting scholar position at the Federal Reserve Bank of Philadelphia Consumer Finance Institute. Marieke's research focuses mainly on individuals' decision making in the field of household finance and empirical banking. Marieke has won the 2019 Michael J. Brennan Best Paper Award for her paper with Emily Breza and Andres Liberman, "The Labor Market Effects of Credit Market Information," published in the *Review of Financial Studies*, and the 2017 Hans Dalborg award for excellence in Financial Economic Research.

Susan Payne Carter is an associate professor of Economics at the United States Military Academy, West Point. Her PhD was in Economics from Vanderbilt University and her BS in Mathematical Economics from Wake Forest University. Her research focuses on applied microeconomics topics, specifically, consumer finance, labor, education, and law and economics.

Peter A. Cornelisse studied under and worked with Nobel Prize winner Jan Tinbergen in the field of development economics at the Netherlands School of Economics, forerunner of the present-day Erasmus University Rotterdam. He obtained MA and PhD degrees from EUR, both cum laude. He worked at the

Turkish State Planning Organization in Ankara from 1965 to 1967 and at the Instititut de Développement Économique et de Planification in Dakar, Senegal, from 1969 to 1971. He was appointed professor of Development Economics at EUR in 1977 and guest professor at Cornell University during the same year. He then switched from development economics to public finance in 1988 and participated in consultancy missions to a.o. Sudan, Egypt, Burkina Faso, Pakistan, Indonesia, and Thailand. Now he is emeritus professor of Public Finance.

Gaël Giraud is chief economist and executive director of the Research and Knowledge Directorate of the Agence Française de Développement. He has also served as a member of the Expert Committee on the National Debate about the Energy Shift for the French government, chairs the "Energy and Prosperity" group supported by Ecole Normale Supérieure, Ecole polytechnique, ENSAE, and Louis Bachelier's Institute, and serves as a member of the European NGO Finance Watch and the Nicolas Hulot Foundation.

Nicole Hassoun is a visiting scholar at Cornell University and professor of philosophy at Binghamton University. She has published widely in such journals as the *American Philosophical Quarterly, Journal of Development Economics, Australasian Journal of Philosophy, European Journal of Philosophy, PLoS One*, and *Philosophy and Economics*. Her first book, *Globalization and Global Justice: Shrinking Distance, Expanding Obligations* was published by Cambridge University Press in 2012, and her manuscript *Extending Access to Essential Medicines: The Global Health Impact Project* is forthcoming with Oxford University Press.

Robert C. Hockett is Edward Cornell Professor of Law at Cornell Law School and professor of public affairs at Cornell University. He is senior counsel at Westwood Capital, a fellow at the Century Foundation, and a consultant for the Federal Reserve Bank of New York, the International Monetary Fund, Americans for Financial Reform, and the Occupy Cooperative, in addition to several federal and state legislators and local governments.

Karla Hoff is Visiting Professor of Economics and International Affairs at Columbia University. She is currently writing *Malleable Minds: A New Perspective on What Makes Economic and Social Progress Possible* (to be published by Columbia University Press). She co-directed the World Bank's *World Development Report 2015: Mind, Society, and Behavior* and served in the World Bank's Development Research Group from 1999 to 2020. She has published papers in the *American Economic Review* that explain how segregation between renters and homeowners may deepen poverty, how cueing a stigmatized social identity depresses cognitive performance, and how Big Bang privatization in Russia impeded the emergence of a political demand for rule of law. She has co-edited two books, *The Economics* *of Rural Organization* (Oxford University Press, 1993) and *Poverty Traps* (Princeton University Press, 2011).

Yair Listokin is the Shibley Family Fund Professor of Law at Yale Law School. His research emphasizes a macroeconomic perspective that differs from the microeconomic perspective that dominates law and economics.

Cheryl Long is departmental chair and Professor of Economics at Xiamen University and Professor of Economics in the Wang Yanan Institute for Study of Economics (WISE). She also serves as associate editor and a member of the Editorial Board of *China Economic Review* (Elsevier) and co-editor-in-chief of *China Economic Studies* (Taylor & Francis). She was previously an associate professor in the Department of Economics and director of the Asian Studies Program at Colgate University.

Luis F. López-Calva, ASG, is the UNDP Regional Director for Latin America and the Caribbean since September 2018. He has nearly 30 years of professional experience, advising several Mexican governments, in addition to UNDP and most recently the World Bank, where he most recently served as practice manager of the Poverty and Equity Global Practice (Europe and Central Asia). He was the co-director and lead author of the *World Development Report 2017* on "Governance and the Law." He was previously lead economist and regional poverty advisor in the Bank's Europe and Central Asia Region, and lead economist at the Poverty, Equity and Gender Unit in the Latin America and Caribbean PREM Directorate, also at the World Bank. From 2007 to 2010, he served as Chief Economist for Latin America and the Caribbean at UNDP-RBLAC in New York. Mr. López-Calva has been associate editor of the *Journal of Human Development and Capabilities*, and he is a fellow of the Human Development and Capabilities Association. He has also been the chair of the Network on Inequality and Poverty in the Latin America and Caribbean Economic Association. His research interests focus on labor markets, poverty and inequality, institutions and microeconomics of development, and he has presented his research at top institutions, including Harvard University; Stanford University; University of California, Berkeley; University of California, San Diego; and the Organization for Economic Cooperation and Development Centre. He holds a master's degree in economics from Boston University, as well as a master's and a doctorate in economics from Cornell University.

Célestin Monga is former vice president and chief economist of the African Development Group and former managing director at the United Nations Industrial Development Organization, senior economic adviser at the World Bank, and the co-author (with Justin Yifu Lin), most recently, of *The Oxford Handbook of*

Structural Transformation (Oxford University Press, 2019) and *Beating the Odds: Jump-Starting Developing Economies* (Princeton University Press, 2017).

Paige Marta Skiba has conducted innovative research in the area of behavioral law and economics and commercial law, particularly on topics related to her economics dissertation, *Behavior in High-Interest Credit Markets*. She has been the recipient of numerous research grants and fellowships from such institutions as the National Science Foundation, the Russell Sage Foundation, the National Institute on Aging, the Federal Reserve Board of Governors, the Burch Center for Tax Policy and Public Finance, and the Horowitz Foundation for Social Policy. Professor Skiba serves on the board of the American Law and Economics Association and the Society for Empirical Legal Studies. She earned her PhD in economics from the University of California, Berkeley, in 2007. Professor Skiba teaches Bankruptcy and Behavioral Law and Economics to J.D. students. She also teaches Law and Economics, Behavioral Law and Economics, and Econometrics for Legal Research in the PhD program in Law and Economics.

Anand V. Swamy is Willmott Family Third Century Professor of Economics, Williams College. His research focuses on land, labor, and credit markets in India. His publications include "The Hazards of Piecemeal Reform: British Civil Courts and the Credit Market in Colonial India," published in the *Journal of Development Economics*, and "Contracts, Hold-Up and Exports: Textiles and Opium in Colonial India," published in the *American Economic Review* (both papers jointly with Rachel Kranton), and "Only Twice as Much: A Rule for Regulating Lenders" in *Economic Development and Cultural Change* (with Mandar Oak). His book *Law and the Economy in Colonial India* (co-authored with Tirthankar Roy) was published by University of Chicago Press in 2016.

Erik Thorbecke is the H. E. Babcock Professor of Economics Emeritus and former director of the Program on Comparative Economic Development at Cornell University. He is the co-founder of the most popular poverty measure used globally by international agencies, governments, and researchers.

James Walsh is a doctoral candidate at the Blavatnik School of Government, University of Oxford. His research interests are in behavioral and development economics. He is affiliated with the Centre for Experimental Social Science at Nuffield, Centre for the Study of African Economies at the University of Oxford, and the Institute of Sociology at the University of Bern.

Index

Figures and tables are indicated by "*f*" and "*t*"after the page number.